Rhetorical Republic

Rhetorical Republic

Governing Representations in American Politics

Edited by Frederick M. Dolan
and Thomas L. Dumm

The University of Massachusetts *Amherst*

Copyright © 1993 by
The University of Massachusetts Press
All rights reserved
Printed in the United States of America
LC 92–41984
ISBN 0–87023–846–9 (cloth); 847–7 (pbk.)
Designed by Milenda Nan Ok Lee
Set in Bodoni Poster Display and Trump Mediàeval
Printed and bound by Thomson-Shore, Inc.
Library of Congress Cataloging-in-Publication Data
Rhetorical republic : governing representations in American politics /
    edited by Frederick M. Dolan and Thomas L. Dumm.
        p.   cm.
    Includes bibliographical references and index.
    ISBN 0–87023–846–9 (cloth : alk. paper). — ISBN 0–87023–847–7
(pbk. : alk. paper)
    1. Communication—Political aspects—United States.   2. Mass
media—Political aspects—United States.   3. United States—Politics
and government.   I. Dolan, Frederick Michael.   II. Dumm, Thomas L.
P95.82.U6R47   1993
302.23′0973—dc20   92–41984
                                                          CIP

British Library Cataloguing in Publication data are available.

Contents

Acknowledgments

We thank Brenda Bright and Willie Epps, Jr., for their help in preparing this volume; Elizabeth Maddock Dillon for research and editorial assistance; Jennifer Culbert, Vicky Elliott, and Ellen Rigsby for editorial assistance; and Anne Norton for the subtitle. We acknowledge the American Political Science Association for permission to publish articles that first appeared in the *American Political Science Review:* B. Honig, "Declarations of Independence: Arendt and Derrida on the Problem of Founding a Republic" (March 1991) and Dana R. Villa, "Postmodernism and the Public Sphere" (September 1992). Finally, William E. Connolly's "Democracy and Territoriality" was originally published in the December 1991 issue of *Millennium*.

—F.M.D. and T.L.D.

Introduction:
Inventing America

Frederick M. Dolan and Thomas L. Dumm

We are presenting the essays gathered in this volume out of a conviction that the struggle over the *representation* of politics in the public spheres of late-twentieth-century America has become the single most important force shaping political life in this country, and that the methods and approaches of political science have proved inadequate for the study of the discourses, imagery, interpretations, and desires attached to practices of representation. Indeed, not only has American political science failed to address what Anne Norton calls "governing representations" of contemporary politics, but it also has done much to obfuscate the political implications of representational practices. It is ironic that in the United States of America, the triumphant product of a spectacular founding fiction, modern political science has chosen to present itself as an attempt to "get real" by turning away from the imaginative productions of political theory and "modeling" the gritty business of competing interests, bargaining, and logrolling as viewed through such methodological lenses as complex correlation study and regression plot analysis.[1] The discipline betrays a longing for precisely what must always be missing from politics, a desire to substitute the putative laws of an imaginary social science for the inherent unpredictability and open-endedness of public life.[2]

The authors brought together here view American politics from a variety of perspectives, but they share the conviction that to approach politics through empirical research on governmental institutions and policy processes, hagiographical studies of constitutional law, and instrumental investigations into who gets what, where, and how is to obscure rather than to reveal the forces shaping political action and judgment in fin de siècle America. For us, Norton's helpfully ambiguous phrase, sliding between adjective and verb, better captures the figures of national identity and national projects that steer and shape American politics. Ours is a republic of words, which also means, necessarily, a republic of fantasies and images. The problem of governing the United States, we submit, is the problem of governing representations: of reinterpreting the phantasmagoric mix of images and tonalities, claims and counterclaims, that shape political discourse in the United States today. And that is to say that government is, strictly speaking, an impossible project—as impossible as predicting and controlling the meanings that will emerge from any text or utterance once it has been submitted to a community of interpreters. That government is "impossible" in this sense does little, however, to inhibit the *will* to control, for political purposes, what is made of words and interpretations. The essays presented here reflect on both the nature of that will and the fate of its representations.

If America is a phantasm, that is because it has always been the dreamscape of European desire, and it is fitting, in the year following the five-hundredth anniversary of Christopher Columbus's voyage, to introduce a collection of essays on practices of representation in American politics with some reflection on the interpretative dimension of the European conquest of America. A point of departure can be found in Edmundo O'Gorman's *Invention of America* (1961), which explores the implications that flow from the simple insight that America could not have been discovered before it had been invented. The trope of discovery, O'Gorman suggests, rests on the assumption that the discoverer knows what he or she is looking for: finding something that was previously hidden and uncovering it reveals the presence of something the discoverer had expected or hoped to find. But America was not to be discovered by Europeans in the way that gold was discovered in California or oil in Alaska. Columbus had no idea what he had "discovered." Not only had he no concept of the existence of the land mass that was to be called America, but he stubbornly resisted the idea when it came to be proposed. What Columbus discovered was India—or, later, once he had reconciled himself to the fact that he had mistaken his destination, Eden. The invention of America, as O'Gorman reminds us, was a gradual and painful encounter of the European imagination with the unexpected: a traumatic confrontation with another world, a human destiny that simply had no place in Christian Europe's Universal History of Mankind. In search of his Oriental Other, a known quantity fulfilling precise functions in a discourse of expansion and colonization, Columbus had stumbled upon the *different*, the wholly unprecedented, a world that had no place on the map of Europe; yet he was relentless in his commitment not to recognize it as such, inventing a new Other in place of the Orient so as not to disturb the fundamentals of the European worldview.[3]

O'Gorman shows how Columbus and his followers' strategy in this regard was to designate the new land mass as an *extension* of the old, just as the word *continent* is a cognate of *continuous*, as in a contiguous or continuous land mass. Before the events we know of as the Age of Discovery, the Earth was thought to consist largely of water. God had planted man on his *Orbis terrarum*, or "island of earth" as O'Gorman translates, a specially created zone comprising Europe, Asia, and Africa that was perfectly suited for human habitation despite the fact that its choicest region, Eden, was now off-limits. Mapping *another* continent demanded theological as well as geographical revisions that would render consonant with Europe's histories, institutions, and myths something that was not supposed to be there. Infusing meaning into this encounter was a matter of governing representation—a complex negotiation of the meaning to be attributed to the land and its peoples; an insistence that the Eurocentric sign govern all subsequent interpretative treatment of the continent. From this perspective, the shock of "discovering" America entailed the gradual invention of the idea of *another world*, another human destiny, another beginning, another fit habitat for "Man." When Hegel, in his lectures on *The Philosophy of History*, called America "the land of the future," proclaiming that "in the ages that lie before us, the burden of the World's History shall reveal itself [in America]," he summed up three centuries of Europe's attempt to understand the unprecedented difference of America as the Other, as Europe's destiny, mirror, past, or absence (87). The New World emerged as an*other* world, not a *different* one; a variation on the European master narrative, not a new genre.

O'Gorman, then, documents the history of a misreading of the different as the Other.[4] From O'Gorman's perspective, however, even more crucial is that the European idea of the world itself was destroyed by this encounter—that is, the world understood, in Clarence J. Glacken's phrase, as a "planned abode for man," a place especially fit for human life. In effect, the Europeans overcame the threat that the unexpectedly different posed to their unified view of the universe by destroying the distinction between the Earth and the World that had secured their identity and replacing it with the idea that the entire universe might be inhabited by those who undertake to make it their own.[5] Those who would be most comfortable in this brave new world were the ones who sought most determinedly to escape from the old order of representation, abandoning Catholicism for an updated Christianity and substituting a labor theory of value for one based on the extraction of gold. Consider John Locke, whose theory of property served as the very fulcrum of the transformation of the world from something Man has inherited into an environment artificially produced by Man. As Hannah Arendt has emphasized, "property" refers, etymologically speaking, to one's own proper place in the world.[6] With Locke, however, what belongs to the human species is no longer a special habitat *given* by nature (or nature's God), but what *individuals* have *made,* in the sense that they have mixed with it all that is "properly" theirs, the ability to fabricate and appropriate. Once property is detached from any sense that the individual belongs anywhere in particular, the very idea of a naturally or divinely appropriate place disappears—if not for Locke himself then, soon enough, for his followers. The New World would then be that portion of the universe as a whole over which Man has successfully extended his dominion. The abolition of rentier and entailment soon after the American Revolution, from this perspective, emerges as a symptom of the accelerated separation of property and place, and of the emergence of a new "governmental state" (in Michel Foucault's phrase), more readily fungible than the old, and also more innovative, more technologically inclined.[7]

In imagining the "discovery" of America as a problem of interpretation, then, it turns out that we have sketched the technological definition of the world—what Martin Heidegger sees as the reduction of the world to a "standing-reserve" of raw material, significant only in relation to the will to order and control ("The Question Concerning Technology" 17–19). But what of the peculiarities that distinguish the political culture that was to emerge in North America? To explore this question, we might ask how the interpretation of modern, Lockean property as a sign of an emerging technological definition of the world might modify the great insight of Louis Hartz, who isolated a peculiarly American and insidious kind of "innocence." For Hartz, the destruction of the indigenous peoples was peripheral to the invention of the United States that took place on the North American continent. Contemplating the Anglo-American conquest of the Indians, Hartz suggests that the subjugation of the continent was not embarked upon with the conscious purpose of a transformative social revolution, because its task was "external and solely external to the social order to which [Americans] belonged" (65). The Indians were "external" in that they were a matter of indifference or unconcern, except as impediments to be cleared away. The newly domesticated Other in America, then, was viewed not as threateningly hostile nor as absolutely different, but as *raw material* to be cleared, amassed, exploited, labored on, and invested. Hartz's notion that in finding America the Europeans found no more than grist for their own designs implicitly construes the founding of the American polity as a technological project.

One may condemn Hartz's insensitivity to genocide, but it would surely be more revealing to pursue why he failed to ask the question of *how* the "other" in America—its forests, its indigenous societies—could be viewed as "mere" otherness, drained of any intrinsic value. For the earliest explorers, as well as for policymakers later, the land and its inhabitants were of course major concerns; relocating the inhabitants and reorganizing their land involved a continual process of interpretation that persists to the present day. Hartz's insistence on innocence emerges as a will to forget that there is nothing natural about apprehending the North American continent as neutral raw material and that the European Americans' inability to respect the intrinsic worth of the North American world itself cries out for understanding.

But there is a further twist to the story, one that returns us directly to our concerns in this volume. According to Heidegger, the emergence of the technological world coincides with the transformation of the world into a representation, a *Weltbild*, a "picture-world." That word order is appropriate because, as he writes, "world picture, when understood essentially, does not mean a picture of the world but the world conceived and grasped as picture. What is, in its entirety, is now taken in such a way that it first is in being and only is in being to the extent that it is set up by man, who represents and sets forth" ("Age of the World Picture" 129–30). The technological definition of the world, and the centrality of practices of representation, are coeval, Heidegger's formulations suggest, because technology emerges as the will to relate to the world in the perspective of the artist, for whom all that exists constitutes mere raw material to be shaped in the process of invention. But as Heidegger adds, "the essence of technology is by no means anything technological." Despite traditional definitions of technology as an instrument for the satisfaction of needs, in fact "we remain unfree and chained to technology," which appears to us as fate, something to which we are "delivered over" ("Question Concerning Technology" 4). And what we are delivered over to are the effects and consequences of our world-picturing, representational practices. Here is another sense, then, in which we might imagine the problem of governing representations as the central political problem—we should not say "for Americans," but rather "on this continent" in the most inclusive sense.

In light of these considerations, we must clarify our contention that America is a republic of words. Of course it is, for all republics have been. But ours is no classical republic; rather, the United States is a postmodern polity, in Jean-François Lyotard's sense of that term, because in American politics what is done with words is *radically* incalculable. Insofar as American politics is shaped in a *plurality* of public spheres rather than by the grammar of a master discourse unquestioningly shared and respected by all, words matter because of their unpredictability, because of what J. L. Austin dubs their "perlocutionary force": their capacity, having once entered the world, to generate effects that cannot be fully anticipated or controlled. The American legislator (or would-be legislator) is no longer in the position of Lyotard's "classicist" who "can write while putting himself at the same time in the position of a reader," but in that of the postmodernist who "no longer knows for whom he writes" and so instead simply casts bottles to the waves to see what sort of ripples they make, what sorts of constituencies form around them (Lyotard and Thébaud 9).[8] American politics is dominated by the perlocutionary force of the utterances that circulate in our public spheres and it has been "from the beginning," for the European "discovery" of America is nothing other than a revelation of difference and contingency that we have yet to face up to. It is the ineluctably postmodern character of our republic of words that stimulates such frenzied efforts to monitor it, to plot the trajectory of its passions and interests, to predict each twitch of the body politic, even though (or rather, because) the attempts of this nation of spin doctors to shape events are inevitably subverted by the perlocutionary force of their own interventions.

As befits citizens of a rhetorical republic, we are left with rhetorical questions, that is, questions formulated without the expectation that they will be definitively answered. Such answers as we have found in the essays that follow are tentative, and subject to revision, not because "further research is needed," but because revision is fitting for an endeavor designed not to foreclose but to open up avenues both for thought and for citizenship.

Notes

1. On metaphysical motifs in postwar American political science, see Dolan, "Representing the Political System: American Political Science in the Age of the World Picture." The irony we refer to here, it should be noted, is neither new nor unique to political science; one of the most pervasive American mythologies figures America as the place where "mere" representation or ideology is overcome and replaced by raw experience. On American literature's persistent attempts to discover "natural" signs of the real, for example, see Kuberski.

2. On the distinctively American fabrication of subjects of agency and instrumental action in the context of a society otherwise too dynamic and robust to bear, see Dumm, *Democracy and Punishment.*

3. Although variations on Columbus's strategy triumphed, we should acknowledge some discordant voices, above all those of Bartolomé Las Casas and Roger Williams.

4. We do not mean to suggest, of course, that O'Gorman's book is the only one to explore a problem that has become extraordinarily urgent over the last few years. For more recent discussions along these lines, see, among many others, Greenblatt, Kibbey, Mason, Rogin, *Fathers and Children,* Simmons, Slotkin, *Regeneration Through Violence,* Todorov, and the essays collected in *Representations* 33 (Winter 1991).

5. Much of the history of this development is discussed in Clarence J. Glacken's classic *Traces on the Rhodian Shore.*

6. For her argument, see Arendt, *The Human Condition* 58–72.

7. On the decline of entailment and rentier in the United States, see Lawrence Friedman, *A History of American Law.* On the consequences for political thought of mobile property in the eighteenth century, see Pocock, *Virtue, Commerce, and History.*

8. In the book from which we quote, Lyotard contrasts the "classical" and the "modern." In subsequent writings, he retains the substance of the distinction but changes the terminology to "modern" and "postmodern." Following his later usage, we refer to the "postmodern." For the rationale behind this terminological change, see Lyotard and Thébaud 16.

Part One   Cold Wars

The essays in *Cold Wars* pose a series of questions about the permanence of the trope of national security. We begin with an intervention by Avital Ronell, who finds in Operation Desert Storm the ghost of World War II as George Bush experienced it. Situating the history of the Bush presidency at both the level of his personal past (through a Lacanian reading of his symbolic lapses and the images of his life as mediated by popular culture) and the technological (extending the network of telephonic communication she elaborates in *The Telephone Book* [1989]), Ronell thinks through the phenomenon of Desert Storm psychoanalytically, the better to recognize the danger of the desire to terminate at the heart of Western *logos*. Seeing in Immanuel Kant's "Perpetual Peace" the paradox of theory worked through to an ambiguous end, she argues for a political theory that intervenes in the real—in the sense of cutting into the psychosis that "really" allows former Vice-President Dan Quayle to suggest that the Holocaust is something that happened "to us." Ronell's essay powerfully rebuts those who would claim that only the most ordinary material interests operate in imperial wars. At the level of representation, recourse to the symbolic becomes a matter of reading the signs made available by the most cautionary of developments of modern thought, the invention of psychoanalysis and the development of mass communications.

If Ronell's tale focuses on the uncanny connections of the symbolic orderings of postwar power, David Campbell emphasizes another register, one on which securing identity is necessarily associated with control over the meaning of danger. The idea of cold wars, for Campbell, becomes a floating signifier that establishes the grounds for a continuous (re)creation of American identity. The genius of cold wars is that, because they are always already under way, the grounds for a secure identity may be given to no one. Campbell traces the peculiar intensity of this problem to American politics, linking the puritan jeremiad, racial purity, and labor struggles to the desire for national security, all of which are episodic eruptions tied to the perceived need to discipline contingency.

While cold wars, it seems, are always with us, the occasional hot one does wonders for reestablishing the symbolic order. Larry N. George shows how the insecurities associated with the collapse of the cold war manifested themselves in the fraternal twin invasions of Panama and Iraq. Drugs, as James Der Derian and Kiarin Honderich emphasize in their study of "narcoterrorism," and as George explores here, have great symbolic value in narratives of control, representing as they do a possibility of letting go that is at odds, to put it mildly, with the pure and stable identity to which conservatives are addicted. George shows how these themes were played out by such conservatives in their attempt, not to keep the cold war mentality alive, but to transfer cold war logic to a postdemocratic polity. George raises the chilling prospect that American citizens are being prepared to accept the terms of postindustrial slave morality: to sacrifice freedom for the wealthy and powerful of the world, who are to be granted a respect far beyond that of democratically elected officials.

If such a slave morality serves to encourage international interventions by the U.S. government while discouraging dissent, it also has chilling effects domestically. Der Derian and Honderich suggest how official stories of "narcoterror" must continuously be deconstructed. As they show in detail, such discourses intensify the culture of suspicion rather than merely exploit it, stimulating domestic surveillance of the most authoritarian kind. Using as their emblematic comparison the story from Stalin's Russia of the child who turned in his kulak father for hiding a pig in his basement, and the proliferation of television shows calling upon Americans to inform on presumptive criminals, Der Derian and Honderich build a strong case for taking seriously the construction of a domestic security state that is, in some particulars, more intrusive than anything imagined by George Orwell.

One danger of cold wars is that they involve secrecy. But revealing the secret is no guarantee that the secret is revealed. Diane Rubenstein employs Lacanian analysis to make sense of what is perhaps the most senseless foreign policy adventure in the last half of the American Century, the Iran-Contra affair. Rubenstein seeks a literal reading of Iran-Contra, that is, one that takes seriously the bodies of the principals of the affair. She therefore examines the inscription of President Reagan's body (cancers of nose and colon), the scatological dimensions of the metaphor of the "leak" (orifices urinary, anal, nasal), and above all the pervasive quality of *silliness* that characterizes the episodes and their denouement. Rubenstein argues that we must not seek to decode the Iran-Contra affair, because the logic of secrecy offers itself as a form of representation, a secret code, a deathbound desire. All codes can be cracked, she seems to suggest, but that assumption is itself a ruse whereby the governmental power of the state is intensified and perfected because its logic of secrecy and unveiling convinces us that we are always at risk in a dangerous world.

1 Support Our Tropes

Reading Desert Storm

Avital Ronell

.01 Going Down in History

According to one version, there was a telephone call that did not take place. This is the version of Saddam Hussein. If the Iraqi troops were remarkably immobilized when they were ordered by George Bush to withdraw from Kuwait, this was because Saddam (so the version goes) was stationed at the reception desk of international politics, waiting for Bush's call. Had that call been completed, claimed Saddam on several occasions, he would have honored the demand of the community of nations for which Bush was the principal operator. But George Bush never placed that call, and Saddam Hussein refused to budge. Instead, Bush called in the tropes—or the armies of metaphors and metonymies, as Nietzsche would say—that were to justify war. For this war, detached from the rhetoric of securing democracy's fragile hold, was about justifying itself: hence the reserve of concepts, such as legitimacy and sovereignty, were called into active linguistic service.

If we begin by establishing the story of a disconnected telephone line, this is for a number of reasons. None of these has much to do with the question of credibility on either side, because that line of questioning has been scrambled by all parties concerned: the war was less a matter of truth than of rhetorical maneuvers that were dominated by unconscious transmission systems and symbolic displacements, which nonetheless have produced real effects. In the first place, the missed telephone appointment that Saddam Hussein has placed at the origin of the war signals at a primary level the electronic impulses that were flowing between powers. Whether or not the crucial telephone call was to be made—Bush was relating full-on to telephonics for the duration of the war—the *atopos* of the telephone created a primal site of technological encounter.[1] This was going to be a war of teletopologies, presence at a distance, which could have been averted, according to the one version, by a telephone call. Saddam Hussein said he would have transferred the locus of power to the Other, provided the Other wasn't going to be a specular other, a mere counterpart and double. No, Saddam Hussein had to hear himself speak through the locus of the Other if he was to cooperate, or at least to feign cooperation, with the community of nations. This is precisely what a telephone call accomplishes: it allows transference to take place in a manner that would supersede a standoff between two egological entities or two continuous subjects; in sum, it programs another algorithm of encounter.

Saddam Hussein, inscribed by Western teletopies and coded by our projection systems, would have answered to his name, he says: he was bound to accept the call, if not the charges. That call, which Saddam said would have made a critical difference in the way the two parties subsequently engaged their lines, never came through. The telecommunicational cast of the Gulf War remains enigmatic (despite so much focus on the participating media technologies) and seems to admit no simple reconstitution of its vicissitudes. For its part, the United States did not put that call through, preferring instead to answer a clearer call to arms. The question is how to trace this call within the dense network of motivation, parapraxes, conscious and unconscious national maneuvers, or even international strategies. The missed call to which Saddam has pointed by no means places him as the principal agency of our inquiry. The point, since there must be one in matters of war, is to take seriously that which disrupted the possibility for communication between US and Them, between US and US. Something is at play here that goes beyond the desire to institute international law, and even beyond our oil addiction. It has to do with compulsion in politics—something that belongs to another scene of articulation. So, in the first place, why did we refrain from including Iraq on the circuit of collective calls? In part because of the different time zones that rendered any simple connection impossible. For George Herbert Walker Bush is a haunted man, and the Middle East remains a phantom territory between the West and its others.

Not that the Middle East was noiseless—ghosts always make their presence known, and sometimes they seem real enough. Except in photo shoots. The call that never came through nonetheless exists. It follows the contours of a disrupted loop or a broken circuit. It presents for us, though in a fugitive manner, an allegory of nonclosure. The Middle East marks the spot to where World War II was clandestinely displaced when its history refused to close upon itself. Political scientists and historians can fill in the blanks better than I could ever hope to, so I will restrict my contribution to pointing to certain mappings of the rhetorical unconscious. This time, when history repeated itself, it was not a joke, but the production of a haunted man to whose systems of repetition compulsion we were all assigned. There was the matter of resurrecting Hitler in the Middle East, and a felt need to control the airspace. The Patriot Missile System perforated two phantasmic oppressions: the Germans had never lost air control in World War II, and George Herbert Walker Bush's was the only one of the three planes on mission to go down that day. When the Avenger plunged into the ocean, young Bush, the youngest fighter pilot in the United States Navy, lost two close friends. Puking from fear and endless seawater, the youngest pilot started attending a funeral whose site he would never be able to pinpoint.

.02 Son of Same

Let me back up. It is not the case *empirically* that the Germans retained air control. But only a naive historicist perspective would disallow the speculative impact historicity genuinely involves. In this analysis, I feel called upon to locate the Gulf War, or the return of the figure of war as such, in the disjunction between empirical history and speculative prolepsis. If we maintain that a major phantasm bequeathed by the Second World War consisted in the desire for a certain closure of air, as it were, this is because one of the dimensions of the war that was left unresolved—unmourned—was both generally, and particularly in the case of George Bush, located off the map, in the air.

How is it that war has returned as the excess of plenitude and the exercise of sovereignty? To be sure, every war is about the presencing of sovereignty, which modern humanism's peace plans, with their absence of grandeur or divine manifestation, have never been able to secure. There is no war—the extreme exercise of sovereign right—that does not claim to disclose a transcendental trace. In this case, technology carried the message from God. But what allowed the sudden remotivation or legitimation of war as the privileged space of national sovereignty? The return of war as a sanctioned figure has everything to do with the return call that at once bypassed Saddam Hussein and destined him as proxy and stand-in for an unresolved break in 1991. What called scores of military phantoms back into action?

World War II invented carpet bombing, creating fire storms. After the experience of mass destruction and victory, however, the Allies concluded that the air war had been ineffectual, even to the point of having increased the duration of the war. The scope of destruction and random targeting would remain in a holding pattern until, at the time of the Gulf War, we took recourse in nuclear and smart bombs, legitimating, that is, their usage. Not only had the air war been ineffectual, but also it had created immense resentment among the civilian populations to whom we henceforth owed restitution. Something else came down from the air as well. When it was decided that the atomic bomb would be deployed, this event was not expected to take on a morally ambiguous cast. The atomic bomb was to accomplish what normally, in the course of carpet bombing, would take three days. The atomic bomb was understood merely to amplify the effects of fire storms. When WWII left the air wide open, we could say that it morally gave notice of an unpaid debt, an account to be settled. For the air had to be disambiguated, rescued, and reterritorialized to a just cause. If a just war were ever to be fought again, it would have to restitute to the skies a moral horizon that would communicate with a failure to close WWII. The smart bomb, which addresses itself to that failure, would outsmart the uneraseable error of WWII; in other words, it would not *smart*. This is not a play on words, though our war includes playing and games. What I am trying to get at is precisely the signifying chains that the phantom of WWII keeps rattling.[2]

The American unconscious has everything to do with riding signifiers on the rebound that, subject as they are at times to retooling, nonetheless return to the haunts of the Same. By retooling, we mean that, while technologizing death, the fundamental idiom still belongs to the tropes instituted in this century by modern warfare. Thus "collateral damage" for instance refashions the industrial production of corpses that Martin Heidegger signaled after WWII, where "friendly fire," while minted by the death denial inclination of California, points to the Pacific and the suicide pact that that side of the war staged through the kamikaze. By the Same we are indicating on another level of discourse that we are guilty of reducing everything to an order of sameness. This is why the very thing responsible for the excess of meaning or otherness occupying the Middle East is being systematically obliterated along the same lines of arrest that had kept Mr. Bush in a forty-year daze. The incredible fact that the Iraqi leader was prompted to pose as Hitler's double (Same), in other words as a by-product of the Western *logos* (it is grotesque to forget that Adolf Hitler was a *Western* production), in itself demonstrates the compulsive aspect of this war.

We are reading a case study of history that presents itself as a symptom. The symptom is that of historical nonclosure and seems in itself to be arrested within a predicament of nonclosure. This war, which masquerades as being "over" (Joyce: "he war," to be read in the Anglo-Germanic space that is opening up before us),[3] has not properly begun to situate its effects: in short, everything was left in the air. This is one reason the war cannot be read according to traditional protocols of historical investigation or even along the lines of strategic or tactical analyses. I am tracing a *phantasmic history.* This is not the result of a whim or an effect of subjective contingency. The phantasmic control systems are out of my hands just as this war left a number of us disarmed. On the eve of German reunification, Goebbels's phrase "new world order" leapt out of his diaries to be recircuited through the ventriloquizing syntax of George Bush. If Saddam Hussein was a prop, it is also the case that this concept functionally suited George Bush. Indeed, we are faced here with the projections of a somewhat more original prop who, in order mythically to fill himself out, needed to rerun through the same war that had knocked him out. This corresponds to a mythic structure of return and second chance that, in life, tends to revert either to the happy few or to the severely neurotic. George Bush was one of them—or rather, two of them. At any rate Bush had always been second and secondary. This was his nature, to be a second nature.

Too young at the advent of WWII, he was destined to be late on arrival. Known as the son of Pres Bush, vice-prez to the undead Reagan, a simulating machine par excellence, he was to become the uncanny president of the end of the millennium. Something went into suspense or responded to the clandestine command, "Freeze!" when he lost his two friends. It was as if George Bush had been arrested, which is why his iconic relation to his wife, for instance, looks as though he had struck a deal with a soul murderer, giving the couple the disjunctive look of a moment in *The Picture of Dorian Gray.*

It has been suggested that George Bush had the luck of encountering the Oedipal taboo head-on: he was permitted actually (symbolically) to marry his mother, thus turning back the interdictory power of the law. With paternal law falling down, crashing out of the sky, the symbolic register is exposed to the most serious effects of scrambling. In the first place, this predicament maintains him in the position of son, ever competing with an ineffectual father (this was played out with Reagan, whom he has meanwhile all but banished from the White House). Second, the prez will have experienced fusional desire and the illicit communions that will have proliferated from this "experience"—we are referring to his special missions directed by God, represented here on earth on the eve of the Gulf War by Billy Graham, with whom Bush spent the night. Perhaps we need to take a closer look at the situation. This look will not constitute the voyeur's gaze into a privately circumscribed space, but will open out onto the unconscious mappings that we are endeavoring to retrieve.

The Bush couple is proud of the generational difference that their union appears to mark. Barbara refuses to mask or suppress the mark of difference that in fact exposes a fusional desire. I am not saying that the male subject should abstain from locating his desire in an "older woman"; that would be absurd and out of sync with the times. I am saying rather that the first couple stages its communion within the precincts of nonhistorical difference. While Barbara Bush has grown into her age—the end of the twentieth century—George Bush will not grow, he cannot age, and this in turn reflects the ahistorical fusions that his tenure accomplishes. (The scandal of difference that the first couple inscribes is displaced onto the family pet, Millie. After Bush was elected prez, the first couple announced the ritual copulation of Millie with a purebred, which, in dog language, means Aryan. Hence the Millie-Vanilli prez who would fuse and simulate histories was to oversee pure generational evolution. Indeed, Millie was so exceptionally evolved that she wrote the autobiography ventriloquized by Barbara Bush. Millie shared not only the couple's secrets but their diseases as well. The phantasms of which Millie Bush is sole receptacle will have to be treated elsewhere.)

While Bush stands arrested, his language spinning accidently out of control, Barbara withers. She is the figure in the couple who mourns: attributing her gray hair—an overnight job—to the grief she suffered over a deceased child (a Robin), she also took a downward plunge a week before the bombing of Iraq started. Sliding downhill on a sled, Barbara Bush breaks a hip joint. The couple is disjointed, a connection dislocated. With the guilty part and partner externalized and maternalized, George Bush can go on with his business unfeelingly. If he cried uncontrollably at the event of his crash, his language oddly obsessed on his unwillingness to shed a single tear over the dead of the Gulf War (he shared this charming attribute with General Schwarzkopf). There is a whole history of pressing tears here on which Barbara bloats and George—well, he sees, he says, he feels, no reason to grieve. With Barbara as shock absorber and Millie as totemic father or expulsed superego, Geo-Bush somnambulizes as he occupies uninterrogated lands of the dead. (Only after the replay, in Christian rallies, he lets drop a tear: major breakthrough for the one who could not mourn.) One thing, perhaps, has become clear for us: the way that the first couple presents itself is not merely a matter for quirky pomo readability. Everything that Bush does is a matter of presencing for a dead center that keeps on replicating itself. Catching up to first place, first couple, first superpower, Bush is still running behind, fluttering and second, America is losing the races; like Bush, it is losing heart, faltering in full regression. Everything that George Bush has done is intended to efface history, or to bring it back to pre–civil rights days, and so forth, in other words to bring it back to the day of the crash.

With GeoBush at the helm we can only go down, crash—or turn around. This is the field of his rhetorical unconscious. Hence the strange and belated evocation of the "line in the sand," which, presenting itself spatially as a deadline, came too late. All of Bush's politics depends on reversing the order of the "too late," reproducing the deadline after it has passed, going back on history.

.03 On Raising the Parataxes

George Bush's couplings appear to demonstrate the principle of non-linkage. In other words, the other is a locus of profound connectivity that first has to be articulated in order to be disavowed. His history as vice-prez is summed up in the notorious avowal of May 1988: "For seven and a half years, I have worked alongside [Reagan] and I am proud to be his partner. We have had triumphs, we have made mistakes, we have had sex." Recovering this lapsus (he means "we have had setbacks"), he elaborates the scene of parataxes by comparing himself to a "javelin thrower who won the coin toss and elected to receive" (Roberts A32).[4] Others have adequately noted the "wimp factor" that dominated Bush's electoral anxieties—being second to the top, at the feminized receiving end—and now he has to turn things around via anal-sadistic military penetrations to equally feminized territories. Curiously, Bush's initial correction reveals the proximity of sex and setback, which is to say the backslide of projected progress, the place of impasse. The substitution of sex for setback, which in this context refers to Bush's secondary position within a structure of the couple, reveals as well the libidinal investment in the setback—which is to say, in the reversal, postponement, delay, which must be surmounted. It further shows that setback for Bush is beyond the pleasure principle and in the service of repetition and the death drive.

On the other end of Mr. Bush's couplifications, on the receiving end, we encounter the absolute *dummy* both in the Lacanian and popular senses of the term. The name of the symptom: Dan Quayle. As dummy par excellence, he ventriloquizes with exceptional precision the breaches in presidential linguistics. He exists, as Bush's political double or other, as that which cannot be; he scans as a sign for the impossibility of becoming-president. As ventriloquizing locus and externalization of the president's inarticulable phantasmata, Dan Quayle dramatizes the executive desire for historical effacement. He is moreover the figure that George Bush has chosen to replace and repeat himself, to fill his space and articulate its contours. Where Bush restricts his elliptical performances of linguistic nonclosure to sex/setback sets, believing also that *"comme ci comme ça"* is a popular Hispanic phrase, and uttering other confusions that name themselves (George Bush's lapses are frequently metacommentaries: the setback names the lapsus he has just committed *comme ci comme ça* the "undecideds," which can go either or both ways, etc.), Dan Quayle discloses himself as if to let the prez speak through an empty body-as-megaphone; he is a broadcast system switched on by the sinister vicissitudes of Bushian desire. When George Bush says, "Read my lips," he means look into the gaping abyss—the yawn—and listen to Dan Quayle. (In French, Bush is pronounced *Bouche,* the word for mouth.) One could offer a compelling, if not compelled reading of Bush and Quayle as a mutant breed of cyburban cowboys, particularly given Bush's simulated address in and from Texas, a hotel in Houston. For our purposes, however, I am going to treat the Bush/Quayle couple as a single entity or utterance machine, with the sole purpose of analyzing their dehistoricizing desire. For all its emptiness and technobody hollows, the prez–vice-presidential machine targets the lack in the Other in a continual setback of friendly fire.

Of the lapses that have been noted in the repertoire of this administration, one in particular puts the *achronos* and *atopos* of the war in uncanny perspective: "The Holocaust was an obscene period in our nation's history. I mean this century's history. But we all lived in this century. I didn't live in this century" (Simms 128). The Bush-Quayle machine has produced a rich utterance that at first sight appears to confirm Mary McGrory's insight that "the non sequitur is the one grammatical [*sic*] form Bush has mastered" (Rubenstein 260). Clearly, this assertion is somewhat ironic, for the non sequitur is precisely that which eludes mastery, marking as it does a gap, the abyss of nonlinkage. Diane Rubenstein has identified this tendency to skip a beat semantically as the binary logic that would oppose the office of presidential speech to the couch of analysand: "For Bush's digressions, non sequiturs, lapses, repetitions recall those of an analysand rather than the narrative closure of an authorial subject [i.e., the President of the United States . . .]. One of Bush's most interesting and parodied linguistic tropes is his use of the word 'thing' " (Rubenstein 261). I shall get to thingification momentarily, though we are already following a logic of the automatons.

First let me gloss the slippage that locates the Holocaust on our shores. In fact the (vice-)presidential unconscious knows how to read, and like the essence itself of the unconscious it stakes out the timeless, refusing contradiction: the Holocaust was a moment in American history says the (vice-)president of the United States. This general assertion is followed by a single subject's intentional inflection ("I mean this century's history"), then it reverts to the general assertion again ("But we. . . ."), and reverts once more to a particularized subject's predicament ("I didn't live in this century"). This subject, as pure subject of enunciation and inscription, is a dead subject who makes claims for not having lived in this century or rather, for not having lived according to calendrical or historical time. Everyone lived in this century ("we all lived"), but the speaker himself did not experience this century, which in his transmission metonymically displaces "the Holocaust." The (vice-)presidential unconscious knows that it does not know the Holocaust, but this unknowing is obtained only as a condition of not having lived in this nation/century. The geo- and chronopolitical map of this administration's compulsion is being disclosed here. The confusion of space and time crucially underscores the possibilization of essential analogy. But beyond the structure that permits our nation to incorporate the grotesque history of Germany or Poland—an outstanding debt for which we inheritors of Nazism still have to pay—Dan Quayle speaks for an administration that will not have lived. As Bush's hologram, this total-recall machine (which lives with all memory but cannot live in time or with introjection) also prints out its participation in the presidential death drive.

If his compulsive program is associated with the death drive, this by no means constitutes a way of putting down Mr. Bush or that which lip syncs him. In fact, it offers a compliment, one that possibly overestimates the presidential reserve of libido. The death drive is understood both by Freud and by Lacan as a normal paradox of bioinstinctual setback for our species. The Bush/Quayle entity may well extend beyond the death drive, which is to say at the limit of the domain of drives (*Triebe*). Going this way or that, they have mutated into a function of thingification where they are placed under instinctual arrest. I in no way intend simply to condemn one man or one man's symptomatology. It may be the case that one has to draw the line somewhere; but, as Heidegger has suggested in another contextual milieu, let us first contemplate that line.

One might easily be drawn into the reactive posturing that elicits condemnation. And yet, this precisely is the time—most "moral" of times—to resist condemnation. Perhaps such a politics of utterance deserves some explanation. Having supplanted rigorous analysis, condemnation, as if to build a roadblock to thinking, has been expressed too often and possibly too recklessly with historically signified villains. I have no interest in attacking one man or his singular decoy—this would be too metaphysical a gesture and would accomplish no more than to locate the origin of event or History in a single (male) Subject. That would be the easy way out: to pin the blame on a proper name that is placeholder for an entire symptomatology of peoples. The question has to be, rather, Why was it possible for George Bush to be president? Why was it possible, at this particular moment in history, for Saddam Hussein to pose as Adolf Hitler? Whether or not you voted, protested, freaked out, or elected one or another mode of passivity, it is a question of our history.[5]

The war is what we share—even if this should be exercised in the mode of repression or according to the injunction to forget. As the (vice-)presidential utterance has disclosed, the boundaries around the place of occupation, according to spatial and temporal determinations, are difficult to fix. This is why it is necessary to resist condemning one person or even one form of substance dependency, such as oil, as having exclusive rights over catastrophic blindness, for condemnation has never brought any serious analysis to term. Thus Jean-Luc Nancy crucially observes that "condemnation, by itself, tells us nothing about what made possible that which is condemned . . . condemnation keeps at a distance, along with the condemned, the question of what it is that made their guilt possible" ("Our History" 106).

.04 $

In an essay that resists treating but names the cases of Paul de Man and Martin Heidegger, Nancy argues that it is our history as such that has been put in question and abeyance by such "cases":

> In any case it seems as if recent history were multiplying individual "cases," for all that they are very different, in order to force us to ask this question [Can our history continue simply to represent itself as History, as the general program of a certain Humanity, a Subject, a Progress—a program that would only have been, can still only be troubled by accidents, by foreign bodies, but not *in itself* and as such?]. It is surely not by chance. For thirty years, self-assurance preserved or achieved at the conclusion of the war (assurance, or the fierce will to be reassured) has caused us to misconstrue the question. In the first place, a marxist self-assurance, whatever its form or consistency. But also, a techno-scientific one; and a democratic-progressivist one. In one way or another, it was the assurance of a certain "destination," come from way back, able to lead us far. But these assurances have worn away, or collapsed, and our history asks how we ever came to this point. The question can no longer be avoided. We cannot be content with affirming that there were "errors," and "mistakes," nor be content with denouncing them. Fundamentally, we all know that very well. Everything that claims to escape this knowledge is only pitiful dissimulation. ("Our History" 101)

Our history asks how we ever got to this point. We are responsible to our history, for which we have to answer. Setback. Cutback. *Finback.* The call for spiritual renewal "already had a certain history behind" it. In the West, history has always been a history of reappropriated crashing—something that we still need to explain, or rather, to respond to as the desire of metaphysics.

The chain of certitudes through which it is transmitted destines metaphysics, in its last spasm, to the objectification of world in technology. When Heidegger writes about our unshieldedness, he reluctantly recruits Rilke, perhaps the last mortal to have experienced in nature the Open. In the grips of technological dominion, where no mark can be zoned outside of us to land in some circumscribed area of non-contamination, man now negotiates the mutation of metaphysics and History at the unmarked frontiers of the technosphere. Since World War II, technology—including computer technology—and the promise of spiritual renewal have been going steady. Can we take a closer look at this hypothetical assertion? FREEZE-FRAME BLOWUP: George Herbert Walker Bush in the open seas, the navy will not come back for him, they were on their last mission and were moving out. Endless open sea. Leo Nadeau used to say the Avenger could fall faster than it could fly. Nothing works—even the parachute proves defective:

> By rote, he found the rip cord, and the chute opened, but it was torn. . . . He was falling fast . . . bleeding. . . .—Doug West. He'd seen the blood on Bush's face, dropped a medical kit. Bush hand-paddled for it. . . . There was no paddle. There was no fresh water. The container in the raft had broken in the fall. Bush was paddling with both hands, puking from fear and seawater, bleeding from the head. He got his med kit and with a shaky left hand swabbed at himself with iodine. He got out his .38 revolver and checked it. (Cramer 74)

He is bleeding. And then it happens, something that will recur incessantly through the peculiar circuitry of the unconscious. In the Open, George Herbert Walker Bush discovers God in technology. The submarine that emerged out of nowhere, the apparition of pure delivery, rose out of the infinite sublime. When the sky crashed into the ocean, God answered the call technologically. God's name, at that moment, flashed onto the sideboard of the metallic surge: it was *Finback*.

Finback was the name of the sub that rescued George Bush. Three thousand miles of ocean. They came to get him. And they filmed him. "And the seaman he saw was standing there, watching with this thing up to his face, a camera, a movie camera. They were filming" (Cramer 80). It was known that the men in the crew loved their job. An unconscious pilot would awaken; he would learn that he was alive, rescued. The future would happen. But George Bush in a sense was destined to remain unconscious. When he awoke, for a brief spell, back then, he cried, he was delirious. He wanted his friends. He was young, he was *hysterical*. No matter what they did, George Bush would never learn that he was alive after that day.

Finback will be the name of this war, but also of the history of metaphysics. Read bifocally, in French and English, it refers us back to an end, the apocalyptic condition for any happening. The end will have come "back then," in the wake of an emerging submarine or in another version of *Finnegans Wake*, in the endless parlor where World War II refused the movement toward its own burial. Finback is the promise of a comeback, a second coming that, like the promise of the infinite, can only take place in finity. Finback means that the end is behind us: "They had behind them, perhaps, in a sense, something that derived from our entire history. Did not the West begin by being, simultaneously, the acknowledgment of its own decline and the demand for its own renewal? Was it not Athens which longed for the time of Solon, and Plato who called for renewal?" (Nancy, "Our History" 108). This is a question of our own history, involving the production of our own identity, and the will to be origin and end to ourselves. "To inaugurate a new era in order to reanimate the breath of a spirit weakened by the accidents to recover a destiny, an epic, the organic growth of the spirit or of man—that is what it means or has meant to possess the *meaning* of history. . . . It knows accidents, precipitous declines, regressions, but its meaning is forever available to it, and it can always reconvoke itself once again to the undertaking of some renewal, some setting straight, some rediscovery" (108).

Locked into the pose of the one rescued, the guilty survivor—he had sent his boys to die—Bush was delivered to a history of denial and compulsive repetition. To be sure, death or pain or catastrophe, each in its singularity, does not possess any historicity whatsoever but can only retrospectively acquire enough velocity to constitute a narrative event. Taking refuge in submersion and repression, history was going to insinuate itself through the untapped disruption that punched a permanent hole in the real. Tightfisted and knotted up by the near miss, George Bush would never depropriate his history enough in order to set forth those conditions that might guarantee a future yet-to-come. He would never be able to let go of the totalized, if lost, meaning that his "precipitous decline" immediately acquired. Instead, he got married real fast, graduated from Yale, and went into the oil business. But oil was not nowhere. Odessa, Texas, was a desert back then, a site of deprivation where George and Bar could repel the aggressive incursions of melancholia. If God and technology continued to go steady in those earth-poking days, there was no breakup in sight. In fact, God and technology were to be engaged in the Gulf War.

.05 Eating Broccoli

George Bush[6] connected the deserts in his life by a thin thread. The temporal structure of this connection was exposed perhaps when in January 1991 he drew a "line in the sand." What kind of figure did this gesture cut? At first glance, it seems straightforward enough. George Bush was issuing an ultimatum. Yet, what concerns us is the rhetorical dimension of this act. A rather ordinary performative speech act, it spatially meant to designate a point beyond which the Iraqis must not pass. The line was evoked, however, *after* Iraq had crossed the Kuwaiti border. The line in fact functioned less as a spatially conceived marker than as a temporally pointing one. What it was pointing at was a deadline. But what sort of a contract was this line drawing up? It was a line that turned back upon itself because it was intended to designate Iraqi withdrawal, a double line of the *re-trait*. In ordinary language usage, a line in the sand does not mean that one is supposed to fall back on the other side of the line, but usually means its opposite. Figuring a deadline, expiration date, and promise, the line in the sand troped instead the time limit of an hourglass. Like an hourglass, however, it was about reversal and turning things around as a measure of time. The line in the sand, catechrestically deployed, posed an ultimatum for what already had transpired in the form of a morally inflected imperative: this boundary crossing should not have occurred. The line, as line of impasse or imperfect past, implemented the signature of reversal and repetition by means of which this war would be authorized.

Still, what is a line in the sand but a sign of its own effacement, a writing of disaster that territorializes the past on the ground of shifting sands? Promised to erasure, the line in the sand figurally says the forgetting to which this war was doubly committed. A figure of immediacy, masquerading in clarity of contour, the line, as word, is that which cannot be kept. In fact, it already points to a word not kept, for the Iraqis had already been granted permission, by diplomatic channels of ambiguity, to cross the line. This in part explains why the line can only point to the suspension of any clear demarcation. Ever pointing to its obliteration in time, it is not a line capable of guaranteeing even its own future, much less *the* future. Nonetheless, it is the line that we were fed.

To the extent that this line at all invites readability, it constitutes a catechrestic metalepsis—arguably the structure itself that dominated the "events" of the Gulf War, where nothing was new under the sky. Let me recapitulate: As a boundary not to be crossed, the line in the sand presented itself as moot, for the war was said to have originated in a crossed boundary. It therefore inscribes a boundary that ought not to have been crossed, a moral line, in fact, that says: This is where America draws the line. As Mad-Maxed out as it may have seemed in the inscription of its fury and spontaneity, this line in the sand pointed us to the past in general, and to the phantom double of this line that ought not to have been crossed. George Bush, youngest fighter pilot of WWII draws the line at this time; he comes of age. Which age?

The line in the sand is, we shall see, not drawn across an indifferently figured body. This body was named a feminine body time and again, a mother's body, and a body subject to rape. A psychology of international relations is taking shape (this is not my invention but a contribution of those who have psychologized and pornographized the "enemy," the invention of those who have made this a war, once again, of the sexes). Where has this land feminization (be)gotten us? Somewhere between the realignment of reunified Germany and Japan, prior to the sexual warfare that informed the Clarence Thomas hearings, George Bush drew a line in the sand. As America loses its bearings, as faltering empire (another useful myth), the president, an eternal son not up to the task, will also have traced out a line of castration. But I want at all costs to prevent precipitous decline and steer us slowly over this heavily symbolized terrain. A great deal has returned to haunt us now, making it hardly surprising that we are inundated by a rhetoric of restoration and reversal. The phantomic return triangulating—once again—Germany, Japan, and America has motivated the pathos with which this administration goes about restoring the national phallus to its proper place.

The narrative of purloined oil wells crudely illustrates the stakes of this dramatic replay. Indeed, as slippery as this may seem, the possession of oil wells marked in the 1940s a critical moment in the strategies of national desire. In the 1940s the State Department described Mideast oil as "a stupendous source of strategic power, and one of the greatest material prizes in the world history," "probably the rightest economic prize in the world in the field of foreign investment" (Beinin 1). After the war, Eisenhower called the Mideast the "most strategically important area in the world." Further, at "the end of World War II, when immense petroleum deposits were discovered in Saudi Arabia, Secretary of the Navy James Forrestal told Secretary of State Byrnes, 'I don't care which American companies develop the Arabian reserves, but I think most emphatically that it should be American'" (Beinin 11). After WWII the Americans acquired Saudi concessions for themselves, freezing out the British and the French.

Regardless of the real import of oil, there is no economy that is not also a libidinal economy, or that does not resignify symbolic deposits of national desire. *Z Magazine* reminds us that in the view of the *New York Times*, "an object lesson in the heavy cost must be paid" when an oil-rich Third World nation "goes berserk with fanatical nationalism" (Beinin 10). *Z* justly remarks that going "berserk" with "fanatical nationalism" is the *Times's* way of describing a Third World nation expecting to benefit from its own resources. In part, though, ownership—the values ascribed to property, propriety, the proper—has gone largely symbolic, which is why the so-called Third World slips into an altogether different space of engagement. This is not to deny the value of those discussions organized around capital motivation—but that alone is not what resurrected the respectability of warfare or created the referential indetermination of what is going on. While Japan, Germany, and America triangulate into a new phase of Oedipal self-patterning—one that does not permit genuine ambivalence but is staked on repression and obsessive replay—we must not allow ourselves to forget the fourth term, or the displacement to what is being called the Middle East, at once the most artificial and originary of historical mappings.

.06 "It is true that tropes are the producers of ideologies that are no longer true" (De Man)

We have until now considered the question from the side of war. Is there another side? In a sense, this war declared itself, when it declared itself, as a war about forgetting War. It was as if it wanted to play itself out on impasse, something accomplished by pressing the RECORD and ERASE function keys. In any case, this reflects the way the war was "covered" by the media, simultaneously recording and erasing its referential track. At the same time as past wars were being done with, this war opened the line of vision for the institution of future wars. A war to end War in order to begin wars, this one wanted to start from scratch (chicken scratch or turkey shoot). It is a matter of civility to declare each gruesome war the last one. Modern warfare has largely been conducted with the stated aim of ending war or of safety checking democratic roadways. Now America is chattering openly about future wars and what we learned from the test site called Iraq.

Let us take a brief technological reality check: third-rate Patriot missiles encountered fifth-rate, merely *ballistic* scud missiles, triggering mythic defense narratives. This is like getting off on a police stick. Obviously, a couple of smart bombs were on the loose, promoting the fiction that a missile always reaches its destination.[7] This fiction is of course crucial: it upholds our history, our metaphysics, our appropriated meaning—all of which are about to meet their destination. But what if they've got the wrong address, and what if the future is not about restoring the phallus—or, for that matter, woman—to a proper place? What is the proper place of this war in our destiny? Why have we mortals never been able to act nonteleologically? And why did destiny shift its site to the nomadic desert spaces where it is said that Moses once broke the tablets of the law, Jesus of Nazareth was pinned to the cross, and the Sphinx asked you, What is man? Not to mention Allah. . . .

No discourse or act of war can put an end to war. War offers community the image of its sovereign exposition to death.[8] Because it stages the infinity of a finitude that encounters its end, war collectivizes and stimulates to life by its horror. Little has matched the pure excess that war draws to its occurrence, as a kind of ransom for the future. As the literature of virility and heroism, war is "the monument, the feast, the somber and pure sign of the community expressing its sovereignty" (Nancy, "Guerre, Droit, Souveraineté—Techné" 37). Each time, it arrives as the "once and for all" of a promised catharsis. Except, possibly, in Vietnam, where war became shameful and our boys, abject. A kind of *conscientious abjection* took hold, and this ran interference with the loaded circuits that coded WWII.

If war has meant so much to us, how are we to let go of its power to fascinate and entrance? There is only the imperative ideal of peace. Peace is not the opposite of war, but its absolute other—something that we have never as such experienced. This in part is because peace, to be what it is, predicates the infinite where war is finite. War in fact aligns itself with the Western appropriation of meaning. Establishing epistemic breaks, a radical possibilization of the Idea in history, of decision, war has functioned as the special megaphone of the Western *logos*. It has been, in our history, a way of achieving resolution through finitizing acts of containment. Thus even this war was waged against the non-finite, uncontrolled effects of past wars in recent history.

War has articulated a readable mode of *decision* to which God, nation, and other transcendental recruits have been called. It is the way the West was won. This has everything to do with truth and the apocalyptic conditions for revealing truth in its transparency. In the history of beings and the history of Being, war is truth. At least, it has been inscribed unfailingly as the necessary road to truth or to a justice rendered beyond the suspension and constitutive blindness that justice in fact figures. The decisive truth of war locates the premises upon which justice can no longer be suspended. This has been our history's way of putting behind us the undecidables. It amounts to nothing less than the Western compulsion to "finish with," that is, to reach the finish line. But this finish line, and the arrogant impatience that drives us toward it, is, we have seen, nothing but a line in the sand. Still, it has been drawn by language and *logos*. Precisely because war feeds the truth machine, aiming for truth, destinal arrival and the clean cut of history, it is our task as thinkers to decelerate finitude's thrust and abide with the inconceivable horizon of an infinite unfinished. What would it mean *not* to close a deal with transcendence, or to desist from following a path of resurrected war aims? What would it mean to follow a politics of radical nonclosure, leaving time as well as borders open to the absolute otherness that must accompany genuine futurity? The line in the sand, as the sign of the figural deconstruction of its literal meaning, promises divisibility as well as infinite granules of pathless randomness and essential aberration that can never be simply appropriated to the sure movement of a path, whether or not it leads "nowhere." The desert commits itself to the abolition of path.

To the extent that we have to renounce "finishing with" and dealing final notice, Western *logos* must learn to open its Faustian fist; indeed, to desert the explosions of otherness that the *logos* has always detonated. For these reasons I have relied upon psychoanalysis to help count the losses. For psychoanalysis, besides reading war, has taught us in this century to be wary of the desire for termination and has exemplarily, if relentlessly, advocated the interminable nature of working through. While it nonetheless posits a term, psychoanalysis also knows about the production of unknown meaning and the ineluctable deviance inflecting normal self-constitution, be this of a nation state or the human subject. In an uncharacteristically simple composition of formulas, psychoanalysis has known from the start that it may be, for us in our history, a matter either of interminable or exterminable. But psychoanalysis has also met the limits of theorizing its knowledge. It reads from layerings of silence and repression, if only to slow down the inclines of the death drive, with which we shall never be finished. Like a woman's work, psychoanalysis's job is never done. In the future, I daresay, the prerequisites for presidential candidacy, besides the restrictions pertaining to age and citizenship, will include a growing demand for health checks and balances, namely, in addition to doctors' reports, appropriate certificates of therapy.

The Gulf War, which was meant to put to rest other wars whose wounds would not close, resurrected the respectability of war as a moment in Western discourse or polemics. While we obviously resisted opening diplomatic channels and producing a choiceful situation, it is not the case simply that we refused to negotiate. Rather, quick polemological tactics supplanted negotiation as a more efficient means of finishing with the problem. It is also the case that video games, with their teleological imperatives, have largely replaced the open-ended reading of books in our culture. Yet to the extent that the war followed, at least in stated principle, strict guidelines, United Nations discussions, telephone treaties, and the Geneva Convention, the war as it was conducted cannot be seen in simple opposition to diplomacy. Of course, as Nietzsche has said about history, it is all a matter of dosage.

.07 Downloading

It was Kant who tried to teach us that peace must be rigorously established. In his uncannily timely *Perpetual Peace: A Philosophical Sketch* (1795) Kant outlines the dangers of a progressive technologization of the troop, anticipating the rhetoric of collateral damage and surgical strike ("man is thrown into the same class as other living machines," "paying men to kill or be killed appears to use them as mere machines and tools," and "subjects are used and wasted as mere objects," etc. [107, 133, 127, 112]). By delicacy of operation and telescoping of futural vision, this work evokes an emphatic sense of being "on location." It is, when reading *Perpetual Peace,* as if Kant had been piloting *Finback* that day, looking forward and back, reading a special clarity from the skies whose open-endedness ought never to have obscured our history. Among the critical interventions that his text makes on behalf of an enduring peace, he warns:

> A war of punishment (*bellum punitivum*) between nations is inconceivable (for there is no relation of superior and inferior between them).
> From this it follows that a war of extermination—where the destruction of both parties along with all rights is the result—would permit perpetual peace to occur only in the vast graveyard of humanity as a whole. Thus, such a war, including all means used to wage it, must be absolutely prohibited. But that the means named above inexorably lead to such war becomes clear from the following: Once they come into use, these intrinsically despicable, infernal acts cannot long be confined to war alone. This applies to the use of spies (*uti exploratoribus*), where only the dishonorableness of *others* (which can never be entirely eliminated) is exploited; but such activities will also carry over to peacetime and will thus undermine it. (139)

It is interesting to note that Kant counts the necessity for ensuring the survival of peoples along with that of rights, offering them each the same ontological peace dividend. This suggests that war exceeds rights while it nonetheless, as the prerogative of power, proceeds from a concept of the rights of sovereignty. As long as there is a national entity war is within the realm of rights, even though it threatens the survival of individual rights or a more transcendental bill of rights. The nation enjoys a sovereign right to go to war, and thus to destabilize the rights for which it may be ostensibly fighting. This contradiction belongs to the essence of the nation state. War, according to Jean-Luc Nancy, in fact exposes the "sovereign exception" that it institutes within the realm of rights. Clearly, what needs to be rethought is the legitimacy of national sovereignty and of everything that is implied thereby. But as long as national identity continues to assert its historical "necessity," what becomes of the ideal of sovereign peace?

The problem that Kant faces in the entire essay involves the deflection of perpetual peace from its semantic hole in the graveyard: Could there be a movement of peace that is unhitched from the death drive? Does the duty we have toward peace necessarily have to have as its background music that radical tranquility which resonates with "rest in peace"? If Kant can only draw a philosophical sketch of peace, this is because his leanings push him toward the edge of undecidability where absolute peace, like war, means you're dead. To get out of the peace cemetry, Kant will have to institute dissonant performative speech acts; in other words, he will have to declare a certain type of war on war.

Kant is perfectly aware of the rhetorical difficulties that face any linguistic mobilization on behalf of peace. To preempt the inevitable strike of war (we earthlings have not known empirically or historically a warless time zone), he will begin parergonally with ironic deterrents. Later on the argument will move into more transcendental fields when, for instance, Kant proposes "the transcendental principle in publicity," which basically opposes all forms of secrecy, saying, "if I cannot *publicly acknowledge it* without thereby inevitably arousing everyone's opposition to my plan, then this necessary and universal, and thus *a priori* foreseeable, opposition of all to me could not have come from anything other than the injustice with which it threatens everyone" (135–236). The transcendental formula of public right comes down to this maxim: "All actions that affect the rights of other men are wrong if their maxim is not consistent with publicity." It is only under the transcendental concept of public right, linked to publicity, that an agreement can be reached between politics and morality. To guarantee this agreement Kant initiates "another transcendental and affirmative principle of public right" whose explanation he however indefinitely postpones, breaking off the essay with the promise for a future unfolding of perpetual peace ("I must postpone the further development and explanation of this principle for another occasion"). The principle in question reads: "All maxims that *require* publicity (in order not to fail of their end) agree with both politics and morality" (139).

Though unfinished, the essay nonetheless names the fulfillment of its terms, namely, the establishment of "perpetual peace, which will follow the hitherto falsely so-called treaties of peace (which are really only a suspension of war)" (139). This replacement of the peace treaty with genuine, lasting peace, Kant assures, "is no empty idea, but a task that, gradually completed, steadily approaches its goal." But was not the hope for peace staked in the abandonment of goal or teleological fulfillment? The disjunction, I believe, accounts for the constitutive incompletion of the text, which performs its inability to reach an end or fulfill a goal, consequently swerving in its performance from the finite repetition of war. Postponing itself perpetually, the text opens out to meet the starry sky that Kant saw above his head, granting flexed suspension. It is within this pause between the performative inauguration of peace and the postponement to which its fulfillment is subject, that Kant can make out the fragile sketch of a perpetual peace. Refusing to end, Kant sends us back to the beginning of this text, which never quite gets off the ground but is all the more powerful for it.

The problem for Kant, and for us, is getting started on the peace march. Kant enumerates his war grievances in the first section and prepares the ground for the installation of a perpetual peace. The first section issues as an instituting injunction that "1. No treaty of peace that tacitly reserves issues for a future war shall be held valid" (107). Kant explains: "For if this were the case, it would be a mere truce, a suspension of hostilities, not *peace*, which means the end of all hostilities, so much so that even to modify it by 'perpetual' smacks of pleonasm" (107). In sum, a peace treaty would be self-annulling to the extent that its raison d'être is expected to crumble. A true peace treaty would constitute the war on war par excellence, and therefore suspend its function as a mere contractual deal among nations. A contract, as Benjamin will later point out in his *Critique of Violence*, always implies its own suspension, or a return to violence in the event that one of the parties should fail to honor its terms.[9] A contract or treaty therefore belongs to the pervasive logic of war, offering little to effect the disinstallation of war in our history.

But if we choose to cite Kant at the unclosing end of the Gulf War, it is also in order to retrieve his frame. For who has not suffered despondency these past several years (the manic victory allowances are in fact part of the experience of despondency, though on the more unsavory side of disavowal)? Who has not felt the *paradox of abortion* performed on the body of history, pregnant with the future?

Kant's frame, in any case, contains its own ironic destruction. If it is to be part of the experience of knowing peace, the essay nonetheless forces him to deliver a few punch lines. A doubling up in laughter (or in pain) marked by the initial breakthrough accompanies the mood of essential peacemaking. The initial breakthrough quickly stalls, however. "To Perpetual Peace," the essay begins; but this beginning is also an end, shadowing as it does the death of that which has not as yet come to be. One can never be sure if we are engaged in a ceremonial performative of clinking champagne glasses or if we are not saying, rather, "In Memoriam: To PP." Precisely because of this chasm of indecision, it is necessary to follow Kant, repeating his gesture, if only to inscribe ourselves by *affirming* castration, which is to say, by putting ourselves in the place of the destitute other without displacing or colonizing this other.

Kant's question begins with the undecidable nature of PP. Is it beyond the pleasure principle, on the side of death and absolute quiescence, or can it be achieved by finite beings? "To PP," as it turns out, is a citation that opens up the undecidable: "Whether this satirical inscription on a certain Dutch shopkeeper's sign, on which a graveyard was painted, holds for *men* in general, or especially for heads of state who can never get enough of war, or perhaps only for philosophers who dream that sweet dream, is not for us to decide" (107). Nonetheless, or even because we cannot decide the readability of the inscription—which is generalizable to the sign of signs, the ensepulchered *seme*—thinking, as if heeding an impossible injunction, must intervene. And what it does when it is called upon to intervene at the scene of absolute undecidability, in the cross fire of life and death, the real and the dream, reading and the impossible, is to name the strength of its own impotence. Writing to peace, as if this were the true but unknown address of the philosopher's dream work, exposes the empty phallus:

> However, the author of this essay does set out one condition: The practical politician tends to look down with great smugness on the political theorist, regarding him as an academic whose empty ideas cannot endanger the nation [*Staat*] since the nation must proceed on principles [derived from] experience [*Erfahrungsgrundsatzen*]; consequently, the theorist is allowed to fire his entire volley, without the *worldly-wise* statesman becoming the least bit concerned. (107)

The theorist, then, can fire away precisely because his words are from the start diverted from a teleological path or aim. But if Kant seems to be launching a war of the worlds containing politician and theorist, it is in order strategically to avert the assaults that theorizing peace ineluctably attracts. In fact, Kant's project in the setup of his essay is to ensure the immunocompetence of his text, which is to say, he is sending out antibodies to neutralize the war-utterance of the political body. For, in times of trouble—and thinking's business concerns making trouble by responding authentically to trouble—the political body always sends in troops to subdue the critical intervention that true philosophical mobilization must contemplate. Kant allows himself to "fire his entire volley" because they are blanks; they are the stuff of dreams and address themselves to that which does not exist in the present. Kant's army of metaphors and metonymies, while participating in the structure of destination, cannot touch the statesman and therefore arrives, if it arrives, as a blank flag of surrender. It is a surrender that protects by establishing the terms of an absolute *differend:* "Now if he is to be consistent—and this is the condition I set out—the practical politician must not claim, in the event of a dispute with a theorist, to detect some danger to the nations in those views that the political theorist expresses openly and without ulterior motive. By this *clausula salvatoria,* the author of this essay will regard himself to be expressly protected in the best way possible from all malicious interpretation" (107).

Theorists, behold! In German, Kant writes that the theorist will know (*wissen*) protection. Where does this knowledge come from? In order to pass beyond the limits of the peace treaty, Kant must initially draw up this legally articulated contract with the politician. Its detachability from the body of the text—the threat of beheading or castration—always attends this essay, which in fact sets out to abolish the conditions for instituting a peace treaty. Because the theorist is fundamentally disarmed by the state, and barred by the nature of philosophizing from producing a referential dent in policy, the politician will have to desist from waging war on polemics or theoretical activity. Nonetheless, what this essay makes clear from the start is that the state practices the duplicitous policy of remaining at once unconcerned with theoretical reflection while menacing it with reprisal for betraying the interests of national security. What is sad for us today is that institutions of learning, linked as they are to the state and other corporate configurations, have tended to internalize this threatened and threaten-

ing posture. Hence the myth or, depending on which side you find
· yourself, the wish fulfillment of "tenured radicals."

Well, at any rate, Kant, in order to protect his text from malicious
interpretation, heads up his essay with a joke, a dream, castration, and
contract. The detachable introduction, which nonetheless enables reflection on a lasting peace to occur at all, ends with a kind of proxy
signing. For, as we know, the politician will not then and not now cosign
this contract that Kant, in his own and our defense, draws up. That is
why I, Immanuel Kant, "the author of this essay," will regard myself to
be "expressly protected" by my performative declaration, which, alas,
may only be a decoy. From what is he performatively protecting himself? From that part of war that politicians have consistently waged on
reflection ("in the event of a dispute"). But this is not merely a professional suit that he brings to bear. What politics may justly deem as
threatening is the interminable, morally anxious, and genuinely ambivalent cast of speculative analysis.

Perhaps the most serious challenge that Kant poses to us today does
not so much concern a regional or local disturbance (wherever that may
be), but one that requires us to reflect upon the singularly repressed
disjunction of freedom and democracy: "Among the three forms of
government, *democracy,* in the proper sense of the term, is necessarily a
despotism, because it sets up an executive power in which all citizens
make decisions about and, if need be, against one (who therefore does
not agree); consequently, all, who are not quite all, decide, so that the
general will contradicts both itself and freedom" (114). Whether standing alone to mark the cleave in which freedom breaks off from itself, or
whether drawing up an unabating contract with the political statesman, the theorist constitutes that figure which drives a cut into the
idealized imaginary of state politics. Indeed, the theoretical imperative
consists principally in making the state back off from its disavowal
systems—as happens, for instance, when the presidential linguistic
machine names the incessant repetition of the Holocaust for this country in the mode of psychotic disassociation.

Postscriptum

Several months after this essay was written, George Bush finally returned to the site of his catastrophic accident. Once again, he was to be
filmed as he uncontrollably threw up the phantoms with which "Japan"
for him is associated.

Notes

1. I have treated the technologically constellated state and the telephone in *The Telephone Book*. One might also consider in this context the terrorism of Stalin's nocturnal phone calls.

2. In "The Differends of Man," an essay on Lyotard, deconstruction, and Heidegger, I have tried to read historical woundings that will not heal.

3. Derrida has explored the polysemous aspects of James Joyce's "he war" in "Two Words for Joyce."

4. On Bush's discourse, see the challenging readings produced in the essay by Rubenstein 259ff. The principle of nonlinkage belongs to psychoanalyical investigations. Consider in this regard the definition of "Isolation" in Laplanche and Pontalis.

5. I am following the protocols established by Nancy for considering this war. See "Guerre, Droit, Souveraineté—Techné."

6. When George Bush proudly claimed that he could now abandon the odious burden, imposed by his mother, of eating broccoli, he signaled the decline of the superegoistic function for him. As prez nothing would be forced down his throat any longer; he could externalize the law without remorse. Elsewhere I have shown what it means for Freud "to learn to love spinach"—an unbearable internalization of mucosity. For Freud's tables of laws, this turn toward the totemized spinach meant he had successfully integrated the superego and the lawgiver. I analyze the utterance "Eat your spinach!"—a once-common injunction issued by parents to their children—in *Dictations: On Haunted Writing*. The spinach episode in Freud's oeuvre functions as an exemplary passage through Oedipus. The more phallically organized broccoli, which Bush has graduated into not eating, suggests rather a refusal of castration: the classical Freudian condition of disavowal, which forms his major character traits.

7. This argument implies some familiarity with the debates figured by Derrida and Lacan in the case of Edgar Allan Poe's "Purloined Letter." For this discussion, see Lacan's "Purloined Letter" and Derrida's "Facteur de la vérité" and "My Chances/Mes Chances: A Rendezvous with Some Epicurean Stereophonies."

8. See Nancy's work on Georges Bataille and community in *The Inoperative Community*.

9. Derrida has evoked some of these motifs in his treatment of Benjamin's essay in "Force of Law."

2 Cold Wars

Securing Identity, Identifying Danger

David Campbell

Introduction

Throughout the 1950s, the National Security Council wrote a series of confidential assessments of United States interests. In 1956, during one of its annual reviews, the NSC Planning Board added a new preamble to the most important national security document. Although it did not alter the general objectives, this rewriting meant that NSC 5602/1 began with the following declaration:

> The spiritual, moral and material posture of the United States of America rests upon established principles which have been asserted and defended throughout the history of the Republic. The genius, strength and promise of America are founded in the dedication of its people and government to the dignity, equality and freedom of the human being under God. These concepts and our institutions which nourish and maintain them with justice are the bulwark of our free society, and are the basis of the respect and leadership which have been accorded our nation by the peoples of the world. When they are challenged, our response must be resolute and worthy of our heritage. From this premise must derive our national will and the policies which express it. The continuing full exercise of our individual and collective responsibilities is required to realize the basic objective of our national security policies: maintaining the security of the United States and the vitality of its fundamental values and institutions.

This preamble was retained without alteration in subsequent versions of the NSC's Basic National Security Policy. Moreover, in the 1959 policy review, expressions similar to this also found their way into the more detailed outline of basic policy that followed the preamble. Added to the list of objectives that must be achieved by U.S. policy was the following paragraph: "*h*. To preserve, for the people of the United States, the basic human concepts, values and institutions which have been nourished and defended throughout our history." This objective thus stood alongside the need to avoid—or if necessary, prevail in—a general war and to accelerate changes in "the Sino-Soviet regimes," as a "basic guide in the implementation of all other national security policies" approved by the president (NSC 5906/1).

What is striking about this and similar texts of foreign policy is the overt concern of the national security state's inner sanctum with political if not polemical formulations. After all, when dealing with NSC documents, we are not concerned with texts being written for public consumption. Although many of these themes would later appear in the rhetoric of partisan speeches and statements, the above quotes are taken from documents repeatedly stamped "Top Secret" and originally intended only for the eyes of a select few. That such a restricted audience, one normally thought to be removed from the more colorful aspects of political life and endowed with the ability to see the world as it really "is," should be actively concerned with the figurative representation of its mission, necessarily requires us to rethink the meaning of foreign policy-making. As a consequence, we should no longer regard those who occupy the secretive domains of the national security bureaucracy as being outside of the cultural parameters of the state in whose name they operate. Most important, examples such as this (among the many available) point the way toward rethinking the relationship between foreign policy and political identity and, as a result, the significance of the cold war.

The Cold War Revisited

While conventional wisdom dictates that the cold war was a situation induced externally by the behavior and beliefs of the Soviet Union, the majority of internal and secret assessments of the early cold war emphasized that, although the threat to the United States and western Europe was most easily represented by the activity of communist forces and the Soviet Union, the danger being faced was neither synonymous with nor caused by them. Moreover, when the nature of the East-West struggle was considered, its terms were as much cultural and ideological as they were geopolitical. As George Kennan argued, "it is not Russian military power that is threatening us; it is Russian political power" (Gaddis 40). Such an interpretation, particularly in the context of war-devastated Europe, led Kennan to proclaim that "World communism is like a malignant parasite which feeds only on diseased tissue" (Moscow Embassy Telegram #511, 63).

Furthermore, the postwar texts of U.S. foreign policy always acknowledged that their initial concern was the absence of order, the potential for anarchy, and the fear of totalitarian forces or other negative elements that would exploit or foster such conditions. It was the (in)famous NSC 68, after all, that declared that "even if there were no Soviet threat" the United States would still pursue a policy designed to cope with the "absence of order among nations" (401, 390). In effect, then, a document as important as NSC 68 recognized that the interpretation of the Soviet Union as the preeminent danger to the United States involved more than the absorption of sense data by an independent and passive observer.

Moreover, assessments of the threat to America and its interests since World War II have identified a wide range of concerns. Despite considerable differences in the order of magnitude of each threat, over the years policymakers have cited world communism, the economic disintegration of Europe, Red China, North Vietnam, Cuba, Nicaragua, Libya, "terrorists," drug smugglers, assorted "Third World" dictators, and, most recently, ambiguity and uncertainty. None of these sources posed a threat in terms of a traditional calculus of (military) power, and none of them could be reduced solely to the Soviet Union. All of them, however, were (and are) understood in terms of their proclivity for anarchy and disorder.

Most important, just as the source of danger has never been fixed, neither has the identity that it was said to threaten. As the preamble to NSC 5602/1 illustrates, the contours of American identity have been the subject of constant (re)writing in the texts of foreign policy: not rewriting in the sense of changing the meaning, but rewriting in the sense of inscribing, so that meanings that are contingent and subject to flux are rendered more permanent. Thus, while one might have expected few if any references to national values or purposes in confidential documents prepared for the inner sanctum of national security policy (after all, do they not know who they are or what they represent?), the texts of foreign policy are replete with statements about the fulfillment of the Republic, the fundamental purpose of the nation, God-given rights, moral codes, the principles of European civilization, the fear of cultural and spiritual loss, and the responsibilities and duties thrust upon the gleaming example of America.

In this sense, the texts that guided national security policy did more than simply offer strategic analyses of the "reality" they confronted: they actively concerned themselves with the scripting of a particular American identity. Stamped "Top Secret" and read by only the select and powerful few, the texts effaced the boundary between inside and outside with their quasi-puritan figurations. Indeed, in employing these figurations, the foreign policy texts of the postwar period recalled the seventeenth-century literary genre of the jeremiad, or political sermon, in which Puritan preachers combined searing critiques with appeals for spiritual renewal. These exhortations drew upon a European tradition of preaching the omnipresence of sin so as to instill the desire for order, but they added a distinctively affirmative moment in which anxiety was the end as well as the means. As Bercovitch argues:

> The American Puritan jeremiad was the ritual of a culture on an errand—which is to say, a culture based on a faith in process. Substituting teleology for hierarchy, it discarded the Old World ideal of stasis for a New World vision of the future. Its function was to create a climate of anxiety that helped release the restless "progressivist" energies required for the success of the venture. The European jeremiad thrived on anxiety, of course. Like all "traditionalist" forms of ritual, it used fear and trembling to teach acceptance of fixed social norms. But the American jeremiad went much further. It made anxiety its end as well as its means. Crisis was the social norm it sought to inculcate. The very concept of errand, after all, implied a state of *un*fulfillment. The future, though divinely assured, was never quite there, and New England's Jeremiahs set out to provide the sense of insecurity that would ensure the outcome. (28)

Whereas the Puritan jeremiads were preached by religious figures in public, the national security planners secretly entreated the urgency of the manifold dangers confronting the Republic. But the refrains of their political sermons replicated the logic of the jeremiad and came to occupy a prominent place in postwar political discourse. Specifically, the articulation of danger contained within the modern jeremiads of the national security bureaucracy transformed the social crises of foreign threats into the norm that constituted the parameters of modern life within the state.

Most important, thinking about the texts of foreign policy as jeremiad-like articulations of danger alters our understanding of the cold war. As a struggle that exceeded the military threat of the Soviet Union, and a struggle into which any number of potential candidates—regardless of their strategic capacity to be a threat—were slotted as a danger, what is understood under the rubric of *the* cold war takes on a different cast. If we recall that the phrase "cold war" was coined by a fourteenth-century Spanish writer to represent the persistent rivalry between Christians and Arabs (Halliday 7), we come to recognize that the sort of struggle the phrase denotes is a struggle over identity: a struggle that is not context-specific and thus, for the United States or "the West," a struggle not rooted in the existence of a particular kind of Soviet Union. In other words, the cold war can be understood as an ensemble of political practices and interpretive dispositions associated with the (re)production of political identity. In these terms, "cold war" signifies not a discrete historical period, the meaning of which can be contained, but an orientation toward difference in which those acting on behalf of an assumed but never fixed identity are tempted by the lure of otherness to interpret all dangers as fundamental threats that require the mobilization of a population.

Illustrative of this was the so-called first crisis of the post–cold war period, the U.S.-led war against Iraq. The deployment of interpretive practices predominant in the post–World War II international environment—which emphasized the zero-sum analyses of international action, the sense of endangerment ascribed to all the activities of the other, the fear of internal challenge and subversion, the tendency to militarize all responses, and the willingness to draw the lines of superiority/inferiority between us and them—against an other unrelated to communism or the Soviet Union, stands as testament to the persistence of certain cold war techniques of exclusion despite radical changes to the historical context. As such, the collapse, overcoming, or surrender of one of the protagonists in the cold war (as conventionally understood) does not mean that the orientation to the world identified as cold war has been rendered obsolete. To be sure, the meaning of cold war(s) will undoubtedly be affected by the conditions of their historical possibility, but the ethical and political challenge posed by this understanding focuses our attention on the need to articulate a different orientation to the world.

That desire cannot be fulfilled by this essay. But by setting forth some of the issues and themes implicated in that aspiration, it is to be hoped that this argument can begin to make a contribution to these challenges. Specifically, by rethinking the taken-for-granted understandings of identity, the state, danger, and foreign policy, we can elaborate more fully the way in which the cold war of the 1950s was pivotal in inscribing the boundaries of American identity.

Identity, the State, and Danger

Identity is an inescapable dimension of being. No body could be without it. Inescapable as it is, identity—whether personal or collective—is not fixed by nature, given by God, or planned by intentional behavior. Rather, identity is constituted in relation to difference. But neither is difference fixed by nature, given by God, or planned by intentional behavior. Difference is constituted in relation to identity. The problematic of identity/difference contains, therefore, no foundations that are prior to, or outside of, its operation. Whether we are talking of "the body" or "the state," or particular bodies and states, the identity of each is constituted through the inscription of boundaries that serve to demarcate an "inside" from an "outside," a "self" from an "other," a "domestic" from a "foreign."

In the specific case of the body, its boundary, as well as the border between internal and external, is "tenuously maintained" by the transformation of elements that were originally part of identity into a "defiling otherness" (Butler 133). In this formulation, no originary or sovereign presence inhabits a prediscursive domain and gives the body, its sex, or gender a naturalized and unproblematic quality. Understanding the gendered identity of the body in these terms means that we regard it as having "no ontological status apart from the various acts which constitute its reality" and that its capacity to act as a regulative ideal is a consequence of the performances that make it possible. As such, the conventional idea that gender is an interior essence definitive of the body's identity needs to be refigured so that we understand it as a discursively constructed notion that is required for the purposes of disciplining sexuality. In this context, gender can be understood as "an identity tenuously constituted in time, instituted in an exterior space through *a stylized repetition of acts*"; an identity achieved, "*not* [through] *a founding act, but rather a regulated process of repetition*" (Butler 136, 140–41, 145).

Choosing the question of gender and the body as an exemplification of the theme of identity is not to claim that the state is analogous to an individual with a settled identity. On the contrary, I want to suggest that the performative constitution of gender and the body is analogous to the performative constitution of the state. The state has "no onto- logical status apart from the various acts which constitute its reality"; its status as the sovereign presence in world politics is produced by "a discourse of primary and stable identity" (Butler 136); the identity of any particular state should be understood as "tenuously constituted in time . . . through *a stylized repetition of acts*," and achieved, "*not* [through] a *founding act, but rather a regulated process of repetition.*" But if no primary and stable identities exist, and if those identities that many had thought of as primary and stable, such as the body and the state, are performatively constituted, how then can we speak of such foundational concepts as "the state," "security," "war," "danger," "sov- ereignty," and "foreign policy"?

It is on the foundation of danger as an objective, independently exist- ing, and readily knowable condition that many of our conventional understandings rest. But danger is not an objective condition. It (sic) is not a thing that exists independent of those to whom it may become a threat. To illustrate this, consider the manner in which the insurance industry assesses risk. In Ewald's formulation, insurance is a technol- ogy of risk, the principle function of which is not compensation or reparation but, rather, the operation of a schema of rationality distin- guished by the calculus of probabilities. In insurance, according to this logic, danger (or, more accurately, risk) is "neither an event nor a general kind of event occurring in reality . . . but a specific mode of treatment of certain events capable of happening to a group of individuals." In other words, for the technology of risk in insurance, "Nothing is a risk in itself; there is no risk in reality. But on the other hand, anything *can* be a risk; it all depends on how one analyzes the danger, considers the event. As Kant might have put it, the category of risk is a category of the understanding; it cannot be given in sensibility or intuition" (199). In these terms, for insurance technology, danger is an effect of interpreta- tion. Danger bears no essential, necessary, or unproblematic relation to the action or event from which it is said to derive. Nothing is intrin- sically more dangerous than anything else, except when interpreted as such.

This understanding of the necessarily interpretive basis of risk has important implications for international relations. It does not disavow that many behaviors in the world have consequences that can literally be understood in terms of life and death. But not all risks are interpreted as dangers. Modern society contains within it a veritable cornucopia of danger; indeed, danger is so abundant that it is impossible to know objectively all that threatens us (Douglas and Wildavsky). Those events or factors that we identify as dangerous therefore come to be ascribed as such only through an interpretation of their various dimensions of dangerousness. Moreover, that process of interpretation does not depend upon the incidence of "objective" factors for its veracity. For example, HIV infection is considered by many to be America's major public health issue, yet pneumonia and influenza, diabetes, suicide, and chronic liver disease were all (in 1987) individually responsible for many more deaths (U.S. Dept. of Health and Human Services, tables 1–6). Equally, an interpretation of danger has licensed a "war on (illegal) drugs" in the United States despite the fact that both the consumption level of and the number of deaths that result from licit drugs exceed by a considerable order of magnitude that associated with illicit drugs. And "terrorism" is often cited as a major threat to national security, even though its occurrence within the United States is minimal (seven incidents without fatalities in 1985 according to the FBI) and its contribution to international carnage is minor (Donner 367).

Furthermore, the role of interpretation in the articulation of danger is not restricted to the process by which some risks come to be considered more serious than others. An important site of interpretation is the way in which certain modes of representation crystallize around referents marked as dangers. Given the often tenuous relationship between an interpretation of danger and the "objective" incidence of behaviors and factors thought to constitute it, the capacity for a particular risk to be represented in terms of characteristics that are reviled in the community said to be threatened can be an important impetus to an interpretation of danger. Specifically, the ability to represent things as alien, subversive, dirty, or sick has been pivotal to the articulation of danger in the American experience.

In this context, it is also important to note that the mere existence of an alternative mode of being, the presence of which exemplifies that different identities are possible and thus denaturalizes the claim of a particular identity to be *the* true identity, is sometimes enough to produce the understanding of a threat (Connolly, *Identity\Difference* 66). In consequence, only in these terms is it possible to understand how some acts of international power politics raise not a whit of concern, while something as seemingly unthreatening as the novels of a South American writer can be considered such a danger to national security that his exclusion from the country is warranted.[1] For both insurance and international relations, therefore, danger is not a specifiable object domain. Rather, danger is the consequence of a certain type of rationality that objectifies events, disciplines relations, and sequesters an ideal of the identity of the people said to be at risk (Ewald 206).

Rethinking danger in these terms alters how we understand the state. Much of the conventional literature on the nation and the state implies that the preestablished identity of a "people" is the basis for the legitimacy of the state and its subsequent practices. However, some of the recent historical sociology on this topic has argued that the state more often than not precedes the nation: that nationalism is a construct of the state in pursuit of its legitimacy. Benedict Anderson, for example, has argued in compelling fashion that "the nation" should be understood as an "imagined political community" that exists only insofar as it is a cultural artifact that is represented textually.

The importance of such a perspective is that it allows us to understand national states as unavoidably paradoxical entities that do not possess prediscursive, stable identities. As a consequence, all states are marked by an inherent tension between the various domains that need to be aligned for an imagined political community to come into being— such as territoriality and the many axes of identity—and the demand that such an alignment is a response to (rather than constitutive of) a prior and stable identity. States are never finished as entities; the tension between the demands of identity and the practices that constitute it can never be fully resolved, because the performative nature of identity can never be fully revealed. This paradox inherent to their being renders states in permanent need of reproduction: with no ontological status apart from the many and varied practices that constitute their reality, states are (and have to be) always in a process of becoming. For a state to end its practices of representation would be to expose its lack of prediscursive foundations; stasis would be death (Virilio 67).

The paradoxical nature of the state endows practices such as foreign policy with a pivotal role in representing its reality in the absence of secure foundations. In this sense, foreign policy is not something that can be understood simply as the external orientation of a preestablished identity; rather, foreign policy is one of the boundary-producing practices central to the production and reproduction of the identity in whose name it operates. This shifts our understanding *from* a concern with relations *between* states, which takes place *across* ahistorical, frozen, and pregiven boundaries, *to* a concern with *the establishment of the boundaries* that constitute, at one and the same time, the state and the international system, the domestic and the external, and the sovereign and the anarchic. Significantly, this means that the constant articulation of danger through foreign policy is not a threat to a state's identity or existence; it is its condition of possibility.

Furthermore, we need to draw a distinction between two understandings of foreign policy. The first is one in which "foreign policy" can be understood to refer to all relationships of otherness, practices of differentiation, or modes of exclusion that constitute their objects as "foreign" in the process of dealing with them. In this sense, foreign policy is divorced from the state as a particular resolution of the categories of identity/difference and applies to all confrontations between a self and an other situated in different sites of ethnicity, race, class, gender, or locale. But this understanding of foreign policy is not totally removed from the state insofar as it establishes a discursive economy from which the interpretations of the second understanding (Foreign Policy) are drawn. This second understanding—Foreign Policy as state based and conventionally understood—is thus not as equally implicated in the *constitution* of identity as the first understanding. Rather, Foreign Policy serves to *reproduce* the constitution of identity made possible by foreign policy and to *contain* challenges to the identity that results (Campbell).

The Cold War: American Identity and the Society of Security

While no state possesses a prediscursive, stable identity, for no state is this condition as central as it is for America. If all states are imagined communities, then America is the imagined community par excellence. For there never has been a country called "America," nor a people known as "Americans" from whom a national identity is drawn. There is a United States of America, and there are many who declare themselves to be "Americans" (though the U.S. census form does not list "American" as an ethnic option), but "America" only exists by virtue of people coming to live in a particular place. The histories of Americans are located in places other than the one in which they live, such that "the flag and the Pledge are, as it were, all we have" (Walzer, "What Does It Mean?" 602).

As with all republics, America has constantly confronted the dilemma of securing legitimacy and establishing authority in a culture that renders transcendental guarantees suspect. Caught in a "Machiavellian moment" whereby the republic encounters its own finitude in the effort to reconcile universal values in particular form, the (re)production of American identity has relied upon a recurrent logic of foundation and augmentation such that performative statements are presented as constative utterances (Pocock, *The Machiavellian Moment*; Honig, "Declarations of Independence"). Each and every republic faces a similar structural requirement, for no matter how powerful or plausible are the claims of nations upon states, in no state are temporality and spatiality perfectly aligned. Each state thus confronts an *aporia*—a gap or rift—in its identity that, just as Derrida argued with regard to language and all acts of founding, cannot be overcome (Honig). But in America, with neither a country nor a people to serve as a foundational referent, the *aporia* in America's identity is magnified.

An important consequence of this enlarged *aporia* is that a seemingly paradoxical relationship between time and space arises. Europeans who encountered the New World went out of their way to deny its historicity, thereby endowing space with a defining role in the constitution of American identity (Mason). With all its qualities understood as present at its genesis, America has been conceived as the land of freedom that derives its meaning from the frontier. Indeed, born modern, " 'American' identity obviates the usual distinctions of national history—divisions of class, complexities of time and place . . ." (Bercovitch 154–55). In this context, the space that is America has taken on such significance that it becomes history. Ironically, this means that the history of America is effectively dehistoricized, for this privileging of the spatial over the temporal in American experience has given history the quality of an eternal present.

Yet, while space is a defining moment of American identity, it is an insufficient condition: the *aporia* of identity cannot be filled by the claims of geography alone. Indeed, the legitimations for the geopolitical identity of America are nonterritorial in character. As an entity that was literally the product of European imagination and in which the "true nationals" and their ideals were always "inorganic" in nature, America has a peculiar iconic quality in which the major conflicts of its identity are ideational. From the religious conflicts of the Puritans, through the witchcraft hysteria of Salem, the loyalty oaths and xenophobic legislation of the early republic, to the prominent place accorded the pledge of allegiance and the flag in modern elections, American politics has privileged the symbolic. As Baudrillard (*America* 118) observed, America begins and ends with "space and the spirit of fiction." Defined therefore more by absence than by presence, America is peculiarly dependent upon representational practices for its being. Arguably more than any other state, the imprecise process of imagination is what constitutes American identity. And in this context, the practices of foreign policy/Foreign Policy come to have a special importance. If the identity of the "true nationals" remains intrinsically elusive and "inorganic," it can only be secured by the effective and continual ideological demarcation of those who are "false" to the defining ideals (Balibar 285). "Only in a country where it is so unclear what is American," argues Kammen, "do people worry so much about the threat of things 'un-American' " (4).

Notwithstanding the ubiquity and persistence of the orientation toward difference signified by the phrase *cold war*, the specific historical context of the (conventionally understood) early cold war in the United States exhibited some features crucial to the (re)production of American identity. To consider what was at stake in this period, I want to examine the standards established by the Truman and Eisenhower administrations to judge the loyalty and security of federal employees.

In a move designed to head off congressional pressure, the Truman administration established in 1946 a Temporary Commission on Loyalty. The commission's report the following year became the basis for Executive Order 9835, which set forth the guidelines for the scrutiny of government workers. The Truman order justified its concern on the grounds that "each employee of the Government of the United States is endowed with a measure of trusteeship over the democratic processes which are the heart and sinew of the United States." It then set the following standards:

1. The standard for the refusal of employment or the removal from employment in an executive department or agency on grounds relating to loyalty shall be that, on all the evidence, reasonable grounds exist for belief that the person involved is disloyal to the Government of the United States.

2. Activities and associations of an applicant or employee which may be considered in connection with the determination of disloyalty may include one or more of the following:

   a. Sabotage, espionage, or attempts or preparations therefor, or knowingly associating with spies or saboteurs;

   b. Treason or sedition or advocacy therefor;

   c. Advocacy of revolution or force or violence to alter the constitutional form of government of the United States;

   d. Intentional, unauthorized disclosure to any person under circumstances which may indicate disloyalty to the United States, of documents or information of a confidential or non-public character

obtained by the person making the disclosure as a result of his employment by the Government of the United States;

e. Performing or attempting to perform his duties, or otherwise acting,
so as to serve the interests of another government in preference to the
interests of the United States;

f. Membership in, or affiliation with or sympathetic association with
any foreign or domestic organization, association, movement, group or
combination of persons, designated by the Attorney General as totalitarian, fascist, communist, or subversive, or as having adopted a policy of advocating or approving the commission of acts of force or
violence to deny other persons their rights under the Constitution of
the United States, or as seeking to alter the form of government of the
United States by unconstitutional means.
(Executive Order 9835, 627, 630)

In 1953, the Eisenhower administration made some important
changes with far-reaching consequences to the Truman loyalty program. Shifting the emphasis from loyalty to security, Eisenhower's administration defined its concern in a novel way and expanded the categories of exclusion. Executive Order 10450, which rescinded Truman's,
began by stating that "the interests of the national security require that
all persons privileged to be employed in the departments and agencies of
the Government, shall be reliable, trustworthy, of good character, and of
complete and unswerving loyalty to the United States." To be sure,
loyalty remained an important issue, and many people considered loyalty and security to be synonymous. But the Eisenhower executive
order marks a clear and identifiable moment in the development of
what Foucault has termed a "society of security." In this understanding,
the state is neither a monolith that exercises power over an independent
social domain, nor a settled identity that simply responds to external
stimuli. Instead, the state and the social are made possible by "multiple
regimes of governmentality," which employ a rationality of security
that calculates the possible and the probable, and simultaneously indi-
vidualizes and totalizes, asking both the citizen and the state what it
means to be governed (Gordon 35–36).

In this context, by replacing a concern for "the democratic processes
which are the heart and sinew of the United States" (the rationale of the
Truman program) with "the interests of the national security," the
Eisenhower program constituted in a different way the object it purported to defend. By diminishing (though not eradicating) the classical
republican notion of the role of a citizen in a democratic polity and

substituting for it an abstracted and reified notion of "the interests of the national security," Eisenhower both extended the domain of the state's interest and increased the intensiveness of its concern. As a pivotal textual moment in the passage from the defense of the nation to the constitution of the national security state, Eisenhower's executive order multiplied the personal dimensions along which threats to security could be observed, thereby amplifying in the name of security the sense of endangeredness that the nation would feel. This is evident in the expansion of categories of exclusion. In addition to the Truman order's classification of danger was added the following:

> The investigations conducted pursuant to this order shall be designed to develop information as to whether the employment or retention in employment in the Federal service of the person being investigated is clearly consistent with the interests of the national security. Such information shall relate, but shall not be limited, to the following:
> (1) Depending on the relation of the Government employment to the national security:
> (i) Any behavior, activities, or associations which tend to show that the individual is not reliable or trustworthy.
> (ii) Any deliberate misrepresentations, falsifications, or omissions of material facts.
> (iii) Any criminal, infamous, dishonest, immoral, or notoriously disgraceful conduct, habitual use of intoxicants to excess, drug addiction, sexual perversion, or financial irresponsibility.
> (iv) Any adjudication of insanity, or treatment for serious mental or neurological disorder without satisfactory evidence of cure.
> (v) Any facts which furnish reason to believe that the individual may be subjected to coercion, influence, or pressure which may cause him to act contrary to the best interests of the national security.
> (Executive Order 10450, 938)

The loyalty-security program in the decade between 1947 and 1957 covered some 13.5 million people, or some 20 percent of the work force. Just under five million were scrutinized for government employment, with the remainder being private sector employees whose work on defense contracts brought them into the program. The scheme cost some $350 million, required over 26,000 field investigations by the FBI to pursue information of a detrimental nature, resulted in over 11,000 losing their jobs, but uncovered no espionage or sabotage (Goldstein 374–75). It was nonetheless a very effective program, though not for the advertised reasons.

No rationalist assessment of the program's impact can fully appreciate the social and political effects it had in inscribing the boundaries of identity. In such an assessment, social control would be the organizing principle, and the conduct of the program would be appraised for its ability to carry out faithfully its aims and scrupulously avoid any digression from established procedure. But in these terms, the loyalty-security program was conducted in a dubious manner. Many innocent people were wrongly charged and either removed from or denied employment, while many who were cleared by the loyalty and security review boards were nonetheless made by their employer to pay the same price that an adverse finding would have incurred. The effects of suspicion thus exceeded the procedures and standards prescribed in the executive orders.

This had an important implication. The global inscription of danger in U.S. foreign policy was something that long preceded the cold war (e.g., the strategies of "manifest destiny" in the nineteenth century), but it was in the post–World War II period, when numerous overseas obligations were constructed, that the identity of the United States became even more deeply implicated in the external reach of the state. What the Eisenhower security program reveals is that concomitant with this external expansion was an internal magnification of the modes of existence that were to be interpreted as risks. Danger was being totalized in the external realm in conjunction with its increased individualization in the internal field, the result being the performative reconstitution of the borders of the state's identity. In this sense, the cold war needs to be understood as a disciplinary strategy that was global in scope but national in design. It was both like earlier instances in which the practices of foreign policy enabled the conduct of Foreign Policy and different from them insofar as the articulation of security involved a new writing of the boundaries of American identity.

In this context, discipline, rather than control, was the program's modus operandi. This is not surprising given that the nature of the "crime" with which people were accused was overtly political and ideological, and bore little if any relationship to a (traditionally conceived) threat to national security. Indeed, what these "crimes" did achieve was not the rooting out of an objective threat, but the reproduction of a standard, an optimal mean, around which those modes of being considered "normal" and those considered "pathological" could be organized (Gordon 20). In this context, consider this brief sample of the charges that brought people under surveillance:

A reliable source has disclosed that at a meeting held at the [____] School in [the housing development] during National Brotherhood Week in 1943–1944, a motion was made by one Mr. [____] that "the Bible should be burned and start building from there," and that you verbally seconded the motion and discussed it.

In connection with your study at the University of [X] in the pursuit of a Ph.D. degree in 1950–51, you wrote a thesis which was based mainly on material from the Institute of Pacific Relations which was cited as a Communist Front organization by the House Committee on Un-American Activities . . . furthermore, it is believed that your thesis is definitely sympathetic with the aims and ambitions of Soviet Russia.

During 1941 and thereafter, at [city, state], and [city, state] and elsewhere, you demonstrated a sympathetic interest in programs, policies and causes of the Communist Party. . . . In this connection you are reported to have made statements to the effect that "the downtrodden masses and underprivileged people are not being treated fairly in the United States." It is also reported that you expressed approval of the political viewpoints of Paul Robeson, a long time member of the Communist Party.

In a sworn statement made before an authorized representative of the Civil Service Commission on September . . . , 1954, you stated that within six months after your appointment with the [agency] in 1942, you were aware that [C], a former employee of the [agency] was a homosexual. You stated that during the period of your employment, [C] had propositioned you on several occasions. Also, that approximately two years ago, you and [Employee] met [C] and [D] in the [____] Restaurant, and after a few drinks the four of you went to [D's] hotel room where you and [C] and Employee [B] and [D] participated in homosexual acts.

He had cohabited for some time with a woman who was not his wife.

Your statements over an extended period of time show your dissatisfaction with the U.S. form of government and your preference for the Russian or other form of totalitarian government.

You were a member of the Consumers Union which is cited as a Communist front by the House Committee on Un-American Activities.

That you: (a) Exhibited a hypercritical attitude toward society that appeared to reflect home indoctrination; (b) Were a member of family considered as extremely radical and sympathetic to the Communist Party; (c) Had a father who: 1. Was a Communist sympathizer.
(Yarmolinsky 1, 32, 55, 115, 177, 244, 291, 296)

When called to appear before the Security Hearing Board, those accused would be asked a range of questions by board members to elicit more information pertaining to the charges. Consider the following sample of the kind of questions that some people were asked: "What do you think of female chastity?"; "What was your reaction upon receiving these charges? Didn't you feel remorseful for some of the things you did in your life?"; "What were your feelings at the time concerning race equality?"; "The file indicates . . . that you were critical . . . of the . . . large property owners?"; "At one time or two, you were a strong advocate of the United Nations. Are you still?"; Do you or your wife regularly attend any organized church services?"; "Have you ever indicated that you favored a redistribution of wealth?"; "Have you ever expressed yourself as being in favor of the abolition of trademarks?"; "Do you think that the workers in the Capitalistic system get a relatively fair deal?" (Yarmolinsky 12, 18, 89, 91, 210, 211).

What indicates most clearly the cold war's status as an episode in the ongoing (re)production of American identity is the way in which the charges and questions pursued by the Security Hearing Board were concerned with the *ethical boundaries of identity* rather than the *territorial borders of the state.* Indeed, the catalog of identity/difference evidenced in these practices covers all the conceivable filaments of the desired American nation: religion, family, sexuality, gender, law and order, civilization, morality, and economic relations. But their concern is not (or only indirectly) with the prospects for a breaching of the state's territorial borders; their main concern is with the feared transgressions of the nation's boundaries of identity.

The role that practices such as these play in inscribing the norms of identity remains relevant to "post–cold war" America, for the Eisenhower executive order on security is still the basis for all security investigations. To be sure, the security and loyalty boards no longer operate, and membership in the Communist party is no longer a disqualification for employment in the government (Lewy). But while no person since 1968 has been denied or dismissed from government employment on loyalty grounds, new norms, such as those associated with drug use, have come to prominence as the preferred grounds for exclusion (Campbell, chap. 7).

Furthermore, aside from the scant relationship between the concerns of these charges and questions and a threat to national security as traditionally understood, what is most striking about the topics ranged across is the way they parallel the issues (even today) tracked by immigration authorities when considering potential residents and citizens.

Indeed, there is a Janus-faced quality to the border inscribed by these and the similar questions asked of foreigners by the Immigration and Naturalization Service: the former look inward to contain difference while the latter gaze outward to screen perceived risks. In this conjunction, then, we find a different appreciation of what is meant by *containment* as the pivotal strategy of the cold war. In fact, there are two meanings of containment integral to this period: "one which speaks to a threat *outside* of the social body, a threat which therefore has to be isolated, in quarantine, and kept at bay from the domestic; and a second meaning of containment, which speaks to the domestic *contents* of the social body, a threat internal to the host which must then be neutralized by being contained, or 'domesticated' " (Ross 331). And at this conjunction of the two conceptions of containment, in an echo of the strategies of otherness found in Hobbes's *Leviathan* designed to discipline the asperity and irregularity of the figure of "man," we find the liminal groups that mark off the border of the state.

This refiguration of containment—away from a practice of Foreign and defense policy toward a strategy central to the constitution of a society of security—can be illustrated by an example that exhibits both the boundary-inscribing qualities suggested above and the conflation of "domestic" and "foreign" issues into one realm of concern. American society in the early cold war period was preoccupied with the relationship between sexuality, deviance, and national strength. The strength of the state, it was argued, depended upon the ability of strong men to stand up to the threats of communism. In this context, "deviant" sexual behavior became a national obsession in the United States after World War II, being one of the categories of risk in the Eisenhower executive order. The Senate issued a report in 1950 entitled "Employment of Homosexuals and Other Sex Perverts in Government," which proclaimed that "one homosexual can pollute a Government office." Within the logic of security, this concern was premised on the notion that sexual indulgence and perversion weakens the moral fiber of individuals, making them susceptible to temptation by outside forces (May 93, 95).

Homosexuality as a symbol for the pathology of deviance has an established history that long precedes this historical moment, however, particularly when it is alluded to by the gendering of people or policies as feminine. During World War I, for example, an elitist patriotic group called the Military Order of the World War was agitated the fact that Bertrand Russell—"the effeminate, pacifist representative of the 'Pink Intelligentsia' of England"—was speaking to women's peace groups in the United States (Heale 82). The appellation "pink" (and sometimes "lavender") to represent liberal, socialist, or communist thought has an obviously gendered connotation, made clear by Richard Nixon when he argued that his opponent in the 1950 California Senate campaign, Helen G. Douglas, was "pink right down to her underwear" (Whitfield 19). And when the liberal intellectual Arthur Schlesinger wrote favorably of "the new virility" of postwar leaders in contrast to the "political sterility" of their opponents, he argued that communism was "something secret, sweaty and furtive like nothing so much, in the phrase of one wise observer of modern Russia, as homosexuals in a boys' school" (Whitfield 43–45).

But "deviance" was not the only object of sexual concern in this context. Just as the Eisenhower executive order listed "immoral or notoriously disgraceful conduct" alongside "sexual perversion" as inconsistent with the interests of national security, so too the culture of the period fretted about the power of female sexuality to entice "normal" men from the moral path. The association of women and aggressive power was evinced by the usual iconography of sensual women that adorned fighter planes and bombers; the calling of saucy women outside the home "bombshells," "knockouts," or "dynamite"; and the placing of a photograph of Rita Hayworth on the hydrogen bomb dropped on the Bikini Islands. The islands then provided the name for the revealing swimsuit that female "bombshells" could wear (May 69, 110–11). Of course, this fear of female sexuality—which resonated with a cultural disposition to understand conflict in terms of the clash between Machiavellian *virtu* and *fortuna*—was not divorced from the changes in gender relationships that the war had wrought, when increasing numbers of women entered the work force. This transformation was accompanied by an increasing emphasis on notions of domesticity, however, and when the war ended but danger was not overcome, domesticity became a prominent feature of the cold war's cultural terrain (Susman). In this context, the nuclear family might be considered part of a strategy of domestic containment: sexuality would be contained through sexual restraint outside marriage and traditional gender roles within it.

Conclusion

America is not exceptional in combining nationalism, eschatology, and chauvinism[2]—all republics have been endowed with a transcendental air by the inexorable role that representation plays in the attempt to

overcome the *aporia* of their identity—but America is an acute instance of this structural quality. With its puritan experience appropriated into an unyielding myth of the nation's existence in sacred time,
the spiritual dimension has never been exorcised from American practices. While an evangelism of fear has been cardinal for the constitution
of many states' identities, the apocalyptic mode—in which a discourse
of danger functions as providence and foretells a threat that prompts
renewal—has been conspicuous in the catalog of American statecraft.
Accordingly, an array of individuals, groups, beliefs, or behaviors have
occupied the position of the Antichrist and been inscribed with one or
more terms from the panoply of tropes of otherness to be found in
American experience. Does this experience make America exceptional,
or does this make America normal? Perhaps America is both exceptional and normal; perhaps in a society of security the exception is the
norm.

In this context, any number of historical events or periods might be
considered as precursors to the (conventionally understood) cold war;
not in the sense that they stand in a relationship of cause and effect, but
rather because they exhibit similar orientations toward danger, the self,
and others. For example, the political controversies of the 1790s, which
involved a series of foreign intrigues in a period crucial for the establishment of the American state, prompted such a severe crackdown on
domestic dissent that Jefferson (who in earlier times had not hesitated
to employ the authoritarian practices of bills of attainder and loyalty
oaths) characterized it as the "reign of witches" (James Smith 184).
Besides, the correlation of domestic insurrection and foreign war was so
ubiquitous that "it was writ large on the birth certificate of the United
States of America," for it was the Declaration of Independence that
charged that George III "has excited domestic insurrections amongst us,
and has endeavoured to bring on the inhabitants of the frontiers, the
merciless Indian savages, whose known rule of warfare, is an undistin-
guished destruction of all ages, sexes and conditions" (Drinnon 99, 97).
Indeed, the manner in which the revolutionary period was marked by
practices later subsumed under the pejorative label of "McCarthyism,"
some 150 years before the Senator of that name came to prominence, is
illustrative of the way cold wars have been central to the constitution of
American identity.

Other precursors to the cold war of the 1950s can be readily identified; prominent among them is the red scare following the First World
War. But neither the contention of the 1790s nor the scare of 1919 were
the point of origin for all subsequent cold wars. The events of 1919 were

no more than another incarnation of the logic present in events such as those surrounding the Haymarket bombing in 1886, which in turn was able to energize social forces because of the sense of danger that was associated with the events of the 1871 Paris Commune (Avrich; Hicks and Tucker). Nor were red scares dependent upon the capacity of bolshevism, let alone the Soviet Union, to act as an empirical referent. Indeed, the appellation "red" invoked the Indian wars of the frontier as much as it did the symbol of the international working class (Slotkin, *Fatal Environment* chaps. 15, 19). When the tropes applied to Indians ("anarchical," "barbarous," etc.) were recycled and ascribed to unionists in the nineteenth century, these figurations derived not from what bolshevism (or anarchism, or nihilism, or . . .) might or might not have been, but from a desire to demonstrate that any group orientation against the emerging capitalist order was a kind of tribalism, a throwback to a savage past, and a symptom of degeneracy.

Indeed, no point of origin can be specified for these cold war modes of representation, because what they represent is the episodic eruption of an ethical power of segregation central to the logic of identity, an eruption that is animated by moral concerns rather than derived from spatial or temporal causes. As the loyalty and security programs of the 1950s made clear, the concern for ethical transgression outweighed (though it was often conflated with) the fear of foreign invasion. To be sure, each episode that exhibits cold war characteristics has elements specific to its location and participants, but in these various historical moments we witness the repetition of certain techniques of differentiation rather than the creation anew of concerns, prejudices, and figurations. As such, the cold war of the 1950s was not dramatically different from earlier cold wars. The danger to the private ownership of property that communism embodies became a code for distinguishing the "civilized" from the "barbaric" (or the normal from the pathological); from this distinction stemmed a disposition that served as the basis for the interpretive framework that constituted the Soviet Union as a danger independent of any military capacity. This is not to suggest that the USSR's military was either insignificant or benevolent, but to argue that because the figurations of the Soviet threat in the post–World War II era were similar if not identical to those that existed prior to 1945, prior to 1939, and prior to 1917, and similar if not identical to those deployed against an extensive range of other "others," the danger said to typify the cold war of the 1950s was not derived solely from the existence of military hardware or the Soviet Union's international position. Moreover, the persistence of these cold war techniques indicates the existence of a well-established discursive economy of identity/ difference in the American experience likely to be drawn upon to enable the disciplining of contingency and the representation of danger in moments of flux, even as we supposedly celebrate the end of the cold war.

Notes

1. I am referring here to the policies of the recently curtailed McCarran-Walter Act, which excluded writers like the Nobel Prize winner Gabriel García Márquez from the United States on ideological grounds.

2. For the claim that it is, see Bercovitch (176): "Only in the United States has nationalism carried with it the Christian meaning of the sacred. Only America, of all national designations, has assumed the combined force of eschatology and chauvinism. . . . Of all symbols of identity, only *America* has united nationality and universality, civic and spiritual selfhood, secular and redemptive history, the country's past and paradise to be, in a single synthetic ideal."

3 "The Fair Fame of the Dead"

The Precession of War Simulacra and the Reconstitution of Post–Cold War Conservatism

Larry N. George

Remember that what remains is not long, and let your hearts be lifted up at the thought of the fair fame of the dead.   —Pericles' Funeral Oration

I knew the origin of war, which was in each of us, and I knew that our concept of the hero was outdated, that the modern hero was the one who would master his own neurosis, so that it would not become universal, who would struggle with his myths, who would know that he himself created them, who would enter the labyrinth and fight the monster . . . the wars we carried within us were projected outside.

—Anaïs Nin, *Diary 7*

A nation is a historical group of men of recognizable cohesion, held together by a common enemy.   —Theodore Herzl, "The Jewish State"

Perhaps, without the bonds of ideological conflict to restrain us any more, our troubles are just beginning.   —Le Carré, *The Secret Pilgrim*

War and Ideological Reconstitution

Bloodshed sanctifies politics; war transubstantiates blood into political power. In nations that no longer anchor political authority in religion, war breaches the membrane between profane politics and the realm of the sacred. During times of political impasse, heroic wars can draw from the same deep symbolic reservoirs that fed ancient rituals of collective victimization, scapegoating, and ultimately human sacrifice itself, to consecrate ideologically partisan tropes and scaffold a renewed national unity. Thus when a state's national identity or its hegemonic political ideology are threatened, political leaders often begin desperately to seek out new foreign adversaries. The resulting aggression typically patterns around familiar narrative modes of catharsis, projection, and sublimation. Under such conditions, both the particular qualities targeted in the designated enemy and the form of exemplary conduct by the nation's heroes can disclose the community's evolving symbolic underpinnings, its ideological self-conceptions, and its political obsessions and anxieties. In this light, the recent U.S. government war on drugs and the military interventions against Manuel Noriega and Saddam Hussein suggest fertile grounds for interpretive speculation.

Literary anthropologist René Girard has observed how in some societies acts of collective, periodic ritualistic violence literally "re-create the community by reenacting a process of community disintegration and regeneration, through a unanimous victimage" ("Discussion" 127). Girard points out that the myths derived from such blood sacrifice are "interpreted as a supernatural visitation destined to teach the community what to do and not to do in the future" ("Discussion" 128). In other societies, foreign military operations serve this function. Such military activities typically adopt what John Lawrence calls "rituals of Manicheism"—symbolic performances of a "highly ideological character," through which communities "differentiate between themselves as the righteous ones and some other group that is utterly unrighteous and unworthy of existing, and so should be destroyed" ("Discussion" 138). In Aeschylus' Athens, for example, faith in the political order, and the essential public *virtu* derived from that faith, were "divinely consecrated and affirmed" by military victory (Jaeger 240): in the words of his *Eumenides*, "Unanimous hatred is the greatest medicine for a human community" (Girard, "Discussion" 126). As Jean Bethke Elshtain puts it, "wars—good wars that unite us—offer a communal endeavor, the sharing of sacrifice and danger. Modern society appears to have found no other way to initiate and sustain action in common with others on this scale" (10). This linchpin function of sacrificial foreign military operations has been a mainstay of conservative political thought, from Thucydides to Edmund Burke and Joseph de Maistre.

Ideological conservatives recognize the power of sacrificial war to reconstitute moral and political categories, and the structures of difference out of which these are woven. They fear the effacement of differences, particularly in political orders where control over political life rests on understanding and manipulating the circulation of politically referential signs, images, and symbols. This becomes especially important as Weberian processes of bureaucratization, surveillance, and technological convergence progressively rationalize the operations of modern economic, military, and administrative state structures. During periods of ideological transition, these structures are targeted as contested terrains, transforming bureaucratic and electoral struggles for control over these institutions into conflicts over whose semiotic order will provide the governing tropes for the succeeding hegemonic ideology. Political energy and capital normally expended on accumulating and exercising conventional forms of power—economic resources, incurred favors and debts, prestige, party or coalitional discipline, and so forth—may shift dramatically toward essentially symbolic means and ends. War is the most productive source of such new symbolic capital.

War performances initiate a dialectic of power and moral reconstitution. Patriotic violence and bloodshed generate moral authority in those who organize it, while the moral legitimacy of foreign military operations is often simply constituted by fiat in the rhetoric of the decision to take action. As George Bush told Congress in his 1991 State of the Union Address, announcing the justness of the U.S. Persian Gulf intervention, "Among the nations of the world, only the United States has had both the moral standing, and the means to back it up" (4). The identification of the cause in which collective, organized violence is to be conducted also articulates the larger moral and political categories through which public authority is subsequently to be exercised. Such categories take the form of chains of binary oppositions, whose grounding is continually undermined by the dynamic of difference and deferral (*differance*) familiar to readers of Derrida. The deferral process spurs the secular political community obsessively back toward reiterations of constitutive violence.

When the powerful tropes of the cold war and nuclear terror, which had held the deferral process in check for decades, dissolved in the late 1980s, the American polity was left suspended over an ideological abyss that echoed in the audible hollowness of Bush's New World Order speeches. In describing what his response would have been to a hypothetical UN refusal to back a U.S. Gulf intervention, for example, Bush affirmed, "I might have said, To hell with them, it's right and wrong, it's good and evil; he [Saddam Hussein] is evil, our cause is right." He later informed American college students in an open letter that "there is much in the modern world that is . . . washed in shades of gray. But not the brutal aggression of Saddam Hussein. . . . It's black and white" (Drew 182). Still later the same year, Bush noted at a press conference that the Iraqi invasion proved that "some philosophers" were wrong in believing that "there's no good or evil" (National Public Radio, "All Things Considered"). As the *Economist* observed following the Gulf War, "All is adrift." Absent a firm, overarching system of meanings, "it is no surprise that George Bush's New World Order, posited on some shining morality, is seen to be so much tosh" (89).

In a fascinating account of the metamorphic symbolism of blood in sacrificial rites of purification, René Girard notes how the

> secret of the dual nature of violence still eludes men. Beneficial violence must be carefully distinguished from harmful violence, and the former continually promoted at the expense of the latter. Ritual is nothing more than the regular exercise of "good" violence. . . . if sacrificial violence is to be effective it must resemble the nonsacrificial variety as closely as possible. That is why some rites may seem to us nothing more than senseless inversions of prohibited acts. (*Violence* 37)

Militarized polities thrive in a context of violent mirroring and projection, where the hated characteristics of publicly designated external foes resemble those qualities that the home authorities most seek to deny in themselves. Such societies obtain and sustain political identity through real or symbolic combat with the Other (Hegel, *Philosophy of Right* 208–12; Elshtain 74–75). The ideal enemy is thus a highly abstract, complex foreign ideological system onto which a range of thematized hate sentiments can be projected. For forty years, the cold war provided just such a moral scaffolding on which a rough national conservative political consensus in both the United States and the Soviet Union, built around an extremely fungible projection-mirroring dialectic, could be suspended.

Political communities caught up in such specular dynamics, but unable to wage war against one another, come to resemble one another in often subtle and unexpected ways. Authoritarianism is reinforced in both societies, as civil liberties, liberal tolerance, and other political virtues resistant to state authority are denounced by conservatives as both extravagant luxuries in time of danger to national security and as symptoms of the presence of the corrupting enemy ideology within the home community. As Andrew Kopkind put it recently, "the epic struggles against fascism, communism, nationalism and tin-pot tyranny have been used effectively to manufacture support for the nation's rulers and to eliminate or contain dissent among the ruled" (433). "The great strength of the totalitarian state," boasted Hitler, "is that it forces those who fear it to imitate it" (Gracie and Zarkov 108). The resulting convergences typically appear as ritualistic political claims and counterclaims directed against the "enemy," but which simultaneously express and *supplement* internal divisions and contradictions within each society. As long as the international enmity persists, the ideological frameworks sustained by the rivalry can continue to sublimate domestic tensions in both polities. When the rivalry dissolves, however, repressed domestic contradictions reemerge, as can be readily seen today in both the United States and the former Soviet Union.

Girard describes a phenomenon he calls the *sacrificial crisis:* the threat to public moral order stemming from the disappearance of sacrificial rites to which a society has become accustomed. The threat takes the form of a "crisis of distinctions," affecting the core of the cultural order, that is, the "regulated system of distinctions in which the differences among individuals are used to establish their 'identity' and their mutual relationships" (Girard, *Violence* 49). Historically, the concern to maintain conceptual and moral distinctions during ideological crises has been the hallmark of conservative thought, exemplified in Ulysses' speech in Shakespeare's *Troilus and Cressida*, Hobbes's nominalist *Logiathan* (the sovereign's gift of word distinctions), and Chaucer's authorship of his own "Troilus and Cressida" in response to the Peasants' Revolt of 1381 as a "cautionary tale for England" (Howard 331–35, 345ff.). The collapse of the cold war has left the United States resembling a society in sacrificial crisis, and recent foreign interventions by American forces can be seen as a reaction more to the danger of a post–cold war shearing of national ideological values than to any real threat posed by Noriega or Hussein.

The reconstitution of public morality through external military violence begins in a series of sacrificial events. As Hannah Arendt observes, the hovering presence of death during combat encourages a patriotic identification that initiates the reconstitution process: "Faced collectively and in action, death changes its countenance; now nothing seems more likely to intensify our vitality than its proximity. Something we are usually hardly aware of, namely, that our own death is accompanied by the potential immortality of the group we belong to and, in the final analysis, of the species, moves into the center of our experience" (*Crises of the Republic* 165). While Arendt stresses the transitoriness of the combat experience, in reality an important moral *supplementarity* exudes from it and flows back to the larger political community, where it reconsecrates the polity and restores, if temporarily, the nation's common moral and ideological scaffolding.

The American mass culture had anticipated precisely such a phenomenological sea change well before the Panama or Gulf wars. Network television in particular had begun to prepare the ground for this shift of affective attention by revising the largely derisory and comedic depictions of foreign military interventions characteristic of the 1970s (especially in "M.A.S.H.") toward a revisionist, tragic representation of war and endorsement of the moral absolutism of the combat unit. Examples here include "Magnum P.I.," "Miami Vice," and "China Beach," the moral formation of whose respective heroes occurred in the crucible of military unit loyalty in Vietnam.

As war approaches, debate over the nation's role polarizes and crystallizes deep underlying partisan and ideological divisions within the society. Once actual combat begins, however, the factional divisions at home are successively, if temporarily, displaced by the parallel moral system originating on the battlefield. In combat and preparation for combat, the absolute moral interdependence of the military unit breaks down prior ethnic, factional, ideological, or other sources of discord among the unit's members. Simultaneously, the ideological or partisan implications of the unit's mission, as of the war in general, are almost entirely subordinated to the immediate tasks of mission success, the preservation of comrades' lives, and the goal of victory. The military unit thus evolves into an abstract and politically content-free moral microcosm—a metonym or miniature simulacrum—of the idealized, reconstituted political society back home. This absolute moral unity of purpose and mutual interdependence is most immediately transmitted back to the families of the combatants, and then stepwise through chains of empathy and through increasingly organized, largely symbolic support systems, until it finally embraces the nation's formal political institutions.

The home community experiences this combat solidarity vicariously, through bombardment by war images and the appropriation of communication media for war propaganda. The imagined war creates what Derrida, in his well-known discussion of writing and onanism in Rousseau, calls a *supplement* (*Of Grammatology* 141–64). The images of distant war generate thanatological political power in the same way that pornography and fantasies of absent sex partners generate libidinal energy in autoerotic experiences. The demonized images of the enemy abroad both supplement and displace potentially divisive political conflicts at home by onanistically satisfying impulses to dominate, repress, or destroy without dangerous direct engagement with the Other.

Sacrificial War

Projection and Condensation
Politically troubled societies ritualistically seek out scapegoats onto whom internal tensions and conflicts can be displaced. The scapegoat myth, as recounted in Leviticus 16:8, governs the Judeo-Christian tradi-

tion from Abraham and Isaac through the Crucifixion and plays several
key roles in the politics of modern nation-states. Most important, scapegoating enables political leaders to elude the restrictions of rational-
administrative political structures. Scapegoating rests fundamentally
on an irrational and unconscious logic—what Girard calls an "element
of delusion"—permitting its manipulation and simultaneous denial by
political leaders ("Generative Scapegoating" 74). The resulting patterns
resemble a collective version of the individual ego *defense mechanisms*
discussed by Freud: repression, displacement, reaction formation, fixa-
tion, regression, and projection.

Among Freud's defense mechanisms, projection—the expression of
an inner tension or fear regarding the self by objectifying it onto and
attacking it in others—most obviously impels sacrificial wars. Kenneth
Burke describes the process well in his discussion of the "perfect enemy" and "the 'natural' invitation to 'project' upon the enemy any
troublesome traits of our own that we would negate," explicitly comparing the individual phenomenon to the common political situation
"when rulers silence domestic controversy by turning public attention
to animosity against some foreign country's policies" (Burke 18–19). As
Girard observes, "A community that actively seeks and finds scapegoats
is usually a community troubled by dissension or by some real or
imaginary disaster. Such a community will establish a false causal link
between its chosen scapegoat and the real or imaginary cause of its
trouble, whatever that may be" ("Generative Scapegoating" 103). Projection has dominated American conservatism in the twentieth century: enemies were sought abroad who represented to conservative
leaders and their constituencies potentially dangerous features of their
own ideologies and political practices.

Ritual political scapegoating also involves what Freud terms condensation: the simultaneous embodiment and representation of several
projected threats and disturbances by a single imagined object. In addition, according to Girard, the sacrificial victim both must be drawn
from outside the community itself and must be in some metaphoric
sense a part of it, so that while the sacrificial object will in some way
represent, resemble, or reflect qualities of the individual or group for
which he or it is being substituted, at least some deep and irrevocable
ontological distinctions must be maintained to prevent what Girard
calls "assimilation" (*Violence* 269–73, 11–12). If the condensation is
encompassing enough, substantial ideological reconstruction can result from the sacrificial violence. As Girard puts it, "beyond a certain
threshold of intensity—all other circumstances being favorable—the

hostile polarization against a victim must empty the group of internal hostility, unifying it so tightly that a cultural rejuvenation can really occur" ("Generative Scapegoating" 90–91). In the early post–cold war context, Manuel Noriega and Saddam Hussein provided attractive targets of projection for a reconstitutive sacrifice precisely because each represented a symbolically dangerous collapsing of several key cold war distinctions. Each *condensed* a variety of ideological themes of obsessive concern to an anxious postwar American conservative movement desperate to find a replacement for the cold war's international political and moral categories and systems of distinctions through which conservatives' own domestic authoritarian agenda had been legitimated.

Doubling, Personification, and Catharsis

The scapegoat ritual entails a process of doubling: the selection of two sacrificial animals, one of which is killed and the other set free to wander into the wilderness ("e/scapegoat"). "The Athenians regularly maintained a number of degraded and useless beings at the public expense," to be sacrificed as needed, in pairs, whenever calamities befell the city (Girard, *Violence* 9). Girard describes how members of prepolitical communities during times of social fragmentation experience themselves as beginning to "twin" into doubled, symmetrical, matching images of their antagonists. The doubling both heightens antagonisms and also renders allies and enemies interchangeable, leading to the collective search for a surrogate victim, a scapegoat. The members of society "strive desperately to convince themselves that all their ills are the fault of a lone individual who can be easily disposed of" (*Violence* 78–80). This doubling process then permits a single person—the sacrificial target (*pharmakos*)—to be substituted for all the divisions in the polity and to serve as "the sole object of universal obsession and hatred."

The sacrificial object becomes, in Girard's term, a "monstrous double." The sacrificial preparation itself involves two steps: the symbolic alienation of the sacrificial victim from the community and then the symbolic reabsorption of the victim through the sacrifice itself. The sacrificed *pharmakos* (victim) must be powerful enough to embody the qualities seen by the community as threatening, but not powerful enough to break out of the sacrificial dynamic itself and constitute a genuine threat to the community. The doubling process is metaphorically central to the exercise of executive or presidential power, as Ernst Kantorowicz discusses in his study of medieval monarchy (*The King's Two Bodies*) and as Michael Rogin has elaborated more recently (*Ron-*

ald Reagan, the Movie, chap. 3). Doubling occurs particularly during times of deep national political division, or when executive power is itself threatened, as when a president or monarch, fearful of assassination, literally "doubles." This has been frequently thematized—in fictional works like Akira Kurosawa's 1980 film *Kagemusha;* in historical accounts of, for example, Saddam Hussein's platoon of identical doubles; and in works of political theory that transgress the history/literature boundary, such as Don DeLillo's *Libra* (141).

During one sacrificial process discussed by Girard and other anthropologists, the *tyrannos* (king) and the *pharmakos* (sacrificial victim) "appear symmetrical and to some degree interchangeable" as an "individual responsible for the collective salvation of the group." In some cultures, it is the king himself who is the ritual sacrificial victim. More generally, however, the sacrificed victim is a person who is in some way a part of the community but nevertheless foreign to it. Sometimes he is a prisoner of war. Often, he is the king's "fool": a bizarre and comical black double of the king who shares with the monarch many formal resemblances, and even personal ties, but who is without dignity or prestige. Sometimes he is encouraged to misbehave, to harm members of the tribe, and to violate the law, which serves both to incite those who will sacrifice him and to allow him in a sense to "avenge" his sacrifice before it is actually staged (Girard, *Violence* 12, 119–21, 274–75, 278ff., 300ff.). A transparent allegory can be seen here in the initial courting of both Noriega and Hussein by successive U.S. administrations, in the subsequent demonization and military interventions against them, and finally in the concern in both cases to ensure quick and decisive military victories, followed by largely symbolic, quasi-legal sanctions.

The practice of *personifying* foreign evil—the increasing attention paid in American political culture in recent years to such foreign villains as Qaddafi, Abu Nidal, Arafat, Pablo Escobar, Noriega, Hussein, and the Soviet coup leaders—thus has two clear additional ideological implications in the American post–cold war context. First, as communism recedes as a plausbile threat in Latin America, the Middle East, and elsewhere, its *systemic* menace is condensed into the objectified evil character of individual villains. This allows crude demonization to reconstruct an ordered discourse of enmity—one as yet visible only in caricature—out of the particular characteristics of these individual designated foes. Second, it permits the reinscription of the Middle East and Latin America as realms of personal heroism and villainy, like the mythologized American West of the nineteenth century, where definitions of good and evil remain in flux and ready for constitution by the just and judicious employment of American arms. Girard's summary here rings disturbingly familiar when the *pharmakos* roles of Noreiga and Hussein are recalled:

> The mechanism of the surrogate victim is redemptive twice over: by pro-
> moting unanimity it quells violence on all fronts, and by preventing an
> outbreak of bloodshed within the community it keeps the truth about
> men from becoming known. . . . The prisoner drew to his person all the
> community's inner tensions, all its accumulated bitterness and hatred.
> Through his death he was expected to transform maleficent violence
> into sacred beneficence, to reinvigorate a depleted cultural order (*Vio-
> lence* 276)

This can be further illuminated by viewing Noriega and, later, Hussein, as the targets of a therapeutic national and international cathartic effort. The process of catharsis involves the symbolic expulsion of a symbolic pathogenic agent from a diseased body: "purgation by the imitation of victimage" (Burke 397). Girard shows how in preindustrial societies, catharsis operates in a parallel fashion at the individual, societal, and mythical levels, indicating the relationship between purgative medical catharsis and, for example, "purging the land of monsters." Internationally, the targeting of Noriega, and more obviously Hussein, can be seen as a global form of this shamanistic practice. Catharsis is thus another form of *pharmaceutical* activity: the ancient Greek *pharmakos* was the sacrificial victim ceremonially paraded through the town streets so that "he will absorb all the noxious influences that may be abroad and that his death will transpose them outside the community" (Girard, *Violence* 287–89).

Regenerative Violence in the Third World

As Richard Slotkin has chronicled, violence against external enemies has always played a constitutive role in the inscription of American moral and political categories. Violence became the means through which early Americans sought to rejuvenate their "fortunes, their spirits, and the power of their church and nation," and "the myth of regeneration through violence became the structuring metaphor of the American experience" (Slotkin, *Regeneration Through Violence* 5). Disproportionately, this regenerative violence has been directed against regions and populations of what is now called the Third World (including for centuries western North America). This violence always contained a symbolic moment, which had to do with keeping at bay moral chaos and indeterminacy, often represented by the "frontier"—the wilderness and the people who inhabited it. For the Puritans, "the wilderness was seen as a Calvinist universe in microcosm, and also as an analogy of the human mind." Indians flitted around the edge of wilderness "like the evil thoughts that plague the mind on the edge of consciousness" (Slotkin, *Regeneration* 77).

This analogy recurs in the Panama and Persian Gulf interventions. For both Americans and Europeans, Latin America and the Middle East have long been seen as transitional regions, sort of half-civilized zones between the Europeanized world and the wilderness of the North American West and Africa. In addition to its natural geographical and economic attractiveness as a target for U.S. intervention, Latin America in particular has traditionally played several competing roles in American popular mythology that are conducive to legitimating intervention. Dominant among these have been the images of unruly children in need of fatherly discipline, of superstitious Catholics and pre-Christian savages, and generally of an emotionally volatile and disordered region requiring the organizational, entrepreneurial, and administrative tutoring of North Americans (Black). These are also obviously the qualities that conservatives fear and detest in their compatriots, and often in themselves.

Conservatism's repressive self and community manifest more general American obsession with moral ambiguity. America has been beset since its inception by an acutely unstable and contradictory moral order. At the center of American political ideology is a lacuna around which revolve two irreconcilable and mutually hostile value systems. As Wilson Carey McWilliams describes it, "at bottom, American culture is incoherent, composed of elements which are incompatible. America descends from Biblical religion, on the one hand, and Enlightenment rationalism on the other. Americans extol both love and individualism, scarcely aware of the contradiction, and while Americans expect well-being and pursue luxury, no people is so likely to denounce 'materialism'" (Myers 297). Henry Cumings put it similarly, describing the country as "poised in an even balance, between extremes of arbitrary power and despotism, on the one hand, and of anarchy and unrestrained licentiousness, on the other" (Bercovitch 137).

American conservatism has been particularly menaced by this tension, rent as it is between the legacies of two competing and fundamentally incompatible political philosophies—free-market laissez-faire libertarianism and communitarian puritanism. The reconciliation between these strains has repeatedly required substantial therapeutic,

pharmaceutical violence. Thus symbolic compulsions have been added
to the various security, territorial, and economic temptations for foreign military adventures. U.S. interventions in Latin America in particular have been symbolically directed against disordering forces here
at home (Dallek 34–46, 65–72, 102–5, 210–16, 277–79). While U.S.
military involvement in the Middle East has been briefer and less acute
than in the Western Hemisphere, the pattern is nevertheless evident
there, as well (Dallek 170–71, 198–205, 274, 279–81). The seeking out
in Latin America and the Middle East of menacing figures who represent projected American fears and anxieties draws on a long history
prior to Noriega and Hussein.

During the first three decades following World War II, anticommunism provided adequate common enmity to weld together the precarious conservative ideological coalition of free-market libertarians and
traditional communitarians. Concealed in this arrangement, however,
was a repressed moment of respect, even envy, on the part of traditional
communitarian conservatives for precisely the apparent authoritarian
successes of the enemy Soviet system. Conservatives secretly coveted
the communists' seeming ability to eliminate domestic dissent, to
control and discipline a large and racially diverse population, to maintain well-funded and capable military forces with little domestic resistance, and to bend the services of the press, schools, unions, volun-
teer organizations, and the family to national purposes. The dark secret
of American conservatism throughout the cold war was that the presence of a Soviet Union that resembled in many ways a doppelgänger—
an evil twin, or diabolical mirror image of what many U.S. conservatives sought politically for America—provided precisely the sort of
external enemy onto which the political anxieties generated by the
authoritarian implications of American conservatism could be readily
projected and battled symbolically (Hitchens). The internecine disputes
among the nation's various competing political elements, and the more
fundamental tensions among the irreconcilable conservative moral systems that underlay public debate, were temporarily repressed beneath
the anticommunist cold war consensus. The end of the cold war thus
threatened conservatives with the evaporation of an enemy that simultaneously provided therapeutic sublimation for their own authoritarianism, bound their precarious coalition together, and granted them
hegemony over the public ideological order and the nation's political
institutions (Unger; Bernstein, "If They've Won, Can Conservatives
Still Be Important?"; Black, "Dearth of Suitable Villains").

Over the past decade, as the designated menace of global communism receded, conservatism's obsessions and contradictions have been refracted through three nested ideological-policy lenses: consumerism, race politics, and foreign affairs. The casino-shopping mall economy of the Reagan years sustained conservatism's mass support for several years, but the fiscal and macroeconomic consequences of these policies have begun to polarize the conservative movement, driving deep ideological wedges between traditional communitarians, libertarians, militarists, and vestigial proponents of supply-side dogmas (Toner; Safire). Reagan's "personality capital" was sufficient to hold the coalition together, but with his retirement, ideological traditionalists, supported by much of the commercial banking sector, were able to wrest control of the movement, forcing George Bush to mediate, ultimately unsuccessfully, among the increasingly hostile factions. As usual, the precession of mass culture simulacra signaled this shift, as the early-1980s fascination with such icons as Nancy Reagan's dress museum, "Lifestyles of the Rich and Famous," "Dallas," and "Dynasty" began to give way to the traditional conservative messages of *Wall Street, Bonfire of the Vanities,* and the highly public Boesky, Milken, Leona Helmsley, and Charles Keating trials. It is in this atmosphere of competing versions of American conservatism, motivated by a desperate search for foreign and domestic enemies to replace the designated dangers of the cold war years, that the late-1980s war on drugs, and the subsequent invasions of Panama and the Persian Gulf, can be readily comprehended.

Twice in this century traditionalist conservative forces have sublimated through prohibitionism widespread popular discontent accompanying rapid and fundamental domestic political-economic transformations and profound reorientations of the U.S. role in the international system. In both instances, the criminalization of a social and medical problem expanded the power of both organized criminal forces and of the repressive state apparatus constituted to enforce the legislation. The most recent of these prohibitionist movements—the drug war of the past decade—has exported the violence associated with criminalization and repression into the international arena, providing fertile opportunities for ideological and political semiosis.

In 1991, the United States deployed military forces to Peru to assist that government in its war against both the Incan-Marxist Sendero Luminoso guerrillas and the Peruvian cocaine mafia. This articulation of the cold war with the drug war had been prefigured in the Reagan administration's accusations of Cuban and Nicaraguan involvement in the cocaine trade, and in the ill-conceived 1990 U.S. naval blockade of the Caribbean. Tom Clancy, a reliable bellwether of trends in militarist circles and among conservative thinking in general, anticipated this displacement by over a year in his novel *Clear and Present Danger*. As urban police and public officials began referring to drug dealers as "narcoterrorists" and "Viet Cong," and comparing American street gangs to the "murderous militias of Beirut," the war on Latin American cocaine emerged as the first obvious replacement for communism as a simultaneous foreign and domestic target for projecting both conservative obsessions and U.S. armed force (*Los Angeles Times*, 9 March 1991, A1; Davis 268).

The traffic in drugs and alcohol has historically provided a recurring menace to America's moral and legal order, around which dormant puritan moral archetypes can be episodically revived and the country's ideological tissue repaired through collective ritual violence. American drug policy, more than in any other democracy, adopts a martial, punitive, and correctional—rather than medical and rehabilitative—disciplinary rhetoric. In the last decade, the drug epidemic has provoked substantial discord among free-market libertarian and traditional communitarian conservatives. To free-market conservatives like William F. Buckley, drug traffickers are simply merchants operating in a commodity sector that has been improperly designated illicit, and thus paradoxically subjected to the unregulated exactions of the actual free market. In the words of Los Angeles poligrapher Mike Davis:

> The specific genius of the Crips [the dominant local gang coalition] has been their ability to insert themselves into a leading circuit of international trade. Through 'crack' they have discovered a vocation for the ghetto in L.A.'s new 'world city' economy. . . . The contemporary cocaine trade is a stunning example of what some political economists are now calling 'flexible accumulation', on a hemispheric scale. . . . As *Fortune* pointed out a few years back, the Medellin group have always been distinguished by their 'businesslike mentality' and their success 'in turning cocaine trafficking into a well-managed multinational industry'. (*City of Quartz* 309–11)

The traffic in illegal addictive commodities forms a parodic doubling, a shadowy mirroring, of competitive laissez-faire capitalism. Prohibition movements appear during periods of vigorous contention between established, oligopolist financial-commercial capital and upstart competitive enterprises. Prohibitionism simultaneously symbolically condenses several resulting threats to political-economic order and narratively transfers the potentially disruptive conflicts to an arena of common animosity: a *pharmakos* (drug/poison/sacrificial target).

Organized crime as a whole is empowered by the market for illicit but sought-after commodities of various kinds: drugs, prostitution, gambling, usury, weapons. The identification and punishment of organized traffickers in these goods and services constitutes and demarcates foundational boundaries of legitimacy and illegitimacy. The structure and practices of organized crime, and especially popular cultural representations of these, reflect in turn the moral and ideological preoccupations of the country at a given time. Much of mass culture's recent *noir* fascination—the *Godfather* series, *Crime Story, Tequila Sunrise, Wiseguy, Goodfellas, Colors, Mobsters,* and so forth—with organized crime and drug trafficking derives from the continual, but ultimately futile efforts of legally sanctioned force of arms to draw distinctions between licit and illicit forms of business activity in a hegemonically conservative social order torn between conflicting market and communitarian values. The power and appeal of "Miami Vice," to take only the most obvious example, rests precisely on the symbolic conflation of drug traffickers and police, and on the visual-audio supplementarity stimulated by the slipperiness of moral distinctions. The 1990 U.S.-Mexican media war over the controversial, Emmy-winning NBC "docudrama" on the Enrique Camarena murders signaled the internationalization of the phenomenon, following as it did upon the highly publicized international "arrest" of Manuel Noriega.

The slippery moral economy of narcotics trafficking and regulation renders the drug nexus available for deployment as a legitimating figure in an ideologically diverse range of politically reconstitutive strategies. In myth, the *pharmakos* appears at first as a benefactor to the community, and only later, during the condensation of the sacrificial ritual, as a threat to be purged, reconstituting in the process moral, ideological, and political boundaries:

> The ceremony of the *pharmakos* is thus played out on the boundary line between inside and outside, which it has as its function ceaselessly to trace and retrace. *Intra muros/extra muros.* The origin of difference and division, the *pharmakos* represents evil both introjected and projected. Beneficial insofar as he cures—and for that, venerated and cared for— harmful insofar as he incarnates the powers of evil—and for that, feared and treated with caution. . . . The conjunction, the *coincidentia oppositorum,* ceaselessly undoes itself in the passage to decision or crisis. The expulsion of the evil or madness restores *sophrosune.* (Derrida, *Disseminations* 133)

This is why both Jesse Jackson and George Bush could construct their respective 1988 campaign platforms around the fear of drugs. The war on drugs is thus better seen as a war *over* drugs: a struggle to decide which system of ideological or political tropes will successfully frame and control the flow of the supplementarity generated by drug trafficking.

Americans' widespread concern over the country's excessive dependence on foreign oil suggests another dimension of the national obsession with addiction, one allegorically linking the Noriega arrest and trial with the Persian Gulf War. (Miller and Mylroie 128, 132, 177, 216; Lee). Addictive drugs also compound the catastrophic condition of many American communities, and the underfunded but rhetorically ostentatious war on drugs temporarily sheltered conservative leaders from accusations of disregard for those communities' desperate needs. Drugs and drug traffickers permit condensation and projection of middle-class parents' fears of dissolving family and social values, and of the fiscal deterioration of the public education system. Finally, drugs symbolize Americans' suppressed fears of their own addiction to commodity consumption, materialism, and the advertising culture.

That the arrest of Noriega on charges stemming from cocaine trafficking, and the war on drugs itself, were of primarily symbolic value is suggested by the gap between the enormous military means potentially available for interrupting drug trafficking and its actually lax use (Woodward 24). The patent failure of the Panama invasion to accomplish any of its drug interdiction goals other than the hit-and-run, symbolically important arrest of Noriega is suggested by reports that eight months after the invasion, "according to Panamanian pilots and dockworkers, the cocaine traffic was back to pre-invasion levels and, if anything, 'more open and abundant than before'" (Ehrenreich). This is confirmed by the indictment of Noriega on cocaine trafficking charges, rather than for his well-documented involvement with heroin (the *pharmakos* of choice until recently). Indeed, the rhetorical structure of the war on drugs, which was condensed in 1989 into the war on Noriega, is disclosed in the peculiar symbolic doubling of the public image of cocaine in the late 1980s.

Cocaine plays two symbolic roles in contemporary American mythology, each drawing rhetorical energy from the anxieties and moral vertigo of the Reagan-era American political economy. The first of these images involves the powdered drug and taps into popular *ressentiment* of yuppie investment bankers, parvenu lawyers, and the idle children of the wealthy. The second image plays on the growing middle-class fear of and guilt over the largely black and Latino inner-city poor and homeless, presumably rendered dangerous and unpredictable by the effects of crack. Popular mythology has focused on an international syndicate of black and Latino drug traffickers, linking South American cocaine exporters with crack-dealing inner-city gangs based in Los Angeles and Miami. The war against cocaine thus condensed and symbolically displaced the fiscally and politically destabilizing consequences of Reaganomics, while Manuel Noriega's hedonistic life-style, racial characteristics, labyrinthine finances, witchcraft practices, and participation in cocaine trafficking effectively condensed several persistent post–cold war conservative American obsessions.

At still another level, the war on cocaine has disclosed a largely unremarked danger posed by drug abuse to the culturally hegemonic postmodernism of American advertising. Fredric Jameson has identified one of the central figures of postmodernism with the detached sensibilities of "intensity" associated with mood-altering drugs (Stephanson 4). Abstractly, the increasing use of drugs over the past generation has tended to undermine the constructed articulations between desire and the semiotic events and objects to which desire has been painstakingly attached in the workshops of American advertising culture. Although the spread of drugs initially stimulated the semiosis of new images, as abuse has reached epidemic proportions, fundamental linkages between productive work, remuneration, consumption, and the satisfaction of material and status needs have been dangerously loosened. The demystification of the market ethic itself jeopardizes the entire complex of ordered meanings rooted in commodity exchange that have served to regulate American society since the deterioration of community democracy and local organizations early in this century. Endemic social, racial, and other political disruptions are both exacerbated and sublimated by the particularly intense *mimetic rivalry*— identified by Girard as the primordial source of sacrificial violence— characteristic of consumer societies, where alternative social forms of status and power acquisition are successively colonized by the commodification process. The drug dilemma thus implicitly threatens economic reproduction itself, while compounding the fissures already fragmenting the conservative coalition, by engendering disputes between advocates of libertarian, communitarian, and military responses to the drug problem.

Sexual Aggression and Foreign Policy
Another threat to American conservatives thematized in the recent Panama and Persian Gulf interventions involves the oscillating status

of women in American ideological narratives and political life. Compounding conventional male sexual fears, transformations in American sexual practices and the attendant ubiquitous commodification of sexual simulcra have freed up new sources of supplementarity for exploitation by political imagineers. The supplementarity of libidinal energy under such conditions replicates the traditional generative function of taboos and repression in sacrificial rituals. Girard notes that myths of sacrifice and scapegoating "are remarkably eclectic in regard to the crimes of sex and violence attributed to their heroes" ("Generative Scapegoating" 83). Kenneth Burke discusses how most revenge and war epics begin with a violation of the family—linking war narratives from the *Iliad* down to the recent invasions of Panama and Iraq, where symbolic sexual threats and symbolic violence to the family played a central role in the mobilization of popular support for both interventions. During the period leading up to and following the 1989 U.S.-Panama "vertical force insertion," for example, a series of incidents depicting Noriega's sexual depravity were widely publicized. These included his "sexual torture" of two of Omar Torrijos's political opponents in 1964 (which had provoked a demonstration by local women) and his beating and rape, while a cadet, of a Peruvian prostitute to avoid humiliation in front of other cadets (*Newsweek*, 15 January 1990, 20).

When the invasion of Panama began, Noriega was in a brothel. After Colin Powell asserted that "We will destroy [Noriega's] Robin Hood image," American soldiers exhibited collections of pornographic and torture photographs found in Noriega's former residence. Bob Woodward's *Commanders* notes how prior to the Panama invasion, the plight of a U.S. army lieutenant and his wife, who had been sexually humiliated and threatened, had caught the Joint Chiefs of Staff's attention more than direct armed attacks on American soldiers (162). At a press conference following the operation, Bush responded to Soviet condemnation of the invasion saying, "Look, if they kill an American Marine, that's real bad. And if they threaten and brutalize the wife of an American citizen, sexually threatening the lieutenant's wife while kicking him in the groin over and over again, then, Mr. Gorbachev, please understand this President is going to do something about it."

The dissemination of war propaganda through rhythmically repeated televised sado-sexual images generates political power through a sort of war onanism, revealing complex symbolic sexual references. The giant but impotent Iraqi SCUDs disabled by smaller but technically more sophisticated Patriots, the postwar dismantling of Hussein's "Supercannon," and the wartime production of condoms with names like "The Saddam Hussein" and "The Stealth Bomber" are only some of the most obvious Gulf War illustrations here. Throughout the war, governing images were targeted primarily to traditionally male psychological concerns regarding the loss of sexual monopoly over women. Recalling Lyndon Johnson's comparison between bombing and sexual relations, Gulf War images such as those generated in repeated accounts of the fate of Kuwaiti women under occupation, the unspoken fear regarding Melissa Rathburn-Nealy (the captured American woman POW), and so forth, focused on rape, the real or implied threat of rape, and retaliation for rape.

Like the issuing of the Meese Report in 1985 (Susan Stewart), the representation of images of sexual violence simultaneously served a pornographic and a regulatory function. Indeed the continual display of high-tech violence and round-the-clock reportage created a sort of obsessive public thanatotic *fetish*.[1] In much the same way that pornography serves visually to reinforce insecure male sexual identity, the two-dimensional aestheticization of the Gulf War symbolically restored the nation's potency temporarily, through objectification of and identification with reassuring images of sado-sexual victory, fortifying in turn the conservative movement's flagging national ideological and political vigor.

Sado-sexual disciplinary strategy seeks to inculcate the desire for pain in the disciplinary subject in order to dismantle the subject's autonomy and independent volition. Evidence that a specifically disciplinary, anti*cultural* American warfare strategy is being developed has emerged sporadically since the end of the cold war. As U.S. officers were drawing up plans for the Gulf War, for example, Air Force Chief General Michael Dugan recommended that *cultural* targets be added to conventional bombing run plans. He "asked his planners to interview academics, journalists, 'ex-military types' and Iraqi defectors to determine 'what is unique about Iraqi culture that they put very high value on. What is it that psychologically would make an impact on the population and regime in Iraq?'" (Woodward 291).

The disciplinary use of force in Panama and the Gulf region, redundant to the point of arbitrariness, primarily brought about short-term symbolic reconstructions, rather than substantial political change, in both theaters. In Panama for example, the *New York Times* reported recently that cocaine "traffickers are boldly hauling drugs at all hours," in quantities some Panamanians and Americans say are "greater than when General Noriega was supposedly giving traffickers safe passage through his airports and harbors." The government of President Guillermo Endara, installed during the invasion, has lost its legislative majority and is still "groping for its bearings," having inherited a six-billion-dollar debt, "a bloated civil service and a thoroughly corrupt and brutal army." Endara himself "has appeared indecisive and disorganized and become the butt of jokes," and has served on the boards of banks shut down for drug-money laundering, although he denies any personal complicity. While some signs of economic recovery from the U.S.-imposed prewar economic sanctions and invasion are showing, unemployment remains around 20 percent. Crime is rampant: "After years of political repression but little common crime, Panamanians have been stunned by bank robberies, holdups of restaurants and all their guests, ambushes of business people traveling from airports, and hundreds of burglaries and auto thefts" (*New York Times*, 13 August 1991, A1, A4). Hostility to the United States is widespread, yet the population's support for the invasion remains paradoxically strong, a symptom of successful disciplining captured well in the following vignette:

> Across this devastated and emotionally and economically exhausted urban war zone, people stood amid the ruins yesterday shedding tears of happiness in spite of their predicament and cheering the Americans whose weapons turned many of their homes into smoldering ruins.
> "Thank you, President Boosh! Thank you, President Boosh!" exulted Alejandro Bullen as he stood shirtless not 20 yards from the still-smoking rubble of the apartment building where he once lived. . . . Lowering his voice and shaking his head, Bullen gazed at the remains of his home, adding in Spanish: "I have lost my home. I have lost everything. But finally I have my freedom. We all have our freedom." (Robinson and Bennett)

The ultimate targets of such regenerative foreign sacrifices are those Americans threatening to defect from the hegemonic conservative coalition. The primary function of disciplining violence and ritual projection is to reconstruct a viable role to be played by Americans in the New World Order. Two new forms of heroism appeared during the recent wars, each suggesting one aspect of the American future as envisioned in these narratives: hyperskilled and expensively trained electronic weapons operators weaned on video war games, and empathetic figures embodying the stoic/early Christian virtues of victims—hostages, POWs, the families of military personnel, and so forth. Neither the Panama nor the Gulf interventions generated the sorts of widely publicized combat tales of bravery under fire typical of most military engagements and subsequent mass cultural national debriefings. As Girard has observed, "whenever a people has embarked on a tragic course . . . no heroes arise, only anti-heroes" (*Violence* 295). Senator William Cohen of Maine, for example, after meeting with Arab coalition leaders told Bush, "We visited the Kuwaitis . . . and we realized that Kuwaitis are willing to fight—until every U.S. soldier has dropped" (Woodward 289). Before the war, James LeMoyne, writing in the *New York Times*, quoted a Saudi teacher: "The American soldiers are a new kind of foreign worker here. We have Pakistanis driving taxis and now we have Americans defending us." A few months later, a Gulf emirate leader was quoted in the *Wall Street Journal*: "You think I want to send my teen-aged son to die for Kuwait? . . . We have our white slaves from America to do that" (Brooks and Horwitz A4)—a phrase that a source in Republican inner circles recalled "dropped like a grenade" in the midst of war planning. Yet the image is sticky.

Throughout the Gulf War the dominant theme brought home by Orwellian "news" media that had become essentially a collective Office of Military Propaganda involved American soldiers coping uncomplainingly with sand in their food and eyes, with scorpions and blistering heat, and miserable living conditions, and arduous labor, and material deprivation. This image, in its heroic resignation and stoic view of salvation through suffering and abnegation is as clear a foreshadowing as we have of the future staked out for ordinary Americans under the New World Order. Combined with the continued militarization of American society, the intensification of public and private surveillance, the ubiquity of misogynistic sado-sexual imagery, the repression of libertarian tendencies, and the desperate, obsessive search for foreign and domestic enemies of our own making, we can begin to see the plot outline of an allegory for America's, and the world's, new moral order. The Gulf emir would not be the first to call it a slave morality.

Note

1. Peter Jennings, in the course of a televised satellite interview with some air force mechanics who were decorating some extremely phallic air-to-air missiles with explicit sexual graffiti, grew visibly uncomfortable as he discussed the

"age-old practice among soldiers of painting their wives' and girlfriends' names" on their "ammunition," and found himself pausing between each word, apparently to keep from laughing aloud, but having the disturbing effect of making sure that the double message of "this one's for you, baby" was neither lost nor rendered too explicit by overt gesture.

4 Jekyll and Hyde

The Political and Cultural Economy of Narcoterror

James Der Derian and Kiaran Honderich

Such a perfect democracy constructs its own inconceivable foe, terrorism. Its wish is *to be judged by its enemies rather than by its results.* The story of terrorism is written by the state and it is therefore highly instructive. The spectators must certainly never know everything about terrorism, but they must always know enough to convince them that, compared with terrorism, everything else must be acceptable, or in any case more rational and democratic.
—Guy Debord, *Comments on the Society of the Spectacle*

"You slaved to create me. . . . Now you turn away. . . . You run away. . . . Coward! I am your other self. Are you afraid of me?"
　　　　　—Classic Comics Illustrated Version, *Dr. Jekyll and Mr. Hyde*

Kulaks and Gulags, Junkies and "Jump Street"

William Burroughs, former junkie and novelist extraordinaire, tells a story about the village of Gerasimovka in the Ural Mountains of the Soviet Union, where over fifty years ago a thirteen-year-old boy named Pavliki Morozov denounced his kulak father to the local authorities for hiding a pig in his basement. This was at the height of Stalin's de-kulakization program, in which at least three million died by starvation and many more were deported to labor camps, because they resisted the expropriation of their produce and farm animals. But Pavliki became a folk hero, and a statue was erected in his honor.

This essay tells a similar story. To be sure, the drug war hysteria in the United States has not reached the level of political persecution that existed in Stalin's era. But we need to recognize that the statues and camps for the war against drugs have already begun to be built. There are more people per capita in prisons in the United States than anywhere else in the world, and the majority are there as the villains and victims of the drug wars. For the last decade the United States has been swept by a *de-narcoticization* program dependent on the kind of fear mongering, class hatred, and racialism that feed the totalitarian urge.

For those who think the threat exaggerated, take a hard look at the signs. Headlines tell similar stories of sons and daughters turning in their parents for drug use, and while stone monuments have yet to be erected in their honor, we can witness the electronic equivalent on television, with the fleeting enshrinement of those battling drugs on such programs as "Call 911," "Crime Stoppers, and "America Crime Watch." It is evident in "fictional" programming as well. An early gem of the genre is the special episode of "21 Jump Street" in which a teenager informs on his drug-using parents to Johnny Depp, whose good looks and agonized soul-searching are supposed to make up for the fact that he is little more than a glorified snitch. Then there is the metaphorical space in between fiction and fact, between domestic security and foreign threat, a "factional realm" where President Bush can hold up for the television cameras a bag of crack cocaine that was purchased in a park across the street from the White House (after the Drug Enforcement Agency lured a drug dealer there for his media debut), and U.S. troops can announce the discovery in Noriega's private headquarters of fifty pounds of cocaine in the freezer (that later turned out to be tamale flour).

Is it possible that we are so deep into a drug war that, as in other historical witch trials, good citizens accuse, condemn, and convict without thought of the powerful cultural, political, and economic forces at work?

The Economies of Narcoterror

As a counter-strategy to the drug war, this chapter pursues an understanding of the political and cultural economy of narcoterror. First, the matter of narcoterror. The use, sale, and legislation of narcotics all involve terror in different forms. One of the fears about drug use is that it is thought to remove its users from the constraints of rationality. We say constraints because to be outside the boundaries of rationality can be a source of great power: a New Yorker faced with a demand by an obviously rational person to hand over her watch or jacket will be likely to refuse—because she knows that it would not be rational for the would-be mugger to escalate to violence, when the potential reward is so small relative to the possible costs resulting to the mugger from violence. The same New Yorker will hand it over without hesitation to a junkie because she believes the junkie to be *irrational*, and therefore not susceptible to the system of incentives and punishments through which law and order normally operate.[1]

While the power of terror may be consciously or unconsciously wielded by drug users, it is also used by other people: in the current case, by politicians, law-enforcement officials, and television executives, to name but a few, all of whom are using the specter of narcotics-induced irrationality to serve their own ends. To judge from their descriptions, one toke or snort is enough to turn any God-fearing Dr. Jekyll into a Mr. Hyde, a being beyond any bounds of rationality or moral codes, whose behavior is therefore both unpredictable and disproportionately, incomprehensibly destructive. Current hyperbole conjures the images of an earlier war on drugs when the American drug commissioner Harry Anslinger gave lurid reports of users driven mad by even the most casual contact with marijuana. As he testified before the U.S. Congress in 1937, "I believe in some cases one cigarette might develop a homicidal mania, probably to kill his brother" [sic] (Hamowy 23).

This representation of drug users has two important implications: First, the flip side of the power invested by irrationality is that it puts its possessor entirely beyond the pale. To take an analogy from recent international events, if Saddam Hussein is portrayed as demonstrably irrational and therefore undeterred by reasonable threats, then no holds can be barred in our attack on him and his population. The other implication is that, as social critic Guy Debord says of terrorism, compared with drug addicts running amok, "everything else must be acceptable, or in any case more rational and democratic" (24). Thus polls report that the U.S. population is quite willing to give up apparently unimportant rights of privacy and speech in pursuit of the War on Drugs.[2]

What of the terror of drug sellers? They begin by breaking laws, but they move beyond that into the realm of terror because of the level of profits involved: this is the point where a political economy analysis becomes crucial. Making drugs illegal, if enforced with any degree of success at all, enormously increases the profits to be made in the drug trade. This is partly because drugs are rationed—depending on where you are in the country, and which drug you are looking for, narcotics are often not readily available to anyone looking for them, which will always drive up prices. Profits are also driven up because, given the contacts, abilities, and personalities required to smuggle illegal narcotics into the country and sell them illicitly, conditions of perfect competition do not obtain.

Illegality, and the increased profits that go along with it, are the prime ingredients of the forms of terror that most politicians and law-enforcement officials have in mind when they talk about narcoterror. One form that arises within the United States as well as in Asia and Latin America is the turf battle: rival gangs, or other groupings of narcocapitalists, battle over highly lucrative markets, using machine guns in place of advertising budgets. Narcocapitalists will also employ terror against any authorities attempting to enforce the illegality of narcotics, whether by shooting police, threatening judges, or other techniques. The increased profitability of many drug markets over the 1980s has enhanced these forms of terror by making sellers rich enough to buy sophisticated weaponry and by enormously raising the stakes in their battles.

The forms of terror practiced by drug sellers differ from the terror associated with use in that they are the results of rational practices of profit-maximizing narcocapitalists—though because of the profitability and illegality of their product they do involve often extreme levels of violence. But the other phenomenon that many people more specifically have in mind when they talk about narcoterror is the connection between the drug trade and groups that were already terrorists for political reasons—groups that have already been popularly defined as beyond any bounds of reason or humanity.

The prime example of this linkage is the Peruvian Sendero Luminoso or Shining Path and its relations with coca growers and processors. Traditionally, the Shining Path have not actually engaged in drug production or smuggling themselves. What they have done, though, is act as middlemen between peasants growing coca leaves and the processors who buy them, helping the peasants to receive better terms than they might otherwise. They have also acted more generally to give "protection" both to growers and to processors. This is done in exchange for a cut of the profits, so the Shining Path has gained both financially and politically by acting as advocate for peasant growers in the cocaine trade. In this example the narcotics trade is helping a terrorist cause in both political and economic fashion. Another example of linkage is the widely alleged involvement of the Nicaraguan Contras in cocaine smuggling in order to finance their terrorist activities against the government and population of Nicaragua. In contrast to the Shining Path case, though, this group of narcoterrorists acted with the support of the CIA.

We have outlined a number of forms of narcoterror, and it seems that many of them might be genuinely frightening to those who have waged the War on Drugs, inasmuch as they represent behavior that is not only violent and lawless but also, as we have emphasized, beyond existing boundaries of rationality and control. True as that is, it is equally true that many of the legislators, enforcers, and other storytellers use, depend on, and have even helped to create, many of the forms of narco-terror.

One story depicts the CIA as the grand masters of these practices: the Contras are just one of the groups whose support from the CIA included anything from a blind eye to active help in drug-running activities. The mutual benefits are obvious, and after a series of revelations from congressional hearings and the Noriega trial, the "plausible deniability" became less credible. The CIA could tap into a supply of easy profits from the arms and drug trade to fund projects for which official support was lacking; and politically correct narcotraffickers could access the political protection and transportation infrastructure for which the CIA is renowned.

To avoid the whiff of conspiracy theory, the Iran-Contra affair needs to be placed in the larger context of past experiences, when U.S. strategic interests intersected with the interests of the drug trade. Some would claim that the United States became entangled in the drug web; others that it helped to spin it. The web-spinning theorists claim that the United States not only inherited the Vietnam War from the French, but also the opium trade, which the French intelligence service, SDECE, had used to finance and win the support of Hmon tribesmen from the Vietnamese highlands in the struggle against the Vietminh guerillas. (See Alfred McCoy; *The Politics of Heroin*, Peter Maas, *Manhunt*; Edward S. Herman, *The Real Terror Network*; Jonathan Kwitney, *Crimes of Patriots*.) Even earlier, from 1948 on, the CIA had supposedly used drug smuggling routes and trade in the Golden Triangle to disguise intelligence and paramilitary operations against the Chinese communists. It is also claimed that some of the players who later showed up in the Iran-Contra affair first perfected the guns–drugs–secret warfare matrix in Laos in the 1960s, when Theodore Shackley was station chief of the CIA in Ventianne; General John Singlaub was chief of the SOG (Studies and Operations Group), which carried out secret raids into Laos; and Thomas Clines, also of the CIA, worked with (then) Lieutenant Colonel Secord to run covert air-supply missions.

The Iran-Contra hearings also revealed other drug connections, like the DEA involvement in the hostage ransom attempt in Lebanon and the CIA use of the Santa Elena airstrip in Costa Rica for the transshipment of illegal drugs and weapons (*Report of the Congressional Committees Investigating the Iran-Contra Affairs* 130–31, 318–21). A substantial body of evidence leads one to speculate that agencies of the U.S.

government have at various times colluded with narcotics trafficking. At the very least, over the last thirty years, narcoterrorism has been mainly perceived as a minor strategic threat and as a sometime ally in the battle against (what was seen then as) the much larger danger of communism. Some, like Mexican political analyst Jorge Castaneda, believe it is the very decline of the communist threat that has elevated the narcoterrorist one: "In a sense, now that the Cold War was nearly over, or coming to an end, the traditional justification of U.S. intervention in Latin America, at least over the last 50 years, had disappeared. And it has disappeared, but there's another one in its place, which is the drug war" (ABC *World News Tonight*, 24 April 1990).

At the level of political economy, it would seem that parts of the violent web of narcoterror—the interdependence between drug runners, addicts, and warriors—could be broken by legalization (Nadelmann 31). Narcocapitalists would not practice terror if narcotics were legal: profits would be reduced, and there would be no need to shoot or intimidate law-enforcement officials. According to Peter Reuter of the Rand Corporation, coca leaf production, refinement, and smuggling amount to less than 15 percent of street costs: the rest is a "pure" and irresistibly high profit (Gelb). The terror associated with drug users might also be reduced by legalization since lower prices would reduce the need for mugging. With or without legalization though, the "moral equivalent" of a drug war focused on treatment programs and economic regeneration rather than a militarized drug war based on eradication and interception would certainly involve lower levels of terror. At a time when only one in five of those who need drug rehabilitation treatment in the United States is getting it, the expensive deployment of high technology and troops to Latin America hardly seems defensible. (According to a 1990 General Accounting Office report, the U.S. military on drug interception patrols detected 6,729 "suspicious" flights, attempted to interdict 661 of them, and was successful in catching 49 of them [Gelb]).

However, narcoterrorism is embedded in another kind of economy that adds layers of complexity and intractability to the problem. In a perverse sense, we have become a state of "terror-junkies." Like the user on his fix, so too the administration depends on the terror of drug runners and addicts to construct cultural boundaries: without terror and unreason it could neither define nor justify normalcy or its battle against deviance. Hence, the drug war cannot be understood without a genealogy of the *cultural economy* of narcoterror: the exchange of images, signs, and narratives that valorize domestic integrity and cohere a pure identity over against an invasive alien. Racialism and xenophobia are the border markers of this cultural economy. From President Bush's 1989 inaugural address likening the drug trade to a "deadly bacteria," to the Rodney King trial, to the treatment of Haitian emigres, issues of rage, class, and drugs have been de-politicized and radicalized into a general hypochondria of the Other.

The Dates, Data, and Dada of the Cultural Economy of Narcoterror

How, then, did we get here? To answer this question we have to engage in a critical history that dismantles and goes beyond the official story of narcoterrorism. We must look into the supposed origins of the War on Drugs and how this particular war came to take on such importance in current domestic and foreign policy.

First, some familiar signposts. Narcoterrorism entered the political lexicon as the violent blending of illicit drug trade and political intimidation in Latin America. In the early eighties, Peruvian officials began to popularize the term by linking the Shining Path insurgency to the narcotics trade; soon after, the military arm of the Medellin drug cartel was similarly labeled.

The war *against* narcoterrorism is equally well marked, with Nancy and Ronald Reagan in 1986 sitting on a sofa somewhere in the White House, giving the American public the first high-level, televised debriefing of the "war on drugs." At a time when Gorbachev seemed intent on unilaterally calling off the cold war and Khaddafi preferred to sulk in his tent rather than execute his threat to bring terrorism home to the United States, narcoterrorism moved up the ranks to become our most immediate and dire foreign threat. The charges flew: Colombian cartels were using drug profits to suborn left-wing guerrillas; the Syrians were growing opiates in the Bekaa valley to fund Palestinian militias; the Nicaraguan Sandinistas were providing transshipment for cocaine and using the money to back El Salvadoran rebels; and, then, in a U.S. court in Miami, General Noriega of Panama was brokering protection deals between Fidel Castro and the Medellin cartel.[3]

In the same period, the cultural economy was selling a similar narrative, although the good guys and bad guys were often reversed: television programs and movies such as "Miami Vice," *Lethal Weapon,* and *Above the Law* took the first step in this reversal by dredging up the drug-running forays of the CIA-proprietary Air America in Southeast Asia and reinstating their clandestine operations to Latin America.

The discursive tactic of "just say no" quickly proved inadequate in the war against the new Public Enemy Number One. A volatile combination emerged: internal terrorism in U.S. cities, involving Jamaican and Colombian middlemen, and the expansionist gangs of Los Angeles, the Crips and the Bloods; international terrorism, by the Mexican *narcos* who killed DEA agents and the Medellin "Extraditables" who assassinated Colombian judges and other officials; and media overrepresentation, topped by the vigilante video *vérité/simulé* of "Cops" and "America's Most Wanted."

Our national security *and* the American way of life now being at risk, narcoterrorism took on the qualities of a synergistic threat that prompted a powerful new mix of material and immaterial responses. In an early riposte, then mayor Koch of New York advocated an air attack on Medellin, and Daryl Gates—the chief of the Los Angeles Police Department who had become infamous for his antidrug sweeps of the city with helicopters and armored vehicles—outdid Koch by calling for an outright invasion of Colombia. In Washington, D.C., the National Guard began to provide air support with Huey and Black Hawk helicopters for a police force losing the urban war (an average of 1.2 murders a day in 1990). At Camp Pendleton, the navy and the Marine Corps staged the latest phase of "RIMCON 90," a war game involving amphibious assault ships, hovercrafts, helicopters, and ten thousand marines, which ends with the capture of El Roja, drug lord and financial backer of an imaginary communist insurgency (Gaines). Overseas, the State Department was supplied with over 150 fixed-wing aircraft and helicopters for use in Colombia, Bolivia, and Peru; the Customs Service and Coast Guard established a Command, Control, Communications, and Intelligence Center (C^3I) in Miami to coordinate surveillance by E-2C Hawkeyes, P-3A Orions, and aerostats (radar-equipped blimps); and the Green Berets set off to train paramilitary forces in Latin America for the war against narcoterrorism (Harvey; Jehl; *Navy News and Undersea Technology* 7; Walker; *Defense and Diplomacy* 48–51; Massing, "The War on Cocaine" and "Dealing with the Drug Horror"). It was only a matter of time before stealth technology was introduced, as a front-page article from the *Arizona Republic* reported that "National Guardsmen in Texas could be fighting the war on drugs dressed as cactuses, sneaking up on smugglers under the cover of night and prickly needles, according to a proposal submitted to the Defense Department" (*Arizona Republic*).

Less humorous and more threatening to civil liberties is the single-mindedness of Democrats and Republicans on the threat of narcoterrorism. Senators Joseph Biden (D-Delaware) and William Cohen (R-Maine) cosponsored a bill to establish a "Counter-Narcotics Technology Assessment Center" (CONTAC). Its task? To "coordinate research into high-technology anti-drug trafficking techniques, including surveillance, advanced computers, artificial intelligence, and chemical and biological detection schemes" (Uncapher). CONTAC would be run by the head of the Office of National Drug Control Policy, Robert Martinez, who is intent on setting up a National Drug Intelligence Center (NDIC), that is, a central computer system that would collate local, state, federal, and military information on narcotics.

How did narcoterrorism come to claim precedence over all other forms of terrorism? One history, the official history, is made up of what President Reagan once referred to as "stupid facts," by which he meant of course the stubborn facts that millions of U.S. users spend between $100 and $150 billion a year on narcotics, creating such a demand that—according to the State Department's 1989 *International Narcotics Control Strategy Report*—over fifty-six countries are ready to service in the capacity of growers, manufacturers, traffickers, or money launderers (15, 19–24). Again, we should not allow the data to obscure the most important fact, that illegal drugs ruin and kill people. But we have heard all this so often that they have become not stupid but stupefying facts: they incur an inertia of helplessness, a mass mood that accepts the official view that only the experts, the police, the forces of law and order, can handle the drug problem. The problem, however, clearly exceeds the capabilities of the best trained TNT (Tactical Narcotics Team) units, which sweep a neighborhood clean of dealers one week only to lose it the next, or the DEA, which was forced out of Medellin, Colombia. The problem is that the cultural economy has so valorized the logistics, demonized the agents, and devalued the victims of the drug problem that we have lost sight of its all-too-human face.

To compensate, some alternative facts and histories are needed. Tobacco, an addictive drug, kills over 300,000 people a year; alcohol kills 100,000 (including those killed by drunk drivers); while the use of all illegal drugs combined—cocaine, heroin, marijuana, angel dust, LSD, and so forth—accounted for less than 4,000 deaths in 1987 (*International Narcotics Control Strategy Report*). Since then, the use of and death by the use of illegal drugs in the United States has declined (although the *New York Times* did report an increase in police officers killed in drug-related incidents to fourteen, out of a total of seventy-eight police deaths in 1988 [3 September 1989, 22]).

Yet in the United States the war on drugs continued to escalate.[4] Our suspicion is that narcoterrorism was finally taken seriously—if not hysterically—partly because it had taken on characteristics of a major transnational conglomerate rather than primitive capitalism, with a commensurate increase in political power (Bush, "Address to the Commonwealth Club of San Francisco"). Until the recent crackdown and amnesty program, Colombia supplied over 80 percent of the cocaine that reached the United States. Right-wing paramilitary squads, Marxist guerrilla groups, and two major drug cartels used drug profits to build up power bases that seriously challenged the sovereignty of the Colombian government. We heard much of how the *narcotraficantes* killed over three hundred judges and court employees since 1981 and, more recently, assassinated several candidates for president. Less often reported was the number and extent of jobs, homes, health services, soccer fields, earthquake relief, and schools supplied by the *narcos*— amenities that the state could not provide (Massing, "Dealing with the Drug Horror"). For many peasants they provided a cash crop, and more important, a transportation system that could get the "produce" to its far-flung markets.

The *narcos* do not—could not—rule by terror alone: their notorious option of *"plomo o plato"* (lead or silver) captures this dual strategy. As war is for most states, terrorism is for the *narcos* the *ultima ratio* of their burgeoning agribusiness empire. Providing a relatively lucrative living for everyone from the subsistence farmer to the ghetto dealer— along with bribes for the underpaid police or military officer—is as important a source of power as the threat or use of terrorism. Colombian president Gaviaria's new policy toward narcoterrorism, aimed at the separation of narcoterrorism from drug trafficking, acknowledges this power. By banning extradition and offering light jail sentences for drug traffickers like Pablo Escobar, he managed to broker a highly tenuous truce between the drug mafia, coca growers, guerrilla groups, and the government (Brooke). That Colombia remains the number-one exporter of cocaine, and that many of the amnestied Colombian "drug lords" have been able to set themselves up in well-appointed "prison-haciendas," also attests to a reorganization rather than a diminution of the corporate power of the drug industry. And, after the prime-time video of former Washington mayor Marion Barry smoking crack was followed by a minor misdemeanor conviction, Latin American leaders have became markedly less receptive to U.S. pressure for extradition or heavy penalties for traffickers.

Even if the United States were to send more Green Berets to the Upper Huallaga valley in Peru, the much ballyhooed solution of beating narcoterrorism by antiterrorism is certain to fail, as are schemes to make interdiction and eradication the top priority.[5] The same plan was used with marijuana, which simply resulted in an increase in domestic production as well as in the potency of the marijuana supply. There are already signs that the Colombian drug cartels, feeling the heat, are moving operations into the Brazilian jungles, and Guatemala has become an important transit and growing site. Even if we could someday develop the equivalent of a Narcotics Defense Initiative to shield the United States from foreign-produced narcotics—one plan calls for diverting funds directly from Star Wars to the drug war ("Democrats Propose Diverting Funds from SDI" 2)—designer and synthetic drugs could quickly fill the void. Narcoterrorism will not be stopped until the supply of and demand for illegal narcotics are stopped, which means that the United States must increase treatment and education, provide businesses and jobs in American cities, and introduce crop alternatives to coca as well as an infrastructure of credit and roads in Latin American countries. For political and economic reasons, that is unlikely to happen in a presidential election year or in the near future. The worst-case scenario, then, would be for incarceration, the preferred drug treatment program in the United States, to be enlarged and exported as foreign policy. The legal principle of *posse comitatus* against the military making arrests as well as taking on policing duties will be further eroded as actions are taken, through sanctions, surveillance, and even perhaps blockades, to contain rebellious inner cities and "criminal" nation-states.

As Old Statues Fall and New Statutes Rise

To conclude, we would like to return to that small village in the Ural Mountains. A few years ago, the inhabitants of Gerasimovka, taking their own private step toward the democratization and restructuring of Russian society, tore down that statue of Pavliki in protest. After the failed Soviet coup in August 1991, Lenin, Dzerzhinsky, and other icons from the communist pantheon have also been toppled.

Yet here in America, the cold war ends and we have plunged deeper into the drug war, with media icons, prison-gulags, and surveillance nets being built every day in its honor. As we were writing this, Congress voted to mandate random drug tests for six million national transport workers. A week before, at the Senate hearings to confirm the next head of the CIA, Robert Gates listed drug trafficking right after nuclear proliferation as the first order of business for a revamped, post–cold war agency. In between, the ever-anonymous "senior administration intelligence official" provided more detail of how this next war will be fought: "Look at narcotics: The imagery technology [the use of satellite photographs] is the same as for spotting a Soviet missile silo. Our collection on the economic and social milieu in which drug trafficking survives, our analyses of trafficking organizations, are all on the same level that we use when we analyze the enemy order of battle" (Wines). We seem to have lost one dire enemy only to construct another—and, irony of ironies, the reformed KGB is keen to help us in the struggle against it. After the failure of the Soviet coup, the newly appointed head of Soviet foreign intelligence, Yevgeny M. Primakov, suggested at his first press conference that the KGB and the CIA "could team up to combat terrorism and drug trafficking" ("After the Coup, What Role for the KGB?" E9).

Perhaps, as we try to keep up with the accelerating pace of the present, there is still something to be learned from those Russian villagers. Against the drug war, there can be no substitute for more jobs and better opportunities in the inner cities. But if we do not want our denarcotization program to turn into a full-fledged political pogrom, if we do not want to face the prospect of tearing down more menacing statues in the future, we must dismantle right now and every day the official stories of narcoterror.

Notes

1. As Edward Hyde discovers, "I have power . . . power to repel. . . . Ha! Ha! I will use it" (Classic Comics).

2. According to a *Washington Post*-ABC poll, 62 percent were prepared to give up "a few of the freedoms we have in this country" to reduce illegal drug use; 67 percent favored random car searches; 71 percent wanted to ban depiction of the use of illegal drugs in entertainment movies (*Washington Post*, 8 September 1989).

3. That these stories were the products of cold war narratives, think-tank half-truths, and uncritical media dissemination can be seen from the transcripts of the October 1991 confirmation hearings of Robert Gates as the CIA director (*New York Times*, 4 October 1991, A12–14; 13 October 1991, 24).

4. The anti-drug budget of the U.S. government was $10.5 billion in 1991, $11.7 billion in 1992, and is projected to be $12.7 billion in 1993. Roughly 70

percent of the budget goes to law enforcement (*New York Times*, 27 September 1991; *Minneapolis Star Tribune*, 6 April 1992).

5. For instance, the State Department's Bureau of International Narcotics Matters spends about $100 million a year, of which only $4.6 million goes to crop substitution and development assistance, while $45 million goes to eradicating crops and $35 million to law enforcement and interdiction (Massing, "Dealing with the Drug Horror").

5 Oliver North and the Lying Nose

Diane Rubenstein

The state system must be protected from Congressional investigations that rob the president of his covert tool which must be veiled from scrutiny to protect from embarrassing consequences. The Iran-Contra revelations, Secord lamented, publicly exposing the inadequacies of the President's "tool," have ensured that "the whole world is laughing at us."
—Frederick M. Dolan

Ollie resisted all efforts by committees to housebreak him.—Ben Bradlee

"the malevolent movements of Uranus and Saturn," astrological reference for the Iran-Contra Scandal   —Kitty Kelley

Public disclosure of a covert operation simultaneously reveals and reveils a president's tool. Revealing and reveiling—separated by the difference of a letter: *a*, the "a" of *différance* and Lacan's little object,[1] *i*, indivisible letter of the self and subject of a predication to follow. The covert operation can be read as a letter (purloined or otherwise) contained in traditional notions of diplomacy (the courier's mail pouch) or the new postage of a media cyberspace (electronic mail, CNN). But how should we read such overdue mail/male?[2] Do we read Iran-Contra as Lacan reads the purloined letter, as the process of the course of a letter in its movement of rephallicization? Or do we read Iran-Contra prefigured in Freud's Wolf Man narrative: as an attempt to preserve masculine self-esteem or aggression against the feminine threat or the passive (homoerotic) wish? America standing tall, holding its own against communist insurgency? The Wolf Man narrative here would be the allegory of a secret, of "a drama of disclosure which veils yet another secret" (Fish 540). Two "ur" texts, which have been subjected to extensive and protracted readings, correspond to the two pleasure zones of Iran-Contra—the phallic and the anal.

Iran-Contra begs for a literally symptomatic reading—somewhere between the president's tool and Oliver North's stool. My reading, like that of Nancy's astrologer, will, by a homonymic displacement, follow the saturnalia of uranus/your anus. Iran-Contra is part of a larger Reagan policy, as Don Regan and others have written, of controlled leaks.

Iran-Contra crosscuts and interrupts a presidential politics of bodily disorder. Read against a backdrop of Reagan's medical interventions—his nose, bowel, and penis—it is eerily reminiscent of the Wolf Man. Reagan's body, like Larry, speak(e)s. The story of Reagan's nose surgery and cover-up recall the fetishistic obstruction of the Wolf Man's private nose language. I would insist on the fetish quality of Iran-Contra: the construction of a fetish—a CIA outside the CIA, a "simulacrum of the national security culture."[3] Casey and North's "off the shelf" covert operation is a part object that compensates for as it denies the fear of castration. It also incessantly reminds us of the apparent reality of castration after the Boland amendment cuts off the purse strings. But if one examines the exact language of Casey and North's wish, there is another erotics of the covert operation: an "off the shelf, self-sustaining, *stand alone* entity" is also a turd/feces. Ollie and Casey's "neat idea" is neat in two senses. It is both clever and anal. This "stand-alone, self-sustained entity" is what Freud designated by *Zwangsneurose,* obsessional neurosis, "a self-sufficient and independent disorder" (Laplanche and Pontalis 281). I would privilege the German term *zwangsneurose* as *zwang* refers to compulsive acts (*zwangshandlungen*) and emotions (*zwangsaffekte*) as well as the more common reference to compulsive thoughts (*zwangsvorstellungen*). But most important for our analysis is that this term that Freud uses points to a *symptom* rather than to a *structure.* Laplanche and Pontalis have noted: "The evolution of psychoanalysis has led to an increasing emphasis being placed on the obsessional structure to the detriment of the symptom" (282). The reading of Iran-Contra that follows reverses this traditional preoccupation with structure, placing considerable weight on the symptoms produced in the disclosure of the covert operation.

The reading that follows is framed by two texts: Poe's "Purloined Letter" and Freud's "Wolf Man," as well as the subsequent interpreters of these works (Lacan, Derrida, Felman, Johnson, and Abraham and Torok). My two "ur" texts are detective stories at one (Poe) or two (Freud) removes. Moreover, we will see that these two narratives oppose differing strategies for reading the covert operation: a hermeneutic versus a hermetic reading. The hermeneutic reading would follow the logic of Lacan's "Seminar on 'The Purloined Letter'" and attempt to locate a meaning of the affair, even if it is only the positing of a lack of meaning as a transcendental signified. The hermetic reading would situate the affair within a national security culture figured as a cryptic text that is so radically designified to begin with that it must be (fantastically) reconstituted in order for interpretation to proceed. Hermetic versus hermeneutic readings underline the question central to this paper: (How) can the covert operation within a national security culture be read? They remind us that questions of interpretation always presuppose a theory of readability at work in a text. I situate this question of the readability of the covert operation at the angle between the "clues" afforded within the detective story genre (or the "symptom-clues" of the Freudian case study) and the explicitly psychoanalytic-literary reading of textual clues.

My argument for a psychoanalytic reading of the covert operation is not a traditional hermeneutic interpretation. Decipherings, descriptings, take place on the level of the *signifier*.[4] The secret is never fully disclosed—it was there in full view, or like the signed presidential finding always already there, locked in Poindexter's safe and burnt upon discovery. In other words, this is not a disclosure of a hidden referential content or ultimate signifier of Iran-Contra. The power of the signifier is apposite to the covert operation—it resides in the signifier's "transparent materiality; invisible in its very visibility" (Muller 363). "The Purloined Letter," like Iran-Contra, displays strategies of open concealment as well as duplicitous discourse. We will also note that for Lacan, signifiers, as opposed to meanings, always point to the unconscious. Psychoanalytic readings, which follow the rhetorical displacements of the signifier (and, after all, arms for hostages is a rhetorical as well as a geopolitical deal), mime the notions of diversions and trace that are crucial to Iran-Contra.

I would also like to caution against any overly facile psychological reductionism. I am not saying that either Ollie North or Reagan is the Wolf Man or that they are Dupin or the minister turning letters inside out. Moreover, I am not saying that we are Freud or Dupin. Rather, I would like to address the uncanny coincidence with these literary "ur" texts that a symptomatic reading of Iran-Contra discloses. Coincidence here refers to "the coming together in a single moment of two entities belonging to two absolutely different ontological realms . . . which consequently can have no strict causal explanation, but which, touching, appear to be motivated by some significant necessity, some deep affinity of meaning . . . normally used to designate the accidental appearance of some resemblance between two heterogeneous events" (Klein and Weaver 5–6). This resemblance with an appearance of motivated necessity is called "significant coincidence" by Jung and refers to an associational contiguity. This uncanny associational link between the language in which the affair is disclosed by commentators and participants recalls many of the same *topoi* mobilized in these "literary" texts. What

I am suggesting then is that this "coincidence" points not to any direct one-to-one correspondences but to different *models* of reading. If the language of disclosure of Iran-Contra recalls "The Purloined Letter" or the "Wolf Man," then the readings of these texts in turn should double as model readings of the event, that is, of covert operations, in the national security culture. My concern is primarily about the readability of the covert operation.

Psychoanalytic readings such as those of Lacan and Derrida are not the only possibilities for a rhetorical reading of Iran-Contra. Iran-Contra can be, and indeed has been, read otherwise. In Rogin's version, it is part of a history of racial demonology and the emergence of a specular foreign policy. Spectacle and secrecy are figured *chiasmically* within a model of historical trauma and amnesia. "Covert actions derive from imperatives of spectacle not secrecy but owe their invisibility to political amnesia" (Rogin, "Make My Day" 105). Fred Dolan situates Iran-Contra as a moment in the history of metaphysics: "Such doctrines as 'rollback,' 'containment,' 'counterinsurgency' must be read as sketches for a metaphysics of contemporary world history as a permanent crisis requiring constant supervision and if necessary, intervention" (Dolan 107). Both Rogin's and Dolan's accounts draw on Freud's theory of fetishism. Dolan's ostensible preoccupation is an analogy between the crisis manager's masculinist subjectivity and that of the empirical political scientist. His claim that the male crisis manager's badge of toughness is the mastery of a reified language is apposite in some respects to that of Rogin. For Dolan, a crisis manager is an adolescent boy whose tough talk screens him from fears of inadequacies, thus enabling him to project power. Rogin's discussion of Iran-Contra is similarly framed by an incident of "tough talking," in this case "Make my day!" as challenge and mastertrope of Reagan's and Bush's racist policies. This tough talk is spoken as Clint Eastwood dares a black man to murder a white woman in the context of a film whose subject is rape and revenge (*Sudden Impact*): "The lives he proves his toughness by endangering are female and black, not his own" (Rogin 103). My reading overlaps with those of both Rogin and Dolan: The male crisis manager is a fetishist (Dolan). The covert operation is a form of therapeutic politics within a larger political culture of motivated disavowal (Rogin).

James Der Derian offers a third reading in his "Arms, Hostages, and the Importance of Shredding in Earnest." Der Derian's reading underlines the modernist frames of both Rogin and Dolan (Freud, Marx,

Heidegger) as its exceeds them, situating Iran-Contra against the hyper-reality of terrorism and counterterrorism. Terrorism is a deconstructive activity, and North is the simulacrum of the national security culture. Iran-Contra takes p(l)ace in a chrono/geopolitical cyberspace—a covert operation in (Mona Lisa) overdrive. Terrorism has a proleptic quality as anticipation of a legitimation crisis to come. Der Derian reminds us that deciphering the contemporary culture of the national security state requires attending to excessive writing/overwriting, briefing and overbriefing, the creation of the false Ollie chronologies, back-dated bills, doctored IBM typing balls, magnetic messages (PROF notes), shredding machines, and signatures on traveler's checks (emblems of both traceability/countersignature and security: "Don't leave home without them"). The fabulous textuality is addressed by Representative Pascell in the Senate hearings when he says that Ollie deserves to be in the *Guinness Book of Records:* "Colonel, you have probably produced and disposed of more government paper than anybody I ever heard of" (*Taking the Stand* 555).

And yet, despite the hyperobtrusiveness of writing, the "epiphenome-nology of terrorism" of the covert operation is to be read in shredding. Der Derian establishes an epistemological equivalence between knowledge and shredding, as we learn from "the smoke rising from the 'burn bags' of the executive branch" (Der Derian, "Arms, Hostages" 81). What Der Derian implicitly addresses as another (cyberpunk) language ("at high orbit and in low resolution . . . and in lower orbit but at higher resolution") is the underlying question of my reading. Reading the covert operation of a national security culture, in other words, requires that we confront the (in)ability of the trace to speak.

The Urinary Politics of the National Security State:
Reading Public Orifices/Offices

"Now, of course, the concern you expressed about leaks is a real one. . . . But let's be clear. The fact that a few members of Congress leak doesn't mean that all members of Congress leak, just as the fact that some members of the Administration leak cannot be fairly said to mean that all members of the Administration leak."
—Senator Mitchell, *Taking the Stand*

Iran-Contra signals a shift from the promiscuous Derridean dissemi-nation (before AIDS hysteria) to the urinal politics of Der Derian national security cyberspace, where archival secretions leak out only to reappear as pub(l)ic narratives. Dissemination in a safe-sex age with the condom deterrence of SDI (nothing gets through this defensive shield) regulates the flow and potentially risky exchange of valorized symbols and information. The archive of the national security state accretes, secretes, and excretes not only flows, but also *piles*, too: "But once obtained . . . [this] archive of the high [political] culture of the national security state, that is, the official currency of discursive practices which circulate, accumulate, *piles* up around the great power" (Der Derian, "Arms, Hostages" 80). Not to worry. These excretory "piles" will be cleared by the "shovel brigade."

I am taking Der Derian literally when he suggests that "we must seek out [the state's] most sensitive secretions" (80). For Der Derian's epistemological equation of knowledge with shredding takes place in a post-AIDS discourse of risk and safe sets: semantic sets as well as ethical, epistemic, and practical sets for responding to crises within the national security culture (i.e., disseminating terrorism). The (im)possibility of safe (discursive) sets to "write/read about terrorism without a teleology" affects the semio-critical reader: "reducing the possibility of any metacritical and ethico politico response to it" (81). My literalization of the post-AIDS metaphors of flows and secretions are an attempt to "excessively reinscribe this story of arms, hostages, and terrorism" (81) via a reactivation of Bakhtinian categories of the carnivalesque (i.e., Rabelaisian laughter) or Bataille's categories of nonproductive expenditure (i.e., expenditure without exchange) or what Baudrillard refers to as the "ob-scene." This new semio-critical strategy of overwriting deploys the ludic and the scatological, which can be read either (critically) as forms of resistance or as (postmodern) excess, which momentarily disrupts the domination of the code. A focus on the scatological in Iran-Contra (as in Rabelais) provokes uneasy laughter. Bakhtin reminds us, "laughter liberates not only from external censorship but first of all from the great interior censor" (Bakhtin quoted in Edelman 128). My flagrant literalization of Der Derian and the Iran-Contra (con)texts of Speakes, Regan, Bradlee, and North posits excessive inscription as a carnivalesque writing of the body. Literalization becomes a form of embodiment, a rhetorical strategy to read a radically designified and designifying text.

The covert operation and its disclosure is indissociable from an administration that conducted foreign policy by leaks and was obsessed by leaks.[5] Regan writes: "Even though I had to admit, surveying the techniques invoked and the results obtained, that this policy of deliberate leaks was an interesting example of management by objective" (283). These "deliberate leaks" stand in contrast to the "indiscreet silences" of Reagan's years on Wall Street, the "indiscreet silences" of insider trading. Reagan offers a catalog of leaks—from the unintended leak to the "officially sanctioned leak calculated to produce a specific effect" (283). This second category was not new to Ronald Reagan—the Kennedys used it—but in Regan's words, "it was raised to an art form under Baker, Meese, and Deaver." Both foreign and domestic informational material were leaked. Regan describes a situation in which there is a "remarkably free flow" of unsourced information out of the White House into the public domain as triads (Gergen, Darman, and Baker; Craig Fisher, Jack Svahn, and Meese) act in concert with media stars such as Bill Plante of CBS and Paul Blustin of the *Wall Street Journal.* "Paradoxically, these secret arrangements . . . created what was probably the most open government in history" (Regan 283).

Regan and Speakes present at times conflicting assessments of the ability of the trace (i.e., the leak) to speak (be traceable). For Regan it is a question of knowing one's partners (and their histories) in this fluid exchange. For Speakes, there is a hermeneutic of generalized suspicion without unequivocal verification. Speakes believes Gergen leaked the story of McFarland's Lebanon trip (after all, he's in a high-risk group), but "they never found out who was responsible for that leak or for any other leak" (Speakes 332). Leaks also remain untraceable as Speakes consults his phone log.

The National Security Council team—Allen, Clark, McFarland, Poindexter—were obsessed by the possibility of leaks, making a fetish of secrecy and keeping the press "in the dark." Poindexter drafts an NSC directive on how to control leaks and punish them, including the use of polygraph tests and the creation of an FBI strike force. Casey's obsession with leaks underscores the link with a new late-eighties McCarthyite hysteria over clean bodily fluids, what Arthur and Marilouise Kroker in "Panic Sex in America" describe as a urinal politics. In this body McCarthyism loyalty oaths are displaced/replaced by mandatory drug testing in the workplace: this recyclage on "the terrain of bodily fluids . . . insists on the (unattainable) ideal of absolute purity of the body's circulatory exchange as the new gold standard of an immunological politics" (Kroker 11).

Yet urinal politics is only one part of the flow. There are other orifices (nasal, anal) that leak and have their (body) part to play in a symptomatology of Iran-Contra. When reporters ask for permission to see

President Reagan's scar after his colon surgery, Speakes says no, deflecting attention to another orifice: "He wants to show you the point of entry of yesterday's (proctoscopic) examination." Proctoscopophilia replaces the trace (scar) as it also displaces the tube in the president's nose. "The first photograph of the President after surgery was artfully arranged to conceal the nasogastric tube that had been inserted in Reagan's nose." Nancy's kiss "strategically covers the tube" (Speakes 239). (We will return to a discussion of the Political Father's Nos/Nose in the next section.)

A cursory list of other "public" figures of secretion would include Cap "the knife's" *Seaspray* covert operation of 1981 (clandestine air support for the CIA), which also prepares Cap to be the "mouthpiece" for the military brass in the Reagan administration (Speakes 101). It would also take note of the letter-writing campaign during Iran-Contra to the onomastically felicitous "Spitz" Channel.[6]

But it is North who has a privileged relation to Iran-Contra body fluid/orifice narrative. First praised for his "tight, hands-on" control of the Achille Lauro command post (two pleasure sites of Iran-Contra), North becomes Reagan's alter ego and national hero. Described by Ben Bradlee as a "cold warrior soulmate" and "Ronald Reagan in miniature" (548), he is psychohistoricized as an alternative son: "the desire for the aging Gipper to latch on to a surrogate son . . . who could play out his dreams." Ron Reagan, Jr., "cavorting about in his underpants [briefs] on Saturday Night Live" (a risky business in a dangerous world) is, in Bradlee's words, "not quite the *Halls of Montezuma* stuff the President had in mind." North, as loose cannon within the self-sustaining entity of the NSC covert operation, returns in the Oedipal narrative as a form of Montezuma's revenge.

Through his senate testimony, taking the stand (or more accurately, stooling on just about everyone else but Reagan), North is able to shed his loose-cannon image. But he is never far from scatological figuration. No longer a "loose cannon" but a "national hero," Oliver North is praised by pundits as not "housebroken" by the committee.

The Name of the Nose

> I never thought I'd see the day when the credibility of a White House
> news secretary would be put in jeopardy because of a pimple on the pres-
> ident's nose.   —John Madigan, WBBM commentator

A bit later, the famous symptom of the nose (= he knows) begins.

The scratched out pimple leaves a hole. Yes, he does know the whole
business about the *hole*.
  —"A Lying Nose and the Tooth of Truth," *The Wolf Man's Magic Word*

Since Watergate, the hermeneutic question that underwrites the narrative disclosure of the covert operation is, What did the president
know? What the president knows becomes the ultimate transcendental
signified, limit or horizon for understanding the covert operation. To
displace this originary question rhetorically to a focus on a signifier that
functions as a bad pun—that is, the president's *nose*—may well seem
extreme or frivolous. And yet, the president's nose (and other bodily
symptoms) are hyperobtrusive in the textuality of the Iran-Contra Affair. The equation of knowledge with nose is crucial in a symptomatic
reading of signifiers disclosed in the exposure of this covert operation. The different implications of these two epistomological equa-
tions, knowledge = shredding and knowledge = nose, will be discussed
in a concluding section. For the moment we will read Reagan's nose and
the disavowal/cover-up of this particular cancer as a transparent literalization of the problem of his presidency and of his policies. It is a
transparent literalization—as plain as the nose on the president's face.
  This body focus is not an extension of the doctrine of the King's two
bodies.[7] It is not an argument to develop the identification of the personal with body politic along the lines of a hysterical somaticization.[8]
Iran-Contra is metaphoricized as a cancer on the Reagan presidency. But
most important for my reading are the uncanny parallels between the
sites of Reagan's nonmetaphoric cancer and the Wolf Man's symptomatology. Both Reagan's and the Wolf Man's sites of bodily dysfunc-
tion include the bowels and the nose. Can these sites be read as allegories of persuasion and disinformation? Do the bowels and the nose
somehow mimic the problems of the larger context of Iran-Contra?
  What is most surprising about narrative accounts by insiders such as
Speakes and Regan is that the pathological policies of Iran-Contra are
discursively framed by Reagan's hospital stays and surgical interventions. Decisions concerning arms for hostages, the signing of presidential findings, the staging of the possibility of nonrecall (deniability),
take place in the hospital ward. We may well ask if the primal scene of
Iran-Contra is not a scene of surgical intervention and writing.
  Regan's narrative account of Iran-Contra begins in the (cancer) ward.
"Nancy Reagan stammers slightly when she is upset and her voice was
unsteady when she called me from Bethesda Naval Hospital on Friday
afternoon, July 12, 1985, to tell me her husband, the President of the

United States, would require surgery for the removal of a large polyp in his intestinal tract" (3). Regan's disclosure of the radical semiosis (i.e., astrology) at the heart of the Reagan presidency is interrupted by details of the colonoscopic examination: "the preliminaries for major surgery included measures such as fasting and cleansing of the bowel" (5). Reagan is operated on, wakes up from anesthesia, becomes president again with a stroke of his dark blue plastic souvenir pen at 7:22 P.M., and after a joke about Bob Dole, asks if there is any word on the hostages (11). Over the next few days, between more jokes and Hollywood stories, the president is finally allowed on July 18 to see Bud McFarland, who has urgent reasons to see the president. This meeting, Regan goes on to say, was "of course the first in a sequence of events that very nearly led to the fall of one of the most popular presidents of the United States" (25). Yet this meeting with McFarland passes out of presidential memory.

Speakes's account of the Reagan presidency also begins with a body focus—that is, assassination attempt. "The gunshots thrust me from a relatively obscure job as deputy press secretary into the spotlight as the spokesman for the President, the White House and the nation" (1). The president is shot, and now Larry Speakes—a therapeutic conversion that is linguistically satisfying. Speakes's identification with the presidential body is direct. Speakes's chapter is simply called "A Cancer on the Presidency" and begins with simple declarative phrases: "It's cancer, it's big, it's black, it's ugly" (230). The hospital is just a setting for Regan; the real presidential obstruction lies not in his colon but outside his body in the form of Nancy. It is a stage, a backdrop in which key meetings take place and are forgotten. But Speakes's narrative (and here I am favoring the un-Derridean move of valorizing Speakes over writing/Regan's *For the Record*) implicitly recognizes the import of a truly symptomatic reading of the Reagan presidency.[9]

Speakes links the deniability of Reagan's surgical interventions with political deniability, the cover-up (of Reagan's cancer) with the covert operation. The analogy between body politic and political policies is apparent to Speakes in Reagan's double disavowal. When Lou Cannon asks Ronald Reagan if he had cancer, the president says: "I didn't have cancer. I had something inside me that had cancer in it and it was removed" (Speakes 237). This "unrealistic" and "incorrect" medical history is compared with Reagan's denegation that he did not exchange arms for hostages: "He believed that just as he believed he hadn't had cancer, but he was wrong each time" (Speakes 238). Reagan believed that he was dealing with third parties and thus not directly negotiating with hostage takers. "Iran" here is in the position of "something inside me that had cancer in it." Reagan's disavowal of his cancer allows for Speakes's charitable reading of either presidential nonknowledge or misrecognition: "I know that the President and perhaps McFarland and Poindexter really believed that, but almost everyone else involved— Americans, Iranians, and Israelis—recognized the shipments for what they were: bribes that were intended to lead to the release of the hostages."

The president's colon cancer allows Speakes to admit that the president does not know. But the president's nose is another story. Just ten days after his colon surgery, Reagan develops a pimple on the right side of his nose. He thought that this was caused by irritation from the nasal surgical tape. We recall that the president tried to cover up this nasal tube—discursively deflecting attention to other zones. He compared his surgery to a wart on the end of a finger (Regan 17), or offered to show the hard-nosed press corps the point of entry of his proctoscopic exam. Why does Reagan prefer the anal orifice or the phallic-digital index? Does Reagan have, in the Wolf Man's words, a "lying nose"?

Yet another nasal cover-up ensues as the scab on the president's nose seems serious enough to be removed. A biopsy is performed under a false name—Tracy Malone, identified as a sixty-two-year-old white female. Tracy Malone is the name of an actual nurse at Bethesda: forty years were added to her real age to make "her" sample fit with those in the president's age group. So far, so good.

"It was on Thursday, August 1, that all hell broke loose," Speakes writes. The scene is an address of evangelical broadcasters and members of the regular White House Press Corps who notice the scar on the president's nose: "What's the scab on the President's face?" Speakes disinforms under orders from Nancy: "The scab is an irritation from the tape that held the nasogastric tube in place." Speakes calls it by a string of euphemisms: "an irritation," "a gathering or piling up of the skin." Nancy engages in denegation: "Who has never picked a pimple?" She argues for the omission of certain words: *cancer, biopsy.* "Why can't we just say. . . . He had a pimple on his nose which he picked at and scratched?" (Speakes 243–44). Speakes refuses to sign the press statement of fifty words that omits the two crucial ones (*cancer, biopsies*), sending "a clear signal, though a subtle one, that I was not staking my credibility on these words." Attribution is generic: "The White House, Office of the Press Secretary," and without the endorsement of Speakes's proper name. However, these elementary semiotics were lost on the press corps ("No one noticed my signal," Speakes 245). Maybe it was not their fault. Having dealt with the linguistic complications of the pseudo-crossing of the bar between signifier and signified whenever Larry Speakes, they could overlook the rhetorical subtlety of his clear signal. In an epilogue, Reagan discloses the "basil cell carcinoma" on his nose on Monday, August 5. (Two more nose operations follow in October 1985 and in July 1987—the month of North's testimony.) Yet Sam Donaldson and Helen Thomas accuse Speakes of having a "lying nose." "They raised questions about my credibility."

This "lying nose" can be read as an emblem of the covert operation and disinformation that takes place in the national security culture figured as a "crypt." As we will see in the concluding section, the lying nose is not a conventional metaphor. The cryptonymic reading of the lying nose displays the radical semantic shift that psychoanalysis effects in language. Although my reading of Iran-Contra appears to proceed by a progression of literalized metaphors: *leaks, cancer, lying nose*, they are neither metaphors nor literal meanings in an ordinary language sense. Ordinary language will not help us enter the crypt, although it does enable us zealously to overwrite upon it (Der Derian, "Arms, Hostages" 81).[10] The crypt, Abraham and Torok (as well as Derrida) tell us, necessitates a different t(r)opography. This new tropography proceeds by "anasemic conversion," it *designifies* along the lines of an *antisemantics*.

The reading of the covert operation as crypt is thus a departure from the Derridean reading as an open letter/postcard. Derridean dissemination designated the process by which thought jumped along looser knots of syntax that resisted being unraveled into final sets of meaning. *Déchemination* (the term deployed in his reading of the postcard) underlines "writing's relentless will to divide and detach itself from sender and receiver" (Conley 82). Dechemination does offer a plausible model of reading Iran-Contra, but both terms—*dissemination* and *déchemination*—advocate *polysemia* over *anasemia*.

Anasemia was the mastertrope of Abraham and Torok's work. Anasemia is derived from *ana*: "upward," "according to," "back," "revised," "backward," "again." *Semia* is defined as "that which pertains to the sign as a unit of meaning" (Abraham and Torok 117). Anasemia is a process of problematizing the meaning of signs in a radically undetermined way. Moreover, the various possibilities contained within the first part of the term, "ana," point to the new topography that cryptonomy designates.

Abraham and Torok's anasemia is perhaps most well known to the English reader through their analysis of the Wolf Man, in *The Wolf*

Man's Magic Word. Instead of the presentation of a catalog of "deciphered hieroglyphic," that is, a dictionary of the Wolf Man's words, they present a "Verbarium": an incredible and stupefying language that "sets language at an angle with itself and shatters all linear correspondence" (Abraham and Torok xxv). There is a tremendous temptation to construct a dictionary of Iran-Contra—a dictionary of euphemisms ("residuals," "management style," "strategic opening," "neutralize") or a catalog of rhetorical tropes (*litotes,* the trope of negative relation and denial; *deprecation,* pleas to obtain something; *imprecation, conmination,* and *apostrophe*).[11] Oliver North's testimony deployed all of these rhetorical devices. (In that respect, North was a model reader of the CIA manual.) Yet I will stress the need for a *verbarium,* a term whose play in English translation repeats the French in another language. "Verbarium" or *"verbier"* in French, recalls the disseminating germs of *"herbier."* "Verbarium" in English contains "barium," the element used to trace the symptomatology of Reagan's body politic. Barium sulfate is an indicator in an X-ray photograph of the digestive tract.

Abraham and Torok's verbarium is constructed between three languages: the Wolf Man was a Russian émigré who undertook an analysis with Freud in German. Abraham and Torok's "discovery" is the importance of English in de-crypting. The Wolf Man had an English governess, and his dream is a rebus that is articulated in the play between these languages. Homonymic displacements, phonic similarity (tooth = truth), enable Abraham and Torok to reconstitute the radically designified text and connect the Wolf Man's sexual knowledge (of coitus *a tergo*) to his nasal obsession (he knows = nose). This approach, relying on poetic as well as polyphonic capacities of language, is not to be restricted solely to polyglots. In other words, a verbarium can be constructed out of the differences *within* the same language. It is this latter possibility that intrigues Derrida in his foreword to *The Wolf Man's Magic Word:* "Already within a single language, every word multiplies its faces or its allosemic sides and multiplies the allosemic multiplication by further crossing formal grafts and combining phonic affinities" (Abraham and Torok xiii).[12]

Let us again take up Reagan's "lying nose." There is a "coincidence" between Reagan's symptoms and the nose language of the Wolf Man. The Wolf Man had an obsessive preoccupation with his nose and teeth, continually seeing dermatologists for treatments of blackheads, swellings, wounds from picking pimples, and imaginary or exaggerated scars. On Easter 1925, between appointments with Freud, the Wolf Man develops a pimple on his nose. He consults a doctor who diagnoses it as an infectious sebaceous gland and recommends a particular course of treatment. The Wolf Man consults another doctor who squeezes his pimple, causing blood to rush out and provoking a feeling of great relief in the patient. (Some interpreters go so far as to say he experiences orgasm.) Nevertheless, a scar remains, and nasal symptoms remain an obsessional idea (*idée fixe*) (Kalinich 175–77).

The somatic parallels between Reagan and Freud's most famous patient include his other surgical site. In the course of his psychoanalysis with Freud, Freud promises him a complete recovery of his intestinal activities (i.e., chronic constipation). The psychoanalysis is so successful that the Wolf Man's bowel enters into the conversation! Stanley Fish reads this as an allegory of persuasion that is as transparently literal as my reading of Reagan's nose. Psycho(anal)ysis is an "emptying out" of preexisting convictions and doubts (Fish 542). A bowel or intestine enters into conversation and something is eliminated (doubt? belief?). Does Reagan's intestinal surgery eliminate doubts about the wisdom of exchanging arms for hostages? Does it raise the possibility of another strategic *opening*—that is, one to Iran, paving the way for North's neat idea? Does the intestinal surgery somehow figuratively mime and enable the necessary elimination of doubt? Does it mime or prefigure an act of persuasion, which in turn authorizes the covert operation—going private, finding channels, and creating the self-sustaining entity?

But what does the president's nose signify? Derrida writes about the Wolf Man's nose language: "The Wolf Man's desire had to become mute." The nose language is provisionally analyzed as a symptom in which no word can yet be read. Nose language/what the president knows in a covert operation in a national security culture is "a sort of writing without language, a billboard or open book covered with unpronounceable signs—not yet a rebus" (Abraham and Torok xl). "Bowel conversation" persuades the president to take part in the covert op. Nose language dissuades in the form of the cover-up.

Indeed, the unpronounceable signs point, like Reagan's lying nose, to the covert operation. A rhetorical reading should be attentive not only to silences but also to parapraxes—mispronunciations. Bud McFarland stumbles over the word *prescience* (saying "pre-science") shortly before he is forced to resign due to unforeseen events (Speakes 334).[13] Casey's image is also that of a bumbling, inarticulate man: "The classic example was that the could not pronounce Nicaragua. He would say Nicawawa. He didn't apologize for it. When Casey would discuss Nicaragua, he would just say 'Nicawawa' and everyone present would know what he meant" (Speakes 114). The nose language is covered with unpronounceable signs, "Nicawawa," yet Larry Speakes de-crypts this writing without language. What was the president's nose as signifier? Speakes proclaims: "The President's nose was Grenada all over again." The press exchange with Donaldson and Thomas recalls the credibility crisis over Grenada as it anticipates Nicawawa: "There was no lie, but they were right. There was a glaring omission" (Speakes 247). Glaring, like Freud's *glanz* (shine) on the nose.

The exchange between Speakes, Donaldson, and Thomas serves as a model for other post–Iran-Contra scandal disclosures. But there is one other body site that Larry Speakes of in the briefing room. In August 1986, the details of the president's bladder exam are disclosed. Under local anesthesia, "an instrument is inserted in the penis and goes up the urinary tract and it has a viewing apparatus where the doctor is able to examine the interior of the urinary tract." The word *penis* is mentioned in the briefing room as the president is doubly debriefed. Larry Speakes is jubilant about his narrative miming: "Public discussion of the president's penis? Yes—it happened—in the Reagan White House, on my watch" (Speakes 249–50).

Filling in the Blank Check of the Covert Operation: Iran-Contra and "The Purloined Letter"

Le manque a sa place.
   —Jacques Derrida, on Lacan's "Seminar on 'The Purloined Letter' "

The disclosure of the covert operation simultaneously reveals and re-veils the president's tool. The president's penis is debriefed (by Speakes) as compensation for the nose language. Let us take up the threads of the Iran-Contra narrative again—with Oliver North and Grenada within the frame of "The Purloined Letter."[14] For it is in reference to the crisis management of Grenada (i.e., the president's nose all over again) that North performs a key gesture of "The Purloined Letter," a gesture that is repeated by two of Poe's most attentive readers: Derrida and Lacan. In Grenada, North *fills in the blank* of American foreign policy.

"More than anything else . . . North's role in the Grenada success established him as a man of rising influence within the national security council" (Bradlee 183). Grenada is North's opening into the epi-center of the NSC crisis management group. After the coup against Maurice Bishop, Bush convenes a special situations group, which plans to divert a twenty-one-ship flotilla headed by the aircraft carrier *Inde-*

pendence bound for Lebanon toward the Caribbean. Sentiment grows for an all-out invasion. Vessey argues that the rescue of Americans would be difficult without securing the whole island, and this need a rationale. Fears about student safety and questions about airport construction prove insufficient legal grounds. North supplies a "neat idea" for a rationale. His solution was to use the Organization of Eastern Caribbean States (OECS) to press for American assistance. This "transparent justification" enables North to "fill in the blank." "North . . . pressed an idea that filled in the last legal blank" (Bradlee 175). North fills in a blank and, along with his fellow crisis managers Fontaine and Meages, places a bet on whether the president will sign the NSC directive for an invasion. Their bets are then sealed in an envelope. Reagan signs off on the invasion.

North, like Dupin inscribing a phrase from Crébillon in his fac-simile of the letter, fills in a blank. If the covert operation, like "The Purloined Letter," is an allegory of the signifier, what role does this blank filling play? A full reading of the Iran-Contra Affair as purloined letter would discuss this role at length. It would fill in the gap, by discussing gender and symbolic determination. If "the shadow of Ollie North hung over the entire Iran Contra deal" (Speakes 345), is this a "great female body" to be read à la Lacan? It would read North's filling in a blank in relation to the plausible deniability of the diversion. No smoking gun is ever found because *a space is left blank*. "The evidence shows that at least one of Ollie North's memos about the diversion had a space for the President's signature and that space was left blank" (Speakes 364). This draft of a memo sent to Poindexter to review was never passed on to Reagan. But does this mean that it never reached its destination?[15] Does the lack have (a) (its) place in the covert operation? Do covert operations circumvent the system of checks and balances, replacing them with blank checks? Was Reagan's euphemistic management style a "blank check"?

But there is a second structural parallel between Iran-Contra and Poe's story. For as Johnson has so brilliantly analyzed in her account of Lacan and Derrida's Poe-tic readings, the letter produces an automimetic effect. The key term of Iran-Contra—*residuals*, a euphemism for the word (*diversion*) that Oliver North does not like to say[16]—re-produces the figuration of Derrida and Lacan. "Residual" is tied to "residue," alerting us to the question of whether or not the trace can speak. "Residual," like "diversion," has two connotations, two registers of meaning. "Residual" refers to the corporate ("of, pertaining to, or characteristic of a 'residue,' 'a remainder,' a qualify left-over at the end of a process") and entertainment. A residual is the money paid to a performer whenever that performance is repeated. As entertainment, "residual" connotes the "always-already" diversionary: what is more diverting than a (repeat) performance? (Residue/residuum also have important associations for a cryptic analysis—a residue is what remains of a testator's estate after all debts and claims are satisfied. Residuum generates reside/residence, a dwelling. A crypt is a dwelling place for the remains.)

If "residual" sets off a chain letter of associational connotations, including the one it hides (diversion), "diversion" literalizes the Derridean enterprise of *déchemination*. Diversion denotes an act or instance of turning aside, as well as something that distracts the mind, relaxes, or entertains. It also connotes a military maneuver of deflection that turns an opponent away or astray. *Divert:* to turn aside, distract, or amuse. Yet this entertaining tactic need not distract us, but rather points to how diversion relates to *déchemination*. Déchemination, as we have stated earlier, describes the way that letters stray from their paths, in Conley's words, "writing's relentless will to divide and detach itself from sender and receiver" (82). *Déchemination* is part of a meshing of figures, and it stands in relation to dissemination as its trace. The break out of the closed space of polysemy is accomplished by another neologism: *tranche/fer* or ax blow. *Tranche-fer* homonymically displaces and recalls transfer (as *déchemination*/dissemination). The relations between these "words" is pun, buffoonery, "parasitical dependence" (Conley 82). *Tranche-fer* (ax blow) is a cutting trope deployed to slice through the intersubjective dialectic characteristic of *transference*.

North's activities partake of *déchemination* and the *tranche-fer* of funds to the Contras. The euphemism "residual" points to the "diversion" it covers up and etymologically includes. This amusing diversion is a *déchemination:* Oliver North fills in blanks, writes "diversion memos" that are destroyed, except for one found in his safe (Bradlee 501). But in this displacement of the letter, in the transfer, the *tranche-fer* comes down on him, too. He is continuously and simultaneously rephallicized and dephallicized, described as a "Marlboro Man without the Marlboro" and re-membered as a "Rebel with a cause" (Bradlee 538). A reading of Iran-Contra in reference to "The Purloined Letter" accounts for the movement of the letter in rephallicizing the male crisis manager to enable him to fill in the blank after a president's "management style" requires him to shoot blank checks.

Dances with Wolf Man

> What we have here is a picture of someone who alternates between pas-
> sive and aggressive behavior, now assuming the dominant position of the
> male aggressor, now submitting in feminine fashion to forms that over-
> whelm him.
> —Stanley Fish, "Withholding the Missing Portion: Psychoanalysis and
> Rhetoric"

> If the commander-in-chief tells this lieutenant colonel to go stand in the
> corner and sit on his head I will do so.
> —Oliver North, *Taking the Stand* (342)

Freud's analysis of the Wolf Man deploys a similar rhetorical strategy
to that of Poe's "Purloined Letter"—a strategy of open concealment is at
work in Iran-Contra as well. Freud offers to reveal the Wolf Man's secret
as he also offers to share his doubts and intellectual uncertainty with
us. Ollie offers full disclosure: "the good, the bad, and the ugly," in a
discursive power play as flagrant as Freud's. Both Freud and North
demonstrate the way denial (*litotes*, plausible deniability) can function
equally as a boast and as a jubilant affirmation. Freud's narrative, like
the textuality of Iran-Contra, is one of things withheld (by doctor and by
patient) and lies told to advance the story and to cover it up (Speakes
358). Oliver North is part of a group at the NSC that "withholds the
missing portion" in Fish's terminology, but with an interesting twist.
North withholds even as he "stools." He takes the stand (he does not
lie). The equivocal nature of North—as "compass point" (and the "magnetic North" that Daniel Schorr and James Der Derian speak of) turns
oxymoronic when we consider his full name. Oliver North, a non-
place—olive trees do not grow in the north. No wonder that Oliver
North is difficult to place. Let us frame him then by his testimony and
by the Wolf Man's case.
    Oliver North is a radically equivocal compass point. He wants, in
Bradlee's words, to "have it both ways on the fall guy issue" (517). He
wants to get credit for being able to "stand up and take the heat," yet his
testimony smears everyone but the president. Now, Oliver North is not
the first person who ever wanted to swing both ways, but what is
peculiar to his case is that he draws a line on taking the fall when it is a
criminal issue. He will take a "political" but not a "criminal" fall. How
do we explain this fear of law? Does it relate to North's wish?

I would conjecture that the law Oliver North is afraid of transgressing is his covert or veiled homoerotic wish. Contained within the often-cited boast of aggressive bravado: "If the commander-in-chief tells this lieutenant colonel to go stand in the corner and sit on his head, I will do so" is a wish to sit on the president's face/head.[17] The indeterminate use of the pronoun "his" could refer equally to the president as to North. Who is sitting on whose head? And why must this be done in a corner (veiled)? North distinguishes between a political versus a criminal fall—in one (political) he is a "hero," in the other, a "patsy." Clearly he does not want to be seen as acted upon. North overtly desires to be a "fall guy" on top, in control. The oxymoronic character of this wish ("a fall guy on top") produces a grammatical lapsus (indeterminate pronoun reference) as symptom. Bradlee reminds us that this was not North's first day in court; he flew back to Vietnam to testify for his friend Randy Herrod, accused of My Lai-type brutalities. North's testimony earned an acquittal for the friend who saved his life, and the description of his courtroom appearance is a prefiguration of the hearings: "Every bit the poster Marine with his high and tight haircut and his summer khaki uniform studded with combat decorations. He was articulate and had a relaxed yet earnest tone to his voice. But where Buckley, Carpenter, and Bender decorously kept their legs crossed, North's legs were *splayed out, spread eagled*. It was the only flaw in an otherwise impressive performance, which did not go unnoticed at Marine headquarters." Oliver North, the (spread)-eagled scout, can be read as the large feminine (passive) body spread over this affair.[18] This oscillation between the passive and hypermale can be read against the hysterical male presidencies of Reagan and Bush.[19]

North's testimony reveals another affinity with the Wolf Man narrative, but this is a characteristic he shares with Reagan and Bush. For the Wolf Man narrative/dream is, in Rapaport's words, "an obscene and traumatic spectacle in a pathological staging of the refusal of an image to be either fully opaque or fully transparent, the refusal to fade and the inability to block yet another *mise en scene*" (62). It is this pathological staging that makes obsession possible. A reading of Iran-Contra through the frame of the Wolf Man, through the window (of vulnerability) that stages the Wolf Man's dream, would situate the covert operation in the seductive power politics of the trompe l'oeil. Reagan and Bush present a politics of the afterimage. Presidential subjectivity in an era of the trompe l'oeil is not the deauthorized "dead" father, but rather a disappearing or fading one—a ghost.[20]

Conclusion

"The Wolfman," says [John] Waters, referring to Freud's famous case
study: "I wanted him to be my friend."
    —Paul Mandelbaum, "Kinkmeister," *New York Times Magazine*,
                                                    April 7, 1991, 38

From then on, that particular pleasure, jealously preserved in his inner
safe, could only be subject to total disavowal.   —Derrida, "Fors"

Derrida makes the argument for cryptonymic readings in his introduction to Abraham and Torok entitled "Fors." *Fors* is a word that is
uneasily translatable: "for," an archaic meaning—outside, except for,
save; and "for,"—always modified, the *for intérieure*, the inner heart(h),
or the figure of a subjective interiority. "Fors," plural, invokes a play
between an "inner safe" and "save," (except for) what is contained and
what is left out. I will briefly suggest that this new t(r)opography would
be a model for an international relations that has displaced Cartesian
coordinates that no longer apply.

Cryptonymy is peculiarly suited for the covert operation as it concerns the secret/secrecy. The secret is given a new topolographical and
metapsychological status. Indeed, *cryptonymy* (a neologism combining
crypto and *metonymy*) is a strange psychoanalytic practice that replaces traditional metaphors of the unconscious (secrecy = latency =
hidden) with a "false unconsciousness" (HUMINT?) positioned as a first
object or backdrop. Derrida writes: "an artificial unconscious lodged
like a prosthesis, a graft in the heart of an organ, within the divided self,
a very specific and peculiar place, highly circumscribed to which access
can nevertheless only be gained by following the route of a different
topography" ("Fors" xiii).

The crypt as presented by Derrida is an emblem of an NSC culture
with partitions and simulated situation rooms (built to look like what
people in the movies feel a situation room should look like). The crypt,
like the NSC culture, is an artifact, in whose partitions are enclosed
enclaves such as the "executive junta." It is a figure of compartmental-
ization: "a place comprehended within another but rigorously separate
from it . . . so as to purloin it from the rest." Through this construction
of partitions, the cryptic enclose produces, in turn, clefts in space. "In
the architectonics of the open square within space, itself delineated by a
general closure, a forum. Within this forum, a place." Inside this forum,
an inner safe is constructed, "a secret interior within the public square."

This inner forum (separated from the outer forum, where speeches and symbolic goods are exchanged) is a safe: "an outcast outside inside the inside" ("Fors" xiv).[21]

I would suggest that rather than read Iran-Contra as the simulation it presents itself to be—"A CIA outside the CIA"—that we ask about its inner safe. A "stand-alone entity" still conforms to the topographic space of Descartes: inside/outside. Iran-Contra is about figuring the national security culture as an "outcast outside inside the inside." And this outcast safe has everything to do with secrecy: "staking a secret place in order to keep itself safe somewhere inside a self" ("Fors" xiv). I find it ironic that North's infractions are themselves symptomatic significers: the acceptance of money to build a security fence. I am alerted to the cryptic language of discussion: all the "spare parts" and "oil-drilling equipment" held in the small cargo area of one plane. Why insist on one single cargo plane? I think of Ollie encrypted in the inner safes of his car (in the many curbside interviews) and of the physical layout of the briefing books at the Senate hearing designed to create a "bunker effect" (Bradlee 497). North's testimony itself displays an encrypting effect. His rhetorical appeals build up rationale and construct a record, a caulked and sealed room.

I read Iran-Contra ultimately as the construction of a cryptic safe that maintains, in a state of ritual miming and repetition, the conflict it is incapable of resolving. The secret fragments the topography of the crypt. (The crypt is no "solution"—it is a strategic compromise.) The difficulty in staking a secret place in order to keep itself safe somewhere within a self addresses the rationale of the covert operation and its operatives: "that we are at risk in a dangerous world."

Oliver North has learned much since then. No longer concerned with security fences and the construction of a cryptic enclave somewhere between his "dynamic unconscious and the self of introjection" ("Fors" xix), North now wears his safe on the outside. As a spokesman for bullet-proof vests, North sheds his marine officer's uniform and repeats the gesture of Poe and Freud (turning signifiers inside out). Resplendent in his bullet-proof vest, Oliver North is (finally) safe.

Notes

Earlier versions of this paper were delivered at the Midwest Political Science Association, Chicago, and the Shambaugh Symposium on Rhetorics as Politics:

Discourses Civic and Academic, University of Iowa, 1991. I would like to thank Barbara Bieseker, James Der Derian, and John Nelson for their comments.

1. Lacan's "little object a" or *"petit objet autre"* is a surplus object, a leftover of the Real, which eludes symbolization, yet it *partially* represents the function that produces it. See Slavoj Zizek's *Sublime Object of Ideology* as well as Bice Benvenuto and Roger Kennedy, *The Works of Jacques Lacan* New York for a further elaboration.

2. "Overdue mail," the *"lettre en souffrance,"* is a trope Derrida uses in "The Purveyor of Truth." See Muller and Richardson, eds. *The Purloined Poe,* 173–212.

3. See in particular James Der Derian's "Arms, Hostages and the Importance of Shredding in Earnest" for this aspect of North/"off the shelf entity" as simulacrum.

4. For another treatment of the covert operation read as a signifier, see my "Hate Boat: Greenpeace, National Identity, and Nuclear Criticism" in Der Derian and Shapiro *International/Intertextual Relations: Postmodern Readings of World Politics,*

5. "Leaks" are addressed in another way relevant to Iran-Contra in Plato's *Gorgias:* "In the same way, he labels fools 'uninitiated' ('or leaky') and that part of their soul which contains the appetites, which is intemperate and as it were the reverse of water tight, he represents as a pitcher with holes in it, because it cannot be filled up. . . . The sieve . . . he uses as an image of the soul and his motive for comparing the souls of fools to sieves is that they are leaky and unable to retain their contents on account of their fickle and forgetful nature" (Plato, *Gorgias* [London: Penguin, 1960], p. 92). This image of the soul of fools as a leaky vessel could be read against Reagan's testimony (Total "non"Recall) as well.

6. Other onomastically felicitious examples include "Armacost," "Secord" (a compromise formation combining *secret* and *record*), "Hall" (as a conduit between McFarland and North via her mother, Wilma Hall, McFarland's secretary), "Cave" (the Iranian translator indispensable to our cryptic analysis). One would also note the difference of a letter—*a*—between Regan and Reagan, which Rogin discusses in " 'Make My Day.' "

7. For a full discussion of the implications of this doctrine for the increasing identification of personal with body politic see Rogin, *Ronald Reagan, the Movie,* chapter 3, "The King's Two Bodies: Lincoln, Wilson, Nixon, and Presidential Self-Sacrifice."

8. The argument for hysterical somaticization (a form of miming?) might be read in the recent medical history of President Bush. Bush, who has self-announced problems with "the vision thing," develops glaucoma!

9. This symptomatic reading reveals an interesting moment of blindness. Speakes expresses a petulant disbelief that the Press Corps sees him as a "mouthpiece"!

10. "The problem confronting all inscriptive readers and semiocritical writers

of this story is how are we, armed with the resurrected data, excessively to reinscribe this story of arms, hostages, and terrorism without overwriting the disorder which gave rise to it?" (Der Derian, "Arms, Hostages" 81). I will suggest another analogy that Derrida addressed at length in "Fors," namely "the possibility of writing upon a crypt."

11. For a discussion of these figures, see "Some literary resources," 94–98, in *Psychological Operations in Guerilla Warfare* (the CIA manual). *Imprecation* expresses "a sentiment in view of the just or homeless". *Conmination* is a similar figure expressing a "bad wish for the rest." *Apostrophe* "consists of addressing oneself towards something supernatural or inanimate as if it were a living being: 'Mountains of Nicaragua, makes the seeds of freedom grow,'" while *interrogation* consists of asking a question of yourself to underline rhetorically what is being said (97). North's testimony makes use of logic figures such as preterition, litotes, and rhetorical questions, as well as the plaintive figures of speech (imprecation, deprecation, etc.,).

12. Alloseme refers to word usage.

13. Noonan also concurs in this assessment of McFarland in a few hilarious passages in *What I Saw at the Revolution*: McFarland would not say "Pass the butter," but "The stationary oleaginous object that is now not within my grasp or the grasp of others within this administration would be desirable, though not necessary, within my sphere and on my muffin" (224). This of course is Noonan's parody. The "real" speeches quoted are actually funnier (223–24).

14. A fuller discussion of the parallels between Iran-Contra and "The Purloined Letter" will appear in a forthcoming work. Issues to be discussed will include parallels between the staging of secrecy and revelation; narrative disclosure as a form of seduction in North's testimony; the veiling of truth as woman and the letter as pure signifier of negation. In short, a full reading of Iran-Contra as purloined letter would situate it in relation to the critical debate exemplified by the essays in *The Purloined Poe*, edited by Muller and Richardson.

15. The question of whether or not a letter reaches its destination is at issue in the debate between Derrida and Lacan (see Lacan, Derrida, and Johnson in Muller and Richardson, eds., *The Purloined Poe.*)

16. Another word that North does not like to say is *profit* (Bradlee 500).

17. Fish's thesis in "Withholding the Missing Portion" also alludes to this wish: "a report by the Wolf Man of what he thought to himself shortly after he met Freud for the first time: 'this man is a Jewish swindler, he wants to use me from behind and shit on my head.' This paper is dedicated to the proposition that the Wolf Man got it right" (526). The context of this remark within North's testimony is reminiscent of Fish's focus on the scatological: a discussion of money is linked to the "clean-up" (*Taking the Stand* 341). The discussion of "sitting on his head" occurs within North's assertion that if the commander in chief dismisses him, he would proudly salute and say, "Thank you for the opportunity to have served." "And I am not going to criticize his decision, *no matter how he relieves me*, sir" (emphasis mine, *Taking the Stand* 342).

18. The position of the purloined letter has been read as an anatomical chart of the female body: "upon a trumpery filigree card-rack of pasteboard, that hung dangling by a dirty blue ribbon, from a little brass knob just beneath the middle of the mantlepiece" (21). For differing interpretations of this female anatomy/textuality question see Marie Bonaparte (130), Jacques Lacan (45, 48), Jacques Derrida (189), Barbara Johnson (237–39), and Norman Holland (311) in Muller and Ricardson, eds., *The Purloined Poe.*

19. On the hysterical male, see Arthur and Marilouise Kroker, eds., *The Hysterical Male: New Feminist Theory* (New York: St. Martin's Press, 1990).

20. For a development of these topics, see my "This is not a President: Baudrillard, Bush, and Enchanted Simulation," in Kroker and Kroker, *The Hysterical Male.*

21. Derrida plays on the new configurations of inner and outer: "the inside as outside of the outside or inside; the outside as inside of inside" ("Fors" xiv). This new topography occurs on the frontier between introjection and incorporation and is, as such, part of a much larger discussion of the critical possibilities in Abraham and Torok's work.

Part Two   American Alterities

The essays in this section explore the significance of discourses that circulate in "alternative" public spheres, many of them addressing the problem of "identity politics." Anne Norton explores the productive tension between the absence of women from liberalism (and liberalism's self-celebration) and the constitutive absence on which American national identity depends, committed as it is to perpetual progress, betterment, and the refusal of what is given. She insists on the positive side of this ambiguity. Given the yawning gap between ideal and real, and the desire to fill it by staging narratives of its fulfillment, those excluded from the full practice of citizenship find vocabularies readily available that enable them to intervene in the discourses of American national identity. To be sure, there is a danger in such strategies. They tend to fall prey to the way in which America's staging of deferral, the essentially *asymptotic* character of American political desire (as in what Sacvan Bercovitch calls the "American Jeremiad"), allows for the simple dismissal of experience that suggests that the ideal has not been achieved. In such a staging the actual achievement is in a sense irrelevant and even threatening to the constitutive lack at the center of the discourse.

However, stressing the measure of "success" misses crucial dimensions of political action that have little to do with success or failure in instrumental terms. William Chaloupka examines the performative, theatrical character of the street demonstration in a world of instantaneous mass communications, pointing out that what is demonstrated at such events is not merely a political claim or demand, but through gestures, slogans, modes of dress, and styles of display, an "alternative public person." The most important element of any street demonstration is the appearance, in an alternative public sphere such as the street, of forms of live and activity that, by their very nature, undermine the self-confidence of the regime. Thus the extraordinary "epidemic" effect of street demonstrations, from Chicago in the 1960s to Beijing in the 1980s.

In contrast to the spontaneous construction of alternative public spheres that attract attention because they suggest the possibility of new forms of action and community—forms that seem to disappear as rapidly and mysteriously as they appear—we find institutionalized, even highly ritualized, "alternative" or "marginal" forums for the expression of dissent and fugitive experiences. The tension between the spontaneity and unpredictability inherent in genuine political interventions and the regulated procedures we associate with official public institutions reaches an especially high pitch in the case of public presentations of "political" poetry in America, as John Dolan argues. The formal demands of postromantic poetry require a public that postmodern society cannot provide, and in response a public for poetry is simulated, among other ways, through the ritual of the poetry reading. As Dolan forcefully shows, such poems have everything to do with the literary, ideological, and sociohistorical isolation of contemporary poetry, and almost nothing to do with a public sphere of any sort, official or unofficial.

Stuart Alan Clarke reconnects the unofficial to the official by exploring race, one of the most explosive sites of symbolic contestation in the American imagination. Attempting to make sense of the contradictory uses to which "the race card" has been put in recent presidential politics (the "bad nigger" Willy Horton figured in contrast to the "good nigger" Clarence Thomas), Clarke employs Gramscian categories to unveil a broad cultural logic of race in American politics. The Horton-Thomas "presentation," as Clarke puts it, organizes two elements of a unified symbolism that frames the discussion of race by stabilizing the increasingly plural articulation of the differences at large in American society. Through a trenchant analysis of the political and economic history that informs the current impasse regarding social welfare and racism, Clarke shows how the presidential party (the Republican party) both controlled and exploited those differences through its invention of a new symbolism of racial indifference—a symbolism whose effectiveness depends, paradoxically, on the continued presence of differences articulated through inequalities in the administration of the political economy. We require a keener appreciation of the symbols that this cultural logic relies upon, Clarke suggests, if much progress is to be made in contesting the new domestic order.

6 Engendering Another American Identity

Anne Norton

The Liberal Tradition in America

In his vision of *The Liberal Tradition in America,* Louis Hartz saw an America shaped by its absences, constituted in lack.[1] Americans are shaped, Hartz wrote, by an absent history, a history they abandoned on another continent. Lacking the inequalities of birth that shaped liberalism in the anciens régimes, they are born free. Shaped by the conflicts of the history they left in Europe, they lack the motive impulse of opposition. Without the hazardous legacy, and the fragile promise, of class conflict, liberalism becomes both past and future to its present. Blessed by an exemption from the inequalities that preceded them, Americans are doomed to the eternal recurrence of the same.

Southerners seduced by a feudal dream of aristocratic domination constituted the only fundamental challenge that Hartz saw to the liberal order. With the defeat of the South, Hartz argued, American liberalism came to enjoy an unchallenged hegemony. Only a late confrontation with the world they had left in Europe would bring contradiction home.

The sharp division of a liberal North and a South in thrall to a feudal dream was twice vulnerable. The construction of a feudal South deprecated the liberalism of Jefferson, Washington, and Madison, the liberalism of Southern political discourse and the liberal structures of the Southern states. The construction of a liberal North disguised the illiberalism of Puritan jeremiads and nativist pamphlets, the illiberal character of Northern racial practice, the conflicts with liberalism in industrial development, and the residue of feudalism in American law. In making African-American citizenship the shibboleth of American liberalism, Hartz masked the intensity and complexity of the contradictions in the American constitution.

Not all Americans were liberal before the Civil War. Not all Americans were liberal after it. The liberal tradition in America emerged from civil war as it had entered it—partial and incomplete. Hartz could argue, however, that the primacy of liberalism faced no serious challenges and revealed no serious fissures within itself in the years following the Civil War. The history of American labor in the nineteenth and twentieth centuries, the Indian wars, the Mormon wars, and the illiberal principles of American immigration law might be dismissed (Hartz did dismiss them) as imperfections. Though the racial order of the 1860s kept much of its force into the 1960s, slavery had been abolished. Though African Americans were not yet citizens in practice, they were citizens in law. Liberalism had established its hegemony.

The history Hartz records protects liberalism's claim to primacy by confining inequality within spatial and temporal limits.[2] This history confines racism to the American South. It confines constitutional inequalities to the American past. The spatial and temporal isolation of racial hierarchies enables us—as it enabled Hartz—to grant our America an absolution, making the South scapegoat and sin eater for a persistent, and persistently undemocratic, American racial order. In this reading of the past, the racial inequalities of the present appear as the wreckage of a defeated enemy: foreign and unsightly, holding no threat to the present order. The artifacts and evidence of the inadequacy of liberalism are transmuted into evidence of liberalism's victory.

Yet even forgetfulness of a history marked by Southern agrarianism and labor radicalism, millenarianism and imperial adventures is not quite sufficient to overcome the "aberrations" in America's liberal tradition. Even the full inclusion of African Americans in that promised future we have yet to enter would not be sufficient to make liberalism whole. The nation Hartz described had no women in it. Hartz could see the triumph of liberalism in America only because he was blind to gender. That absence shaped Hartz and *The Liberal Tradition,* as it has shaped America and the liberal tradition. Recognition of that lack puts in question not only the American liberal tradition, but liberalism itself.

American women have never lived simply as liberal citizens. Liberalism held them in a separate sphere. Within the liberal nation, women lived in the remnants of another order. The world of nineteenth-century women was, in Carroll Smith-Rosenberg's famous phrase, the "world of love and ritual." Within that sphere, authority remained paternal. Birth and marriage determined one's place in a complex of hierarchies. Rank was held in one's body, secured by the rituals of the church and the laws of the state. Women's loyalties were (women's loyalties remain) personal. Women were held (women are held) to an ethic in which honor surpassed performance. Marc Bloch described the order inhabited by American women better than Louis Hartz. Women have lived not in the shadow, but in the structures, of the feudal order.

The work of feminist historians, like other work in social history, revealed the presence of difference in the Americas. The often unrecorded subaltern conducted their lives within institutional structures, cultural conventions, and constitutive categories in contradiction to the announced principles of the liberal order. Initial investigations cast these structures and practices as mere aberrations. The subjection of African Americans was seen as an artifact of the Confederacy: archaic, foreign, illegitimate, already defeated. The subjection of women has been similarly seen as feudal residue, like Hartz's feudal South: romantic, anachronistic, and illiberal.

The subjection of women, however, is neither archaic nor foreign to liberalism. The participation of women in the liberal revolutions of the eighteenth and nineteenth centuries was rewarded with more limited influence, more thorough formal and informal regulation. The great liberal revolutions marked the triumph of liberty by securing a more exclusive fraternity. Women who had stormed the Tuileries with the *sansculottes* found themselves denied admission to Jacobin clubs.

In the subjection of women, as in the establishment of democracy, Americans could claim to have surpassed Europe. Tocqueville observed, and commended, the stricter confinement of women in America; their more thorough exclusion from public discourse and political influence: "In America, more than anywhere else in the world, care has been taken constantly to trace distinct spheres of action for the two sexes. . . . You will never find American women in charge of the external relations of the family, managing a business, or interfering in politics" (Tocqueville, *Democracy in America* 601). The American woman "is never allowed to leave the quiet sphere of domestic duties." Americans, Tocqueville wrote, "hold that a woman's mind is just as capable as a man's of discovering the naked truth, and her heart as firm to face it." They "think nothing more precious than a woman's honor, and nothing deserving more respect than her freedom" (602–3). Yet the Americans,

Tocqueville wrote, have never "supposed that democratic principles should undermine the husband's authority . . . they never deny him the right to direct his spouse" (601).[3] "Thus, then, while they have allowed the social inferiority of woman to continue, they have done everything to raise her morally and intellectually to the level of man. In this I think they have wonderfully understood the true conception of democratic progress" (Tocqueville 603).

Tocqueville's analysis, like Hartz's assumptions, places the conventional subjection of women at the center of the liberal project. Hartz merely assumed the absence of women from politics; Tocqueville praised it. For Tocqueville, the gendering of democracy in America is a distinction, simultaneously differentiating and elevating American identity. Gender hierarchies are presented in Tocqueville not as the legacy of Europe but as the achievement of America, not as a feudal aberration but as a liberal principle. Americans evince their subtle and progressive understanding of liberalism in gendering the body politic male.[4]

Closed Bodies, Open Minds

Language is the field of our being. Our thoughts are cast into language before their conception, we are born into language before we are born to the world. Our bodies are not simply flesh. They bear meaning before they are borne in the womb. They are incarnate, for in them the word precedes the flesh. Leg and arm and head and heart existed for us before we had legs and arms and hands and heads and hearts to occupy them. Our bodies are already constituted before we enter them. Whatever shape the body takes, the meaning of that shape is there before it.[5]

The classic texts of liberalism present conceptions of contract, individuality, and liberty that inscribe subjection on the woman's body. Liberalism marked bodily integrity as the sign and security of liberty. Liberals undertook to protect man's bodies, even from themselves. Hobbes made contract the guarantor of bodily integrity; the sovereign the security of that state, and proscribed even attacks upon oneself. Man might live with his body closed to the intrusions of others, and in that safety he would find his freedom. Hobbes, and Locke after him, made the body fence and shelter for the mind. Men free from fear could look beyond survival. Men with their bodies inviolable, protected from assaults by other men, could think for themselves. The closed body sheltered the open mind.

The open body was the body subjected. The body that was open to the assaults of others held a mind occupied by fear, beliefs subject to coercion. Any body that depended on another for subsistence might be made the other's subject. An intrusion that could touch the stomach would touch the heart. Opening the body closed the mind.

The bodies borne by women were open bodies. Their bodies opened in the conception and the birth of children. Their bodies were occupied by others. The law held their bodies open to husbands. The bodies of men might be opened by violence, marked and made subject, but women's bodies were seen as open from their birth. They could be properly closed only when they were coupled with men's, or confined in the fictive body of the household.[6]

Liberalism vested rights and authority in the body and provided protection to it. One held rights in, and acquired property through, the body. The law recognized the importance of the body's presence in its provision for *habeas corpus* and in securing the right to confront one's accusers in the flesh. A plethora of laws aimed at securing those ends named in the Constitution: "to provide for the common defense and promote the general welfare."

Not only individual but collective power and title originated in the body. Authority and legitimacy originated in the people assembled. Thus Rousseau writes that the state itself must defer to the authority called up by the present bodies of the assembled people. The privileging of speech that Derrida observed in the high regard of liberal regimes for epics and anthems is the sign that liberalism locates itself in the body, achieving the synthesis of representation and authority "in the self presence of its speech" (*Of Grammatology* 134).

Liberalism acted through the law to acknowledge and to secure the integrity of the body as security for the integrity of the mind sheltered within it. It endeavored to close off the bodies of men to one another, to maintain them in a state thought to be inviolable and impenetrable. The bodies of women, which were thought to be naturally open, were closed off civilly, in marriage and the household.[7] Liberal systems of law maintained the commom law doctrine of *couverture* that made wives the property of their husbands. Women's bodies, naturally open, achieved the closure that assured their integrity only when they were "covered" by their husbands, and the law.

The state of the liberal individual, endowed with rights, bearing a mind thought to be open in a body closed to the intrusions of others, was "biologically," "naturally" foreclosed to women. The liberal individual was singular. Pregnancy would make some women's bodies momentarily plural. The necessity of closing the bodies of women made their plurality constant, encompassing women in the names and will of their fathers and husbands. The liberal individual was autonomous. Women could not be permitted this autonomy, lest they act against the interests of those they held in their bodies or those who held them in the household.

There is, of course, another set of bodies made subject by their openness. Liberalism's conception of the political consequences of corporeality required not only the exclusion of women from the public sphere, but also the stricter regulation of male sexual conduct in the private sphere. Men who opened their bodies to other men lost the inviolable, impenetrable interiority of the body that secured rights. The subordination of male homosexuals differs from that of women, however, for it was seen as determined not by providence but by election. Male subjection was "unnatural."

The bodies of women and male homosexuals, alike in the openness ascribed them, different in the understanding of its origin and duration, were alike in another respect as well. The open body was the body of indiscriminate, unbounded desire. Women, Rousseau warned, have "insatiable desires." Were they not restrained by shame and the law, "men would be tyrannized by women. . . . For given the ease with which women arouse men's senses and reawaken in the depths of their hearts the remains of ardors which are almost extinguished, men would be their victims and would see themselves dragged to death without ever being able to defend themselves" (*Emile* 359). The open body is the body of desire—the desired and desiring body. All bodies are subject to desire: to erotic desire and to hunger, the desire for food. The feminine body, already marked as open, becomes the mark of irresolute desire. The ascription of insatiability to women exceeds and supplements liberalism. Thus Freud asks, What do women want?" having already determined, categorically, that women are always wanting something. Desire, as Freud's question suggests, marks the presence of an *aporia.*

The Promise of Disembodiment

The nominal integrity of the male body is no more (though no less) than that. Men's bodies are also open and plural. They desire, and they are the objects of the desire. Desiring, they experience incompletion, lack, irresolution. They eat, and they share in the collective corporeality of pregnancy. Because they eat, they are neither impenetrable nor inviolable. The classical republicans, the early and late Southern agrarians, and the Populists recognized that the economic structures of an emergent capitalism put the security of individual provision—and therefore, individual liberty—at hazard. Their concern for securing universal access to the means of provision was entirely consonant with the liberal arguments that had made the closed body security for the open mind. These too-corporeal republicans failed, however, to recognize what contract had accomplished. The merely nominal integrity of the male body was taken as currency for the open mind.

With the advent of contract, men had entered upon civil society, and in doing so had imposed upon themselves the authority of representation. "Things inanimate," Hobbes argued, "cannot be authors, nor therefore give authority to their actors: yet the actors may have authority to procure their maintenance, given them by those that are owners, or governors of those things. And therefore, such things cannot be personated, before there be some state of civil government," (*Leviathan* 162). The establishment of civil government, however, makes representation authoritative and impersonation legitimate. The advent of civil society is the advent of representation. The interests and the will of the people are represented by contract and sovereignty. Representation replaces the body. Through it, the presence of authority can be secured in the absence of the assembled people. Representation becomes the medium of politics and commerce: money becomes currency for goods and value, title currency for rights and property, contract currency for will.

Individuality, in an embodied liberalism, has the status of an attribute. It presents itself as merely a trait or quality, a representation of one aspect of a person, that each held in common with all other men. Where representation has authority, liberalism is disembodied. Individuality is no longer an attribute of embodied men, but a status or condition, detached from the bodies that were once its source.

The liberal individual, bearing rights, holding an open mind secure in a closed body, became an abstraction. Individuality, once an attribute of certain bodies, became an abstraction assignable to any body, and to no body. Corporations, lacking the embodiment—much less the bodily integrity—that individuality once designated, acquired that status in law. Men, who had once held rights in their bodies, who had made their bodies the title and the means to citizenship, now supplemented those (natural rights) with the creation of literary selves. The idea of individuality overcame the represented bodies of men, replacing that which it purported to represent. Individuality acts as a supplement.

Disembodiment removed liberalism one step further from the inscription of rank at birth that had marked feudalism. Disembodiment moved liberalism one step closer to the rule of reason. African Americans once held as slaves could be held to be equals. Women, once held to be constitutionally inferior, could be ascribed constitutional rights. Individuality, and the rights of man with it, could be extended to any body. The promise of disembodiment became the promise of liberalism.

With the promise of disembodiment, liberalism held out the promise of history erased. A past of humiliations and impotence would be forgotten, the long record of slights, subjection, and subordination set aside, never to be recalled. This was the promise of color-blind, gender-neutral, liberalism. This was to be the "radical future of liberal feminism." Yet this promised, still unseen, utopia was understood by many of those to whom it was extended not as liberalism's great promise but as its profound defect. Liberalism offered forgetfulness as overcoming. One might think that people whose histories were marked by rape, by mockery, by condescension, or by the whip and the yoke might be grateful to see their histories forgotten. They were not. Disembodiment did not erase desire.

The subaltern in America have been marked by a common desire to reclaim their histories. African Americans have urged memory upon their people, calling upon them to remember slavery with Emancipation, redemption with Reconstruction, the failures of the civil rights movement with its triumphs. It was not merely, as Martin Luther King, Jr., declared, that "unearned suffering is redemptive." The willingness to surrender the past was seen as self-denial, the rejection of kinship with those who had likewise had their subordinate status written on their bodies.

Women have been among the most assiduous of the subaltern historians. The silence of the canonical histories sent women back to the archives; the absence of women in the institutions of the state impelled them to social history and a broader understanding of politics. Their vigilant, resurgent recollections affirm a presence in the past. The recognition that the nation has temporal as well as spatial boundaries prompted the recognition that the contest for inclusion in the present entails an insistence on inclusion in the past. The recollection of women's history carries with it a rejection of the invitation to inclusion in an "American" identity that fails to acknowledge the presence of women in the past.[8]

These are the desires, and the projects, of aporetic identities. Women and African Americans know themselves to be ignorant of what they have been. They are still more ignorant of what they may become. They are led by lack to want, by want to desire, and by desire to question. Their lack puts the promise and the claims of liberalism in question. Their efforts to uncover a silent, sequestered past reveal America as an aporia.

Property

The denial of history that disembodied liberalism carries with it has led to the misunderstanding of other categories central to the liberal tradition. Property is identified, in American liberalism, with security and freedom. Property was acquired by men through their bodies. They made material things their property through use, making their own the land on which they stood, the food they ate, the things they held in their hands. They acquired rights to property by mixing their labor with it. Property served, therefore, not merely to protect the self, but to extend it in the world. It made men free of the dominion of nature, and other men and gave them dominion in the material world. Property serves as a fence, walling out the vicissitudes of nature, protecting the individual from the assaults and incursions of other men. "This makes it Lawful," Locke wrote in a famous passage, "for a man to *kill a Thief*, who has not in the least hurt him, nor declared any design upon his Life . . . because using force, where he has no Right, to get me into his Power, let his pretence be what it will, I have no reason to suppose, that he, who would *take away my Liberty*, would not when he had me in his Power, take away every thing else" (297–98). In this passage, Locke reveals to us a crucial transformation in the meaning and use of property. Once the means for the material protection of the body, property becomes the body's sign and surrogate, the first medium of representation. Property stands for the body. Assaults on property are consequently read as assaults upon liberty and life. In this transformation from a means of protection to a means of representation, property becomes a supplement to corporeal individuality in the fullest (Derridean) sense.

   Property served to protect men from nature and other men, to enhance their enjoyment of their corporeal condition, and to extend the boundaries of their material dominion in the world. It enabled them, too, to transcend the limits of their bodies: to recognize attacks on their liberty and lives before they touched their bodies, to represent themselves and maintain their authority in their absence. Property thus served to protect men's freedom and expand their dominion, to protect their bodies and enhance their pleasure. As property became a legal and cultural surrogate for the self, it also became the medium for the self-made man: a means for the materialization of individual power, taste, and authority.

Property served others differently. The historical experience of women makes a mockery of the identification of property with security and freedom. "Security of property" meant, for men, a more secure freedom. In the history of women, as in the history of African Americans, "security of property" often meant only a more secure bondage.[9] Property enabled men to expand their dominion in the world. It subjected women to the dominion of men. Property provided men with a language of commodities in which they could make their construction of themselves manifest. The language of commodities served women differently, attaching to their expressions of individuality and to their aesthetic judgments affirmations of their dependence and inequality.

Public and Private

The private realm that property defined protected men and subjected women. The household, in which men enjoyed an extended identity and material dominion, confined and diminished women. Within the household, men were protected from the intrusions of the state. Women were not. The state intruded into the household to secure the subjection of women; subordinating them to the authority of men, particularly their fathers and husbands, and tolerating (when it did not explicitly permit) assaults on their bodies. The state entered the household to hold women's bodies open to their husbands, legally precluding the possibility of rape in marriage. The state entered the household to close women's bodies to themselves, forbidding (at diverse times) abortion, birth control, and midwifery. The household prevented women from entering the state, but it did not prevent the state from entering them. Within the household men enjoyed a comprehensive identity, subsuming women and children under their name and their authority. Women were diminished in name as they were in agency and action.

The distinction between public and private thus did more than mark out a zone in which men would be free from the intrusions of the liberal state—and it did less. It made it possible for men to exercise, in the private sphere, the aristocratic authority that liberalism had replaced in the public sphere. The old saying "A man's home is his castle" is more than metaphoric. The boundaries of the home secure men and invest them with the signs of—and the means to—the forms of domination and political rule that liberalism had nominally overcome. The doctrine that the private sphere was outside politics silenced critics of liberalism's failure in the private sphere.

The nominal separation of public and private worked as an earlier dichotomy had, establishing a (merely) narrative quarantine. The myth of the feudal South had isolated the American racial order temporally and spatially—in the South, in the past. The signs of persistent and pervasive racial inequalities were transmuted into the artifacts of a liberal victory. The division between public and private has a similar form, and similar effects. The dichotomous distinction of public and private isolates gender hierarchies spatially, in the home. Liberalism can thus be ascribed both a perfect political hegemony—for politics is confined to the public realm—and an absolution from responsibility for the inequalities of the public realm. The contrast of public and private is transmuted from the evidence of liberal failure to the proof of liberalism's triumph.

The Resurrection of the Body

Rather than accepting the promise of liberal disembodiment, feminism has brought the body back in. Feminist historians and feminist theorists have concurred in seeing in the body the site of women's oppression. Feminist issues have had, in consequence, a striking physicality. Abortion, rape, wife beating, incest, pornography, and anorexia all mark the woman's body as a political place. Feminists debate among themselves the meaning and status of the body, the limits and the uses of sexuality and sexual pleasure, the construction, effects, and significance of maternity, and the significance of images of the woman's body; yet they concur in seeing it as a site of struggle. These issues are joined in a manner marked by the same presence of the body; in the use of images of the body, in the reliance on physical presence.

Both of these aspects of feminist physicality have been present in the debate over abortion. The opponents of abortion have made their presence a tactic in demonstrations at abortion clinics. Their employment of photographs—and, on occasion, the bodies—of fetuses also calls on us to acknowledge the body. Those who maintain the rights of women to abortion have revived the location of rights in the body. They have opposed the employment of the aforementioned photographs as evidence of a willingness to open women's bodies to the intervention of the state as they open them to the public gaze. For all those involved in this debate, the body has been weapon and battlefield. With the return of the body in the controversies and the controversial discourse of abortion comes a recognition of the political power of the image, of sight as power, and new questions concerning the legitimacy of representation.

The issue of abortion presents further challenges to liberalism, for it obliges liberals to confront an instance where individuality does not have the unity, singularity, and integrity that liberalism ascribes to it. It raises a series of questions that recall to liberalism the concerns of the body and the consequences of corporeal difference. Is the pregnant mother one or two? Is that which falls within the confines of one's body, that with which one has mixed one's labor, property? Can an intrusion into another's body be productive? Can it issue in the other's authority? It obliges liberals to acknowledge that laws are not—and cannot be made—gender neutral. It obliges liberals to acknowledge, in the flesh, the demands of difference.

When the body is brought back into liberal politics and liberal discourse, it brings history with it. The turn to history has turned the attention of American scholars to history in the present: the legacy of historical process in contemporary institutional structures.[10] Liberalism disembodied is not merely liberalism deaf to the voice of history. It is liberalism blind to the structured inequities of our own time. Liberalism disembodied is not simply, as its proponents promised, liberalism freed from fealty to illiberal criteria. It is liberalism bound to a denial of present, material, conditions. The demand for context links the projects of historians with those of the critics of liberal theory.

The resurrection of the body in American liberalism would rewrite the theories and policies that govern individuals as subject and sovereign. A liberalism once again invested in the body would be a liberalism brought again to the recognition that the conditions that bodies are subject to are matters of the most profound significance. A liberalism mindful of the body would simultaneously revive the recognition of individual singularity and inflect our understanding of politics with a consciousness of the inequalities that inform the practices it comprises. This would be a liberalism mindful of difference—of the consequences of different histories, of the differing conditions of poverty and wealth, of the differences of meaning inscribed on male and female, black and white.

Mindfulness of the condition of meanings that history inscribes on bodies also obliges us to recognize that neither the state nor politics more broadly keeps to the narrow boundaries liberalism has set for it. The state intrudes into the homes and bodies of women. In the practices of everyday life, in the purchase of commodities, the organization of labor in the home, and the superintendence of labor at birth, in the marriage contract and the presumption of a prior sexual contract, women and men experience the constitution of identities and relations of power. Politics overwhelms the distinction between public and private. The distinction between public and private survives, however, to indicate (if only briefly and allusively) the simultaneous presence of disparate political orders.

The disparate orders that govern men and women as citizens, as men, as women, in the workplace, in the home, are neither discrete nor impenetrable. They are articulated in complex arrangements of interdependence. Each expresses an aspect—but only an aspect—of the complex of contexts, historical forces, institutional effects, drives, desires, language, and lack bound together in our corporeal singularity. Attention to the place of woman in liberalism and the experience of women in America has made the temporal more complex. The linear, progressive conception of history, on which the idea of the American liberal tradition depends, is put in question with the acknowledgment of women's separate spheres. With the recovery of women's history, contradictions emerge to sully the clean division of times into periods and politics into orders. The enormity involved in dismissing the contradictions governing the condition of women in the liberal tradition has obliged us to think again: of liberalism, of America, of the division of time into periods, and of the fusion of identities in individuals.

American women lived not in the liberal order but in another; a separate sphere in which rank was written ineradicably upon the body. The liberal America of Louis Hartz was, however, the nation in which this order was embedded. The concerns and the condition of those to whom loyalties bound them were the concerns of liberals. Culture, education, and observation made women liberals as well. Fraternity might be categorically foreclosed, but liberty and equality remained aspirations. For women, as for African Americans, subjection brought with it a doubled consciousness.

"We are not a perfect people": Double Consciousness and the Idea of the American Mission

The double consciousness of the subaltern is created not merely from the contradiction between the nation of their experience and the nation of their compatriots at the center. It also emerges from the distance between the nation of their experience and the nation of their aspirations, the nation they know and the nation they desire. In this, it reflects a constitutive feature of American identity, the consciousness of lack, of desire, of an unknown end. America is a nation in question.

All Americans know two nations as their own. The first is the nation we inhabit in the flesh, the nation of our experience, the nation of our memory. History has made itself material in this present, providing the structures that order our lives: the hierarchies we know; the laws we obey or disobey; the institutions, practices and processes that represent us. This history has imprinted our bodies, marking us with the past. The second nation is the nation of our imagining, of our aspirations and anxieties, the nation we fear, the nation we desire.

America remains unsettled. Tocqueville was haunted in his time (as we are in ours) by the fear of an America impelled by greed, unable to set race aside, overtaken by mediocrity. The authors of *The Federalist* feared a nation unable to resolve its differences, a nation of warring, insignificant factions. Americans find expression for the anxieties of the present in images of a nation to come—a postnuclear desert, a toxic wasteland, an urban empire of the underclass. These are the nation of our fears.

America remains unfinished. American politics, rather than merely lauding the achievements of the past or evoking the grandeur of the present, also calls up this absent nation, this state of grace we have yet to achieve. "This is not a perfect party," Jesse Jackson declared at the 1984 Democratic convention. "We are not a perfect people. But we are called to a perfect mission." We are made Americans not in our allegiance to the present, but in our longing—and in our work—for the absent nation. In their rage at lack, in the passion of want, the subaltern conceive the nation they desire.

The distance between these nations becomes simultaneously the field of our history and of our constitution. American history, in this understanding, is "how one becomes what one is."[11] The present nation stands as an indictment of our defects, the evidence of our inadequacy. This is the nation we are called to overcome. This is the nation Langston Hughes evoked when he wrote, "Keep your hand on the plow" ("Freedom's Plow" in *Selected Poems* 291–97).

Hughes belongs with Whitman, Benét, Lindsay, and Ginsberg, in the company of poets who articulate (that is, announce and analyze) a vision of America. Their poems on American identity are alike in their aporetic character, in their use of the form of the jeremiad, and in their reliance on differences—in historical time, in geographic space, and litanies of different cities and occupations—to convey the *res Americana*. In "Freedom's Plow," Hughes captures the power of American longing. The poem counterposes building and dreaming, the ideal and the work, the utterance of words in a historical context and the meaning immanent within them. Thus he quotes the Declaration and observes that "there were slaves then," but observes that the slaves "silently took for granted / That what he said was also meant for them." Hughes measures the distance between the "great thoughts" of the people and the manner in which they "faultily put them into practice," but he counsels,

> If the house is not yet finished,
> Don't be discouraged, builder . . .
> The plan and pattern is here
> Woven from the beginning
> Into the warp and woof of America

The poem ends, as jeremiads do, with an exhortation: "Keep your hand on the plow! Hold on!"

This exhortation was taken from a slave song. For over a century these songs have been the work songs of the American mission. They have informed the discourse of African-American, and thus American, politics from before the Founding to the present. They conveyed the means and the ends of resistance to slavery in the antebellum period. They were the anthems of the civil rights movement. Yet we have too often neglected to read them as political texts. W. E. B. Du Bois placed a bar from the Sorrow Songs at the opening of each chapter of *The Souls of Black Folk*. The songs are richly allusive, bound to canonical scriptures and national history. The refrain "we shall overcome, someday" calls on us to consider the American mission in different terms—terms less religious and more philosophical. Yet these songs receive little commentary from the theorists. Hughes presents his poem as a commentary on the canonical texts of the regime. Benét, Lindsay, and Whitman saw their poetry as political texts. All refer to specific political events, and all served in their time to impel political action. Yet when these poets are read, they are read as the objects of political analysis and only rarely as analysts themselves. The distinction between prose and poetry, like the distinction between public and private, has legitimated the exclusion and dismissal of a wide and revelatory range of American political discourse.

Bercovitch, echoing Weber, calls on us to see the mission as an aspect of the Protestant ethic in the spirit of capitalism. Mindful of Hegel, we have looked upon the Puritans and the Whigs and their successors as impelled by a sense of their world historical importance. Through them, the scriptural ideal would make itself real in the world. In Whitman, Benét, Ginsberg, and Hughes, in the words of men and women whose names are lost to us, the mission comes from other mouths. The diverse conditions of the bodies that announce the mission invest it with a different meaning.

Langston Hughes placed his borrowed passage in its historical context, in the mouths of men and women working in the fields, embodied and enslaved. In conveying his sense of American identity as incomplete, as "promises—that will come true," Hughes foregrounded his blackness and spoke in a woman's voice. It is as the Negro Mother that Hughes speaks of the American mission, "carrying in my body the seed of the free."[12]

People would recognize, before and after Hughes, that America was incomplete. Others, before and after him, linked that incompleteness to the places occupied by blacks and women. For most, however, blacks and women serve merely as signs. For Hughes, they are prophets and the builders, those most fully engaged in the American project, most occupied by the unfinished business of America, most mindful of the American dream. For Hughes, the subaltern are significant not because they mark the defects of the present nation, but because their structured subordination, their lack, invests them with the national mission.

America remains in question. The once sequestered histories of the subaltern have put the triumph of liberalism in question. With this once settled certainty in question, America becomes an aporia. There is no predestined victory, no perfect mission to return to. Americans find themselves lacking the easy resolution of the jeremiad. There is only want and the consciousness of lack, the question Is it possible? and the desire.

Notes

1. I have foregrounded Louis Hartz's account of American identity with regard to its intellectual and disciplinary standing among accounts of American identity, and second because Hartz foregrounds the liberal tradition. Thinking of women in America, I will argue, challenges conventional understandings of both American identity and the liberal tradition.

2. I do not regard Hartz as the primary author of this history, though I think he may be its most discerning reader and clearest exponent. It is an American history, whose broad outlines are widely accepted. The importance of the Civil War in Hartz's account, and the meaning given that conflict, owe much to the posthumous authority of Lincoln, who successfully wrote the triumph of liberalism into the inchoate history of the war.

3. Nancy Cott notes in *The Bonds of Womanhood* that Tocqueville probably exaggerated both "the young unmarried woman's independence and the wife's willingness to bend to subordination," but also commends his perspicacity in recognizing the paradox of voluntary self-abnegation that marked marriage in the American democracy (78). Carole Pateman observes in *The Sexual Contract* that the position of the marriage contract in liberal theory and liberal practice similarly rests—when it is presented as voluntary—on a similar paradox of disinterested self-abnegation.

4. One might well ask whether Tocqueville regards this subjection as conventional. He writes, rather ambiguously, of "the great inequality between men and women which has up till now seemed based on the eternal foundations of nature" (600). He is careful to ascribe the view that "the natural head of the conjugal association is the husband" to "the Americans," rather than claiming it for his own (601). While he explicitly rejects the view that would "make of men and women creatures who are not equal only, but actually similar" (601), he always presents the subjection of women as the work of opinion or convention rather than directly ascribing it to nature. Perhaps most striking is his characterization of the inferiority of women as "social" rather than "natural" (603). Whether Tocqueville accepts or questions the natural inferiority of women, his identification of their continued subordination with the success of democracy is further evidence for regarding the subjection of women as a liberal principle rather than a feudal artifact. If Tocqueville does, as I suspect, regard the subjection of women as conventional, then his conception of democracy in America may have an antifoundationalist cast that invites further investigation.

5. See Gadamer, *Philosophical Hermeneutics* 3–17. Gadamer's account bears a family resemblance to Althusser's account of hailing or "interpellation" in "Ideology and the Ideological State Apparatus" in *Lenin and Philosophy.*

6. The reading of the woman's body as open considerably antedates liberalism and has been subject to diverse evaluations and systems of governance. The assessment of the open body as vulnerable and defective is, for reasons that I will discuss below, intimately related to liberalism. Other interpretations of the woman's body as open are discussed in *Zone* 3, 4, and 5; Julia Kristeva, "Stabat Mater," in *The Kristeva Reader* (160–86); Rudolph Bell, *Holy Anorexia;* and Francis Barker, *The Tremulous Private Body.*

7. This consideration of the meaning and importance assigned to the body can account for the shifts that Carole Pateman identified in the postions ascribed to women in the work of Thomas Hobbes (*The Sexual Contract* 39–54). Hobbes

initially marks men and women as equal, yet makes the marital state one of subjection. If one notes the importance Hobbes gives to maintaining bodily integrity, and his identification of corporeal with political independence, one can account not only for the natural equality and marital subjection of women in his thought, but also for his statement that "every woman that bears children becomes both a *mother* and a *lord*" (*De Cive* chap. 9). In a passage that in its ambivalence reveals both Hobbes's wit and his attention to the body, he writes, "birth follows the belly."

8. This understanding of the motive power of history returns us to Hartz's argument that the American liberal tradition was rendered stagnant and immobile by liberalism's unchallenged hegemony. In returning to Hartz, however, we must also recall that the historical contradictions necessary to overcome this immobility have been with us from the beginning. They came not from an international order forcing itself in upon the United States, but from within America.

9. The entire apparatus of slavery, from the apologies of Locke to the Fugitive Slave laws, rested on property. Property rights were used by businessmen in the 1960s to defend their denials of service to African Americans. They are cited now by those who argue that affirmative action must give way before the right of corporations to protect themselves from costs said to be unduly burdensome. The common law doctrine of *couverture* made women the property of their husbands. Statutory law, for the greater part of American history, gave the use, governance, and often title of women's property over to their husbands and fathers. Additional examples of classes and categories whom property served to subject rather than to free are easily proliferated. The liberal conception of private property, held by individuals, was employed by early American settlers to deprive and displace native Americans. For John Quincy Adams, among others, the right to property might legitimate the appropriation of Indian lands, if not the annihilation of Indian lives: "What is the right of a huntsman to a forest of a thousand miles over which he has accidentally ranged in quest of prey?" (quoted in Rogin, *Fathers and Children* 6). Property rights, belatedly invoked, were held as obstacles to the return of the expropriated property of Japanese Americans.

10. As this passage suggests, moments of intellectual confluence occur in the work of structuralists and feminists. Theda Skocpol's work is exemplary in this regard. The turn to history in the work of the new institutionalists is both influenced by and particularly open to feminist scholars and feminist scholarship.

11. The phrase is, of course, Nietzsche's. The idea of the American mission and the attendant form of the jeremiad have been described by Sacvan Bercovitch in *The American Jeremiad*.

12. Hughes, "The Negro Mother," *Poems* 288. See also "Mother to Son," 187. Hughes writes in a woman's voice in more mundane contexts as well, for example in the poems concerning "Madam Alberta K. Johnson."

7 Suppose Kuwait's Main Product Was Broccoli?

The Street Demonstration in U.S. Politics

William Chaloupka

The events of 1989 and 1990 in China, Eastern Europe, and South Africa reached us as a sequence of images, mostly televised glimpses, the *mise-en-scène* of postmodern revolution. Mandela walking from prison and, later that day, addressing a crowd of supporters. The Berlin Wall under the wrecking ball of what can only be described as a band of reveling party goers. A simulated lady liberty in China.

For me, one image stands out, in some (contestable) way enclosing, containing each of those events. It is a familiar image, available to each of us as a text that we could reinterpret. A lone Chinese student steps in front of a column of tanks in Tiananmen Square. As the lumbering, awkward tanks try to turn, first one way and then the other, the student easily blocks them. He is more agile than the tanks; for the moment at least, his visibility is a ghost shirt. Finally, the tanks stop trying to turn, becoming, for brief seconds, a world-class mark of frustration. As if wanting to escalate the play just a bit more, the student climbs the lead tank and appears to be trying to speak to it. Words against metal. A few of his friends appear in the frame now, pulling him back into the crowd. Perhaps he could yet be safe; the next few days in the square hold his fate.

Or, more to the point, the protester's gesture goes into orbit. One of its reentry points was, of course, U.S. politics. At the first opportunity, President George Bush—a sophisticated China hand from way back, he will tell you—praised the student's courageous action as an expression of the students' thirst for freedom. Bush saw the student as confirming the most basic elements of democratic social thought. The president's reading of this gesture was a commonplace one, in those hyperreal months between Beijing and Bucharest. In each instance—in Asia, or Europe, or Africa—following stunning disruptions and, often, transformations that were just as surprising, every political development was almost exclusively described in terms of the values that supposedly drove movement.

In one story after another, from increasingly improbable places, we heard of an almost uncontrollable yearning for freedom, breaking out in one remote locale after another, pushing one network anchor after another to yet more frenzied travel, in an odd inversion of the term *anchor*. Commentators spoke of communism's demise or capitalism's triumph, readings that held only as long as one suspended notice of South Africa or the Palestinian *intifada,* for example, or the notable lack of interest in capitalist ideology among the Chinese students. Others, perhaps sensitive to those exceptions, spoke more generally of the collapse of outmoded (governmental, political, and social) systems.[1] That abstraction had other problems; a net wide enough to capture both communism and apartheid would be wide enough to capture other outdated political modes, as well. In short, the explanations offered for these remarkable events lacked specificity, leaving enough anomalies unexplained to let us reopen the issue; what is happening in these scattered, yet somehow connected events?

My own reading of the episode with the tanks—and of this entire sequence of events—diverges from the most commonplace explanations. By gesture and posture, the student had appropriated more than one genre, and it was this "intertext" that made the interaction with the tank so stunning, so captivating of our gaze, on the screen.[2] Without doubt, this was a story of "bodies and tanks"; his body improbably stopped the machines of oppression. But the student's action made other references, as well. The dance of student and tank column was more Charlie Chaplin than Locke or Mill, more cinema than physics, more play—dangerous, self-obliterating play, to be sure—than ideology. Bush's reading of the image was opportunistic, a rushed effort to re-inscribe a truly perilous moment with an explanation that fit into the plot he had in mind. Bush saw no signal that order itself was at stake, no sign that irreverence had sought and reached new levels. He did not notice the genie leaving the bottle, entering the (television) tube, and starting to move around the globe.

My response emphasizes something he excluded: a subtly but importantly different kind of freedom, carried by the actual political mech-

anism that accomplished each transformation—the street demonstration, on television. The floating, propelled network news anchors
narrated these events as if they had no vehicle at all, other than a very
abstract ideology of freedom and a simplistic functionalism of collapsing systems. I do not disagree that protesters expressed values of liberation, nor that systems could reasonably be called outdated. Without
doubt, the rhetoric of freedom flowed abundantly, before turning sour
and unmistakably opportunistic with the onset of the Persian Gulf
crisis in August 1990. But to emphasize only the liberal ideology of
these events would be to miss their media—the practices, vehicles, and
genres that carried what was, in each case, a very light ideological load.[3]

It should not be too surprising that the mode of change received so little direct attention during this period. In prevailing modernist thought,
it is the "content" of messages that matters, not the "vehicle" that
carries them. This exclusion carries an ideology, as do all such important exclusions: modernism prefers to accrue "developments" incre-
mentally and progressively, in the manner of engineered technological
change. Western radicals have often agreed with the modernist preference for content; when black poet Gil Scott-Heron announced in the
1960s that "the revolution will not be televised," his message was
subversive and compelling precisely because it mirrored a liberal judgment. Television, whatever it was, was not real and could not be the
field of emergence for something as dramatic as a revolution. As appealing as he was, Scott-Heron was also wrong.

His error speaks to more than an inclination to trivialize "the tube."
The other side of his equation—denoting radical political change as
"revolution"—suggests another exclusion. Not only has modernity
privileged "content," it has also generally lodged that political "substance" in institutions.[4] In this setting, terms such as *liberation* and
collapse acquire institutional codings. For some time now, liberty has
implied institutional terms: rights, participation, and even taxation
rates. In political discourse, values have long been described and delimited by the institutional mechanisms supposedly associated with them.
"Freedom" is inscribed as "electoral function," and "equality" becomes
due process, a description of juridical rules, for example. But in the late
1980s, this linkage of value and institutional context underwent a
transformation. An extrainstitutional reading of each value emerged
from the streets, but more important, on the screens of televisions
everywhere, all at once.[5]

Escaping the institution—at least for an ecstatic moment, now and
then—the late eighties threatened, on one giddy occasion after another,

to declare independence from any context at all. The key feature—the (self-referential, context-defying) pace of transformation—was largely ignored because it was a nonfeature from most established points of view. Each of these events shared an unmistakable pace, unaccounted for by liberal theory or most journalists' commentaries; changes raced forward at breakneck speed, each challenging the last as if a land speed record was at stake.[6] The pace of transformation is nowhere inscribed in a liberal ideology that naturalizes a "drive for freedom" but has always preferred a rate more glacial than instantaneous. Accumulating collapse requires structural signs—legitimacy failures or economic pressure or gathering institutional distress—that could not accumulate at the racetrack acceleration pace of the late 1980s. But while institutional regimes contain their own logic and rhythm, challenges to them can carry different kinds of logic and can unfold with a different rhythm.

That speed itself becomes a clue.[7] Reading these events from a postmodern frame—deliberately setting aside the modernist and liberal frame we have privileged for so long—the pace at which events are represented hints openly that *what is seen* now lags behind its mode of presentation and emergence. Specifically, these transformations might not raise issues or resolve questions about modes of government so much as they problematize modes of representation. They wrench representation away from institutions, deconstructively moving it, resituating it as a regime of truth and visibility—as rhetoric, in a broad sense.

Given the populist rhetoric of all demonstrations, it seemed safe to assume that these new events were representational. "The people" are represented in the demonstration, the populist asserts; "the people, united, will never be defeated." An economy of representation accompanies each demo, in this populist story. The difference between turnout and majority, discounted for danger or other inconvenience, amounts to an event's political weight. The demo, as even a political scientist might grudgingly now admit, is only another representative form in their (small) bag of independent variables—a political tactic enabled by (and operating under) free speech provisions of a constitution, as mediated by a judicial mechanism. But the populist reading of protest almost always misses what the event is about. Political science texts can explain that demonstrations have effects, but they cannot quite explain how that effect works or how it might be calculated, given the tiny proportion of any population that demonstrates.[8]

This liberal rhetorical link of demo and representation has other problems. As *constitutional representation*, the demonstration is inevitably defective: simplistic, too ill behaved for a congressional hearing, too damaged to be a citizen's act. (If this sort of demonstration presented a food processor at a department store, representing it for sale, we would be entertained, but we would not learn what the gadget did.) Rather than merely grading the demo down for its "bad citizenship," I would study politics at this point of severe disjunction between the citizen role and the protester role. These two styles are (tellingly) different, as are their goals and their standards of efficacy. Liberal democracy strives to produce one kind of citizen, an actor in a well-established context of legalistic, constitutional authority.

The "protester," by contrast, constitutes herself along different lines. She appropriates a subtle, second meaning of "demonstrate." In most uses, the word *demonstration* suggests objectivity: to demonstrate is to point out, to make known, to describe and explain, to prove through deduction. The protester's usage moves toward the contingent realm of strategies and emotions. Her demonstration does not establish objectivity and logic (demonstrating the relationship of gravity and eggs, say) so much as it "shows up" the objective order, assertively getting in its way.[9] The protester acts against the citizen's connection to authority, threatening to expose illegitimacy; her demonstration is "a show." (This is more evident in French, where *démontrer*, to demonstrate, immediately recalls *montrer*, to show.) The protester—publicly but irreverently—shows that the way we live is necessarily at odds with prevailing knowledge. The protester's action thus may be minimally programmatic by intent, not defect.

By contrast, the citizen demonstrates that he has interests, complaints, and proposals—he is the one who petitions the government. When the citizen strays from this carefully circumscribed role, his action is soon discredited. The citizen demonstrates the severity of his concern; the protester demonstrates herself, her life, against a framework (not merely one of its consequences or artifacts). She shows irrepressible bodies, engaging through humor, outrage, and a distinctively expressive urge, not by her compliance with rules but by resistance: *In your face, deal with me.* That demonstration shows life as not encompassed by civic philosophy, as not represented in political institutions. Every "official story" begins to take on a suspicious tone after the demonstrator has done her reading of them; such stories might be at odds with the rowdy, transgressive urge that actually makes life lively. This is not to idealize or reify the protester, whose aim against any idealism or reification aspires to be true rather than lasting or even accurate. The protester exposes—shows, presents—misbehaving, poorly disciplined, ecstatic ways to live, against various (constitutional, philosophical, theological) meanings that work against life-as-lived. The only way the protester can address the institution is at the margins (in the street, over there in the park). Furthermore, by privileging pace, the demonstrator invites charges of "impatience," on the always aesthetic (hence shaky) grounds that this impatient beat fits the song best.

In this essay, I will take the position that the televised street demonstration is an important intrusion of the rhetorical onto the political scene. By "rhetorical," I recall not only speech acts performed by demonstrators, but also the role that a demonstration necessarily reenacts, owing to its form, its oppositional role, and its status as moral interruption and subversion. Democratic theory necessarily subsumes the rhetoric of the demonstration, imposing a scheme of representation on it that admittedly fits in some ways, but not in others. I am suggesting that an alternate "rhetoric of the demonstration"—one that emphasized visibility, the interplay of communication networks, the increasingly problematic representational forms, and the actual reasons for its habitual impudence toward power—might clarify our era's oppositional politics.

To be blunt about it, I think my reading produces a better understanding of what that Chinese student was doing with those tanks than does George Bush's reading. The student's protest made sense within this alternate rhetoric, announcing his own freedom (constituting it) in a way not entirely contained by ideology, plan, or program. He campaigned for the vitality of intertext, for an irreverent disassembly of institutional order that had controlled him simply by determining the conditions under which he could be seen. Turning into Chaplin for a moment, the student *demonstrated.*

The Demonstration as Form

The history of protest is intertwined with the history of revolution, crossed with the sociology of crowds. Joseph Gusfield began his review of social movements—the capsule within which the study of demonstrations is usually encased—with a reminder of "France in 1789, Russia in 1917, and China in 1949," but quickly moved on to "Civil Rights movements . . . ghetto riots, and . . . utopian settlements, to list some from among many." Essays in his book trace the origins of social protest through such diverse events as the Abolitionists of the mid-1800s, nationalist movements in India, German Nazism, eighteenth-century food riots in Europe, Marcus Garvey's Universal Negro Improvement Association, various labor movements, and millenarism.

The notion of leftist social protest, so commonplace today, may be a relatively recent development. In *Political Man*, Seymour Martin Lipset notes that "before 1917 extremist political movements were usually thought of as a rightist phenomenon. . . . After 1917 politicians and scholars alike began to refer to both left and right extremism, i.e., Communism and fascism" (128). Having claimed the demonstration, however, the left frequently moved it to a secondary importance, always preferring to privilege "content"—the people, their interests, the forces opposed to them. One widely read book (by Boyte) that promotes various "citizen movements" of the left barely mentions the role of the demonstration and fails to index any synonym of demonstration, protest, march, or sit-in.

Gusfield's definition of social movements emphasized their purposes and goals, distinguishing them from such things as soccer riots and trends that may be secondarily related to a social movement. In general, social scientists have analyzed the demonstration in functional terms, emphasizing what makes protests similar to other kinds of political activity (especially in the way they compose themselves and the way they accomplish policy goals).[10] One consequence of politicized campuses in the United States during the sixties and seventies may be that analysts of the demonstration are careful to discuss political context, distinguishing social movements from public opinion, voluntary associations, or "elementary collective behavior."[11] In short, even if the most attentive social scientists have for some time distinguished between "crowds" and protests, they have still tended to employ the terms and categories of political science and pluralism to discuss the phenomenon.[12]

As a form, the demonstration lost its appeal for both politicos and theorists in the 1980s, and perhaps even earlier, when the antiwar movement ebbed into the era of Watergate in the United States. In retrospect, that disappearance may have had more to do with Ronald Reagan's successful counterrevolutionary tactics, which Michael Rogin summarizes as a demonization (*Ronald Reagan, the Movie* 1–43, 272–300). The year 1989 was a turning point in the demonstration, with events focusing attention on this political genre and outcomes reminding us again of its (always problematic) efficacy. Given this chance to revisit an old familiar form in view of the vital and flourishing literature on representation, several themes immediately emerge.

Resistance and Institutionalization
On its face, the demonstration is always rhetorical; it *demonstrates*—shows, exposes, replays, tests—in ways distinct from other forms of politics. The narrative form of the demonstration is the assertion, performance, or claim, more than the explanation or totalization. It poses a partial, situated, contextual intervention, and thus confronts knowledge/power connections that otherwise remain implicit, as Foucault has so convincingly argued.

Perhaps the most important distinction between the demonstration and other forms of political speech lies in the tendency of the demonstration to *show* (a position or concern or commitment) without *institutionalizing* that representation. At the least, it leaves traces of ambivalence in any institutionalization; the leap from representation to law would remain problematic, ready to be overturned by the next demonstration. For Americans, this aspect of the demonstration may be best encapsulated by the career of Martin Luther King, Jr., who reacted to legislative successes for the civil rights movement by moving to another basis of moral challenge, the Vietnam War, rather than by consolidating institutional advantage. That move was controversial, even within the civil rights movement, and caused no little consternation within the Johnson administration (Lewis 297–312 and Halberstam 187–211).

Suppose Kuwait's Main Product Was Broccoli[13]

King's assassination illustrates another key feature of the demonstration: its ambivalence. Other political forms presume success; after all, they are grounded in nature and truth. Institutionalized, the values of liberal democracy attain the status they expected to attain. If that institutionalization fails, nature and truth collapse. The demonstration, on the other hand, expects to fail, as any system based on escalating risk and instability must. In that sense, the flagged viability of the demonstration during the 1970s and 1980s—and then the spectacular failure of the Tiananmen demonstration, among others—did not signal the ultimate demise of the form. Institutions such as Soviet communism are subject to collapse; such an institutionalized "truth regime" can be disproved or discarded. But the demonstration is not "disproved" by its failures, as is clear in the eastern European response that Tiananmen helped provoke.

(Obviously, many protesters do not understand this aspect of the demo; asked to participate, some will always ask, "How do I know this will do any good?" Their confusion between demonstrating and, say, expending effort to study for an exam misses the point of the enterprise. But their misunderstanding does not always undermine the demo, which thrives on such ambiguities, vaulting from them to yet more subversions, more engaging transgressions.)

Any discussion of the demonstration thus has to confront its negation. The wit and verve of the demonstration necessarily diminishes, sooner or later, or is susceptible to cancellation, in the case of assassination or other armed interference. In the United States, demonstrations became more predictable and ritualized during the last two decades. Mass gatherings in Washington, D.C., became formulized and ceased even to presume that they could be dangerous. Environmentalists, human rights advocates, and antihunger activists mastered the demonstration-as-rock-concert genre. The women's movement, at least partly founded in demonstration, moved quickly away from the form, leaving it to their opponents, the antiabortion advocates. But none of this "disproved" or "signaled the demise" of the demonstration; when Randall Robinson's TransAfrica movement revitalized the form with small but highly visible demonstrations at the South African embassy in Washington, the demonstration reappeared, presenting itself (for arrest) as if nothing had happened in the interim. The demonstration had not died as a failed institutionalization of truth sometimes expires; it waited, as it were, in videotape vaults around the world.

Popular Will

There are other ways in which the demonstration endangers the regime of truth so carefully composed by liberal democracy, a regime by which a *popular will* composes and expresses itself, and is then transformed into law. Not only is the demonstration nervous about the step into institutionalization, as mentioned above; it also hesitates to accept the standards that underlie "truth production," Foucault's phrase for the process of moving authority into language practices, and hence into people's lives. Early on in the development of the televised demonstration (in Chicago, 1968), the participants had already announced the terms of success and judgment of the form they were inventing when they chanted, "The whole world is watching." The crucial majority was formed by the gaze, not by an action or presence or even proposal. The credulity of their chant upset the liberal processes of "popular will"; social force could now emanate from bodies-in-view. The institutions of electoral "representation" began to face a test stronger than anything since the class warfare of a previous century.

Casting themselves as outsiders bent on "telling truth to power," demonstrators are always attempting a reversal, a contesting of established patterns. This is a subtle and unstable aspect of protest; it can just as easily be recast as an attempt to remind the regime of its professed values, of its origins. It is this instability that marks the demonstration as a potential outcast from the sober and serious pantheon of *critical theories*. The ability of the demonstration to capture attention is not (necessarily) underwritten by seriousness and focus, by some ability to capture a discourse of truth honestly told. This unreliability of the demonstration turns out to be its source of legitimacy; the demo resists power, even the categories that power imposes.

Gesture and Slogan

This also raises the issue of the slogan, which is surely at the core of every demonstration. Todd Gitlin reminds us that early SDS gatherings went so far as to debate and then orchestrate their picket sign slogans, better to focus the "substance" of their intervention (Gitlin 32–54). The demonstrators noticed and complained when those slogans were not used in news coverage. The chant, a less organized form (implying a spontaneous vox populi) became the privileged instance of the slogan. Derogatory press reports of demonstrations always note that organizers contrived unimaginative and excessively organized chants. More supportive press reports select particularly transgressive or humorous slogans as evidence of a demonstration's mood.

> **Some baby in Baghdad**
> **died for your car**

The demonstration does have majoritarian ambitions, displayed when it reenacts a "repopulation" of the streets. But its use of gesture and slogan also deconstructs majoritarianism, which is redeployed as spectacle. Knowing that no majority of any population ever demonstrates, those who reenact this political ritual still speak of a "massive popular expression." In fact, the demonstration rearranges each of those terms—*massive, popular,* and *expression.* Massive comes to mean "large enough to command attention, or to resist attempts to marginalize." Popular refers to a certain sort of attention to exclusions from other political arenas, whether government or media. Expression straddles the (now problematic) line between the expression of political will familiar to liberalism and the projection of spectacle more familiar to postmodernism. The demonstration reenacts and redeploys each classic modernist political term—*vanguard* and *elite, exception* and *margin, popular* and *population.* And, as 1989 reminds us, this practice clearly retains some kind of efficacy.

As a consequence of these moves, the demonstration necessarily remains distinct from the act of governing, not only by its announced hesitance about such acts, but also by its form, by the way it generates truth. This hesitance is notable because it is not only a negative, anarchistic aspect, but also a positive and moral one. Political scientists have occasionally recognized this, in the rehabilitations of populist democracy that followed the civil rights movement. But now the demonstration must be viewed as more than "input" to some exterior, stable political system; it is clearly capable of being transformative. This is an important development for postmodernism, which has so often been accused of apolitical nihilism. The televised demonstration is a key moment in the postmodern response to that critique. This is the core of any conceivable postmodern politics of objection.

Another Version of the Public Person

Every scheme of visibility and power implies a setting, carrying with it strong assumptions about the "audience" it meets, the roles that audience can play, and the responses that link the audience with whatever forms the object of their gaze. The dominant set, in liberal society, is citizen-as-audience watching government-as-mirror of the citizenry. This circuit is strongly self-referential and circular, which may help explain its remarkable stability. Liberal "responsibility" encodes that circular relationship. Government "responsibility" implies a willingness to respond to citizens, who in turn deserve to be heard in proportion to the "responsibility" of their claims. It is the citizen's responsibility to frame demands in terms the circuit can handle: appreciative of power's problems, careful, partial (not absolute), and patient rather than impulsive.

By stepping outside the bounds of these sociopolitical "manners," demonstrators present a different model of the citizen, even if that presentation is incidental to their central project—the articulation of demands, the insistence that attention be paid. The demonstrator is, in other words, an alternate citizen, a different kind of public person. As soon as one notices that difference, the entire context of the social contract is up for grabs. The demonstrator, in her most effective moments, is nothing less than a rival version of the popular will. This version emphasizes everyday life, as the Situationists first explained, and presumes to contrast the common practices and attitudes of that life with the restricted, self-controlled version required by Western representative democracy.

Straight white Jewish woman seeks peace

The demonstration implies an entirely different sort of participant. This is one of the important insights of Peter Sloterdijk's *Critique of Cynical Reason*. The demonstrator, by demonstrating, is at a distance from the citizen (even though they can claim citizenship when necessary, reversing course to their own advantage). The demonstrator positions herself as a *cheeky* citizen, to appropriate Sloterdijk's term. Looking for the unacknowledged foundations of enlightenment, Sloterdijk notices a certain mood not contained in the liberal circle discussed above: "I want to try to name a source of enlightenment in which the secret of its vitality is hidden: cheekiness" (99–100).[14] This unacknowledged, cheeky precedent of Western enlightenment provokes and problematizes that seemingly functional self-control—liberal responsibility—that was the enlightenment's more public and direct descendant. The measured, naturalistic pronouncement on values and possibilities meets a foe from outside its frame, one that uses the "apparently irrelevantly provocative gestures" (Sloterdijk 101), which Sloterdijk traces back to Diogenes' attack on a prematurely enshrined harmony between life and doctrine.

Sloterdijk's explanation of the importance of this "subversive variant of *low theory*" is almost schematic: "The process of truth splits into a discursive phalanx of grand theory and a satirical-literary troupe of skirmishers." In European philosophy, Diogenes initiates a specific "resistance against the rigged game of 'discourse.' . . . Since philosophy can only hypocritically live out what it says, it takes cheek to say what is lived. In a culture in which hardened idealisms make lies into a form of living, the process of truth depends on whether people can be found who are aggressive and free ('shameless') enough to speak the truth." Although such a skirmish could never assume success—it is, after all, an antiscience—it surely knows what success would mean: "Those who rule lose their real self-confidence to the fools, clowns, and kynics" (Sloterdijk 102).

Sloterdijk uses the Greek *kynic* and *kynicism* to refer to this cheeky cynicism, a posture that intervenes with considerable precision into the realm of power. He carefully explains that an "essential aspect of power is that it only likes to laugh at its own jokes." The unwillingness to share a giggle—to laugh at its own expense, as the saying goes—is central to the workings of power. We are left to chuckle only at the opponent or the dispossessed. Kynicism confronts this aspect of power as no other approach can. It does so in terms any demonstrator can understand: by intervening with the body, "bodies as arguments, bodies as weapons." This concern for the body, for how one lives rather than how one idealizes, is characteristic of the kynic, who puts himself or herself into the physical metaphor of the reminder, the presence of the open secret that power and its discourse are incomplete (Sloterdijk 109, 99).

The New World Order Has an Old World Odor

Almost by definition (by tradition and usage) then, cynicism cannot be defined as a pure condition, an essential presence in Western political life. Like any other positive development, cynicism is available for capture; it can become a site for contesting an era's character. As modern order learns to operate, to perform its basic functions, it learns to deal with the reversal of its own ideological idealism produced, in turn, by so many of those operations. Order can respond to the cynic by becoming more cynical than its critics. "The cynical master lifts the mask, smiles at his weak adversary, and suppresses him. *C'est la vie. Noblesse oblige.* Order must prevail. . . . *Master cynicism is a cheekiness that has changed sides*" (Sloterdijk 111). This "master cynicism" denounces the efficacy of protest, but does it cynically.

One of the defining triumphs of American protest, reported only long after the fact, was Richard Nixon's obsession with the demonstrations taking place within view of the White House during the Vietnam War. Surely, most of those demonstrators were convinced that the White House would refuse their message, but they repeatedly spoke to the void, intervening with their sometimes ill-clothed and unwashed bodies, in Diogenes' explicit tradition. Nixon (the master cynic) announced that they were irrelevant, a matter for no concern. But the kynics bothered Nixon so much that he worried endlessly about them, and eventually positioned buses to block his view. Nixon specifically enacted Sloterdijk's description of the master cynic's demise: "Those who rule lose their real self-confidence to the fools, clowns, and kynics."

This repositioning of the critical impulse—to the margins of discourse and beyond the bounds of seriousness—rearranges the map of public space. Different locales are privileged, and for different reasons. The street, the space of everyday life, is an important site, but it is not the only such key site. Also playing "an essential role in the history of cheekiness" are "the carnival, the universities, and the Bohemians" (Sloterdijk 117). These sites have no constituted, legalistic authority, but manage to provide a place where the kynics can stand apart, formulating their assault on the pompous power inscribed in the absolutism and idealism of Western philosophy. Being located away from "legitimate" locations of power is obviously no handicap: how could the kynics and the demonstrators function anywhere else than at a margin, a cusp, a thoroughfare? Their commitment to maintain a marginal position allows these locations to accumulate a countertradition, a history of cheekiness.

One obvious objection to Sloterdijk's schema is that demonstrators have long sought to cloak themselves in the legitimacy and moral force of a Plato, rather than his public tormentor, Diogenes.[15] In a sense, Sloterdijk's kynic is at the margins of the marginal—camped out at the fringe of the demonstration while the serious spokespersons intone severe moral critique, nearer its core, at the microphones. But in another sense, the kynic is where the actual force of the demonstration resides, no matter what happens at the microphone. The oral histories of demonstrations (the next day, over coffee) linger over the jokes and funny signs and slogans, the outrages and improprieties, more than the speeches and carefully coherent position papers.

Furthermore, even the most solemn demo speeches sometimes revert to a cheeky, joyous impudence. The aestheticized performance of a Malcolm X or a Martin Luther King, Jr. sets the genre of the contemporary American demonstration, and their performances were continually ambivalent in form. A bit too loud, a touch too joyous, occasionally naughty in their choice of metaphors, these performances know they are transgressive, even while they accomplish their announced aim to speak truth to power. We recall King's "I have a dream" speech, for example, as all moral force, but some of its power flows from its songlike qualities, a feature King drew reference to when he made explicit reference to "the old Negro spiritual." Even this most serious, legitimacy-pursuing speech—perhaps King's most carefully prepared text[16]—had its playful, kynical moments. One of its most sustained metaphors transposed the social contract into a moral checking account, reversing the familiar role of poor blacks writing checks that bounced, and playing with the implicit connection between the liberal social contract and capitalism itself.

Knowing that he could not directly address capitalism in this most visible speech, King still knew he could address it indirectly. He recasts the Declaration of Independence as a "promissory note," now issued to blacks as a "bad check, a check which has come back marked 'insufficient funds.'" But the innocent recipients of that fake payment (e.g., his audience that day, which by this point in the speech are laughing loudly at the playful reference to the forbidden terms of the economic system) "refuse to believe that the bank of justice is bankrupt." Even the form of their complaint—the insistent, visible public demonstration—enters the play, when King reminds them that there are many "demands" that are legitimate in society: "So we have come to cash this check, a check that will give us *upon demand* the riches of freedom and the security of justice."

In the United States, the master cynic tries to dismiss this aesthetic aspect of the demonstration as a characteristic of black culture, but the kynical performance of the demonstration has long since carried beyond black communities. The naughty, funny shows staged by Abbie Hoffman offer the most outrageous examples, but the irreverence also can be found throughout Woody Guthrie's work, passed down to his son Arlo, whose "Alice's Restaurant" is surely a kynical masterpiece. Anyone who has ever attended a large American demonstration—by whatever left group, on whatever issue—cannot have missed the cheeky core of the action, on placards, in costume, in the joy of kynics gathered in the street.

> **No testosterone!**
> **Give estrogen a chance**

As U.S. populism moves to the right, there have even been instances of right-wing kynics. Randall Terry's Operation Rescue, a militant anti-abortion protest movement, explicitly used the kynical form. Placing themselves at the doorstep of their adversaries, Terry's group practices an "in your face" confrontational style surely learned from predecessors on the left. The blood, pain, and bodies are disrespectfully flung in the face of power. To be sure, Terry's movement is weak on ideology—portraying pregnant teenagers and the people who help them as a power establishment is quite a leap—but the demo is not primarily a "consistency game." The demo will likely remain a practice of the political left: disrespect for power and discipline are not typical conservative attitudes, after all. Still, Terry's case suggests the independence of the form, not entirely subsumed by ideology and not thoroughly attached to an interest group or institutional structure.

But if the U.S. left inadvertently communicated the demo form to the right, it has also sent it around the world, to other destinations of ambivalent ideological character. The form is often established more clearly in such international mirrors; what stands out in Beijing or Moscow can often be what has been misunderstood or simply brushed aside in the United States, closer to its source. In one such case, the *New York Times*, true to form, reported this aspect of a major Moscow demonstration, even if that newspaper seldom finds the cheek in domestic gatherings. A front-page article on the major, March 1991 demo in Moscow's Pushkin Square was subtitled "Rally Takes Kremlin Terror and Turns It into Burlesque." The reporter cited "a grinning marcher" with a sign reading "Is Communism done yet? Or is it going to get worse?" The *Times* described the gathering as "ebullient, peaceful . . . an impish violation." Reenacting the Chinese student (and Chaplin), "the people moved through the falling snow . . . savoring the simple act of public assembly. They took pleasure in circumventing an armada of water canon, military trucks, and combat troops and police of every description in the center of the city, a stunning gathering assembled by the Kremlin in fear of public disorder" (Clines).

The *Times* could hardly have noticed, but it still presented evidence that Moscovites had already begun to import more from the United States than Pepsi, Big Macs, and MTV. They had begun to notice the unique and practiced form of the demonstration. Not only entrepreneurs, it would seem, have headed to Moscow; via the tube, a new sort of public person—cheeky, kynical, and out in the streets—had also made the trip.

Meta-Revisionism

Even at its best, the demonstration yields ambivalent results, uncomfortable at any specific achievement, unlikely to pause for long before pressing on. It should not be surprising that dominant perspectives easily redefine eras of protest, after the fact, as having failed. They could not go on, and they did not. Theoretically, this is easy enough to understand and accept; Albert Camus had long ago explained it well enough: "Rebellion is, by nature, limited in scope. It is no more than an incoherent pronouncement" (Camus 106; see also 13–22, 105–11).

Politically, the self-destructive structure of the demonstration has been harder to accept, especially during modernity's reign, when institutionalization meant the same thing as success. For a demonstration, success must surely be coded as entering into memory, surviving as a ready model, available to be replicated (simulated, repeated) at a later date. The kynical dimensions of civil rights protests—even the most "high serious," respectful gatherings at the steps of the Lincoln Memorial—do not much survive in the subsequent two decades of legislative response. Even these protests survive as memory, however, to reemerge as founding events of contemporary black culture and as international precedent. It is even easier to see campus protest and antiwar movements as primarily cultural, since these events never had much of a legislative legacy. These movements survive as attitude and gesture; it is hard to imagine anyone thinking them fulfilled by, say, the War Powers Act, or even by the occasional Peace Studies department at an American university.

This "failure" of the demonstration is always too incomplete to satisfy its opponents, the always strong "master cynics" of Sloterdijk's schema. With good cause: remaining outside the institutional scene, protest retains peculiar efficacy, no matter how temporary its existence may appear. The demo intervenes in power, confronts it, and changes it in that confrontation, reminding the kynics of their role. To traverse the path from demonstration to power is to have already altered society, no matter the institutional outcomes. But, since this alteration is at best only imperfectly institutionalized, traces of change remain a memorized text, available as a site where the meaning of history can be contested, revised repeatedly. This aspect of the demonstration—its propensity to open its history as a text for revision—not only confirms Baudrillard's view of history as hyperreal and commemorative; it also flatly contradicts his vision of the "disappearance of politics," opening new fields of political activity (Baudrillard, *Simulations* and "Revolution and the End of Utopia"). Although revision has always been the handmaiden of history, it surely gained new life when the important historical precedents escaped the institutional frame.

Yellow Ribbons, Troops, and Marches

Recent events surrounding the Gulf War present a crucial example of the odd efficacy of the demonstration, as well as its ambivalent legacy. In an important sense, one of the causes of the Gulf War was surely the need to revise the history of Vietnam. And the core of that revision involves a demonstration.

In this reading, the hysterical "support the troops" frenzy of the Gulf War—and its much longer aftermath—specifically engages this revisionist project. After all, the summons to "support the troops" (explicitly tied to a massive yellow ribbon redecoration of the American cityscape) is itself an odd war cry. It is explicitly more limited than calls from previous conflicts; "support the war," "the Great war," "the war to end all wars"—all those slogans refer to a policy or an objective. "Support the troops" almost begs alternate completions of the sentence; "even if the project they are conducting is dubious, at best." Indeed, the Tony Orlando (!) song that inspired the yellow ribbons is about an ex-con, not a soldier. But this emphasis on the troops not only encodes ambivalence about their status and project; it also announces a second purpose to our involvement. Not only did Saddam Hussein need to be stopped—a newly discovered project, it seems, in the summer of 1990—but perhaps as important, "the vet" had to be reinscribed, rewritten to exclude the kynical vet who found a voice, through the vehicle of a demonstration.

Read My Apocalypse

The kynical soldier has a long history, as the dark humor of the battlefield attests. Nonetheless, through the vehicle of the demonstration, the kynical veteran of the Vietnam War found new ways to cause trouble, even after leaving the battlefield. Oliver Stone's film, *Born on the Fourth of July*, emphasized the importance of one particular demonstration. The silent Vietnam Vets Against the War (VVAW) demonstration at the 1972 Republican convention in Miami was extraordinary in itself, "speaking" with a thunderous silence. Other actions by the VVAW, throughout the country, spread that eloquent silence, making the antiwar vet a fixture of the Vietnam era in the United States. Through these protests—the real parades honoring returning vets—the kynical vets had captured the legacy of Vietnam, if only for a while. Interestingly, the Ron Kovic book depicted by Stone's film had emphasized the "last patrol," the convoy of cars driven cross-country by California vets going to Miami for the protest. The most dramatic account of the demonstration itself was written by Hunter S. Thompson, whose description is worth quoting at length:

> [The Vets] were moving up Collins Avenue in dead silence; twelve hundred of them dressed in battle fatigues, helmets, combat boots . . . a few carried full-size plastic M-16s, many peace symbols, girlfriends walking beside vets being pushed along the street in slow-moving wheelchairs, others walking jerkily on crutches. . . . But nobody spoke; all the "stop, start," "fast, slow," "left, right" commands came from "platoon leaders" walking slightly off to the side of the main column and using hand signals. . . .
>
> I left my car . . . and joined the march. . . . No, "joined" is the wrong word; that was not the kind of procession you just walked up and "joined." Not without paying some very heavy dues: an arm gone here, a leg there, paralysis, a face full of lumpy scar tissue . . . all staring straight ahead as the long silent column moved between rows of hotel porches full of tight-lipped Senior Citizens, through the heart of Miami Beach.

The silence of the march was contagious, almost threatening. There were hundreds of spectators, but nobody said a word. I walked beside the column for ten blocks, and the only sounds I remember hearing were the soft thump of boot leather on hot asphalt and the occasional rattling of an open canteen top. (387)

Given the importance of the VVAW, it was a matter of crucial importance when Kovic, a leader of that demonstration, spoke to the (ostensibly moderate, perhaps even conservative) Democratic convention that nominated Jimmy Carter, only four years later. An important boundary had been transgressed. The kynic—having successfully cast a pall over one convention—had attained the rostrum at another, only four years later.

Once empowered, if only briefly, the kynical vet did some damage. A Vietnam memorial was soon commissioned and built in Washington: a gleaming black trench wall, menacing the State Department's back door. As planned and originally constructed, the monument had no reassuring, unifying narrative—it had, instead, a text of individual, singular names, listed by chronology of their death (not alphabetically, which would have implied a false unity, making it a bit too easy to find a specific name). No other American monument has ever become such a site of contestation, finally requiring an amendment—a heroic statue—to tame it. The fight over the Vietnam Memorial was but another sortie in an ongoing battle over the kynical vet. Rewriting the history of Vietnam-era demonstrations played large after Reagan's little simulated wars in Grenada and Panama, and Bush's large simulated war in the Persian Gulf.

The promise to honor "the troops" when they returned from the Gulf was an attempt to bring that contested era to an end, at long last. Interestingly, the last act of this contest would be a grand rhetorical turnabout, something even flashier than the "night into day" fireworks displays that marked most Gulf War celebrations (as well as the war itself, in night-vision video form). Fanatically welcoming the troops of Desert Storm (sometimes even calling them "Storm Troopers," to deploy exuberantly yet another revision), the yellow ribbon folk hoped finally to close the contest by pinning the antiwar demonstrators with the blame for dishonoring returning Vietnam-era troops. Never mind that this reversal was dubiously founded.[17] As Thompson explained, the antiwar movement had almost unlimited respect for the VVAW, with good cause; "There is no anti-war or even anti-establishment group in America today with the psychic leverage of the VVAW" (Thompson

392). At any rate, only the vet who returned with a keen kynicism intact would have wanted a parade conducted by demonstrators, whose parades are typically unpredictable and disrespectful. Indeed, it probably helped that the yellow ribbon tied together a false case. To exhaust the memory of the kynical vet, the memory of the VVAW, nothing less would really do. This was the master cynic's run on the kynic's stage.

Conclusions

By way of concluding this venture into the uncertain, inconclusive terrain of the demonstration, I will admit that not all demonstrators are kynics, however. The ones too literal, too consistent, have some difficulty understanding why their approach works so poorly. The tendency to remain linked to the message, to an ideological vision that would fit within modernism, is too comfortable for some demonstrators to abandon. Even the best analysts of the demonstration are sometimes confounded by this problem. In his discussion of the mass media and the new left, Todd Gitlin focuses on the way the media constituted SDS. Gitlin is sophisticated enough to understand that this is an interactive process; some reporters are sympathetic, and some on the left are more able than others to appropriate the media's ability to spread a critical message.

> **We're tired,**
> **We're cranky,**
> **We don't like the government**
> **—"Stragglers for Peace"**

Ultimately, however, Gitlin stays with the project of analyzing messages and codings, just missing the larger rhetorical event—the intervention that a demonstration composes, not entirely dependent on ideological message and direct influence on power. Culture and counterculture play a very slim role in his analysis, though surely that was part of what "the whole world was watching." Gitlin knows there is a difference: "The New Left of the 1960s, facing nightly television news . . . inhabited a cultural world vastly different" from earlier left movements. But his bottom line is literal and ideological: "To put it simply: the mass media have become core systems for the distribution of ideology" (2).

The best of our demonstrators, however, have always understood that the message—the ideology of the demonstration—composed only one of its dimensions. The status of this intervention includes an edge toward performance and action, remaining subtly uncomfortable with the stability and reliability of ideology. The demonstration knows that it cannot go on forever; that is the modernist's ambition, the impulse that creates institutions and professions and habits of continuity. The demonstration—this oddly efficacious, but ambivalently realized rhetorical reenactment of modernity's demise—does not survive; it recurs.

Notes

1. For a longer list (and an analysis somewhat more grounded in interest and elite control), see Penley and Ross viii–xvii.

2. The term *intertext* implies a level of analysis between related texts, perhaps observing what happens when genres mixed, promoting margins or fields over depth or structure.

3. Well after the fact, the only major voice to have emerged with intellectual credibility is that of Vaclav Havel, whose work might not turn out to be hostile to this analysis. See Havel, *Power of the Powerless* and *Disturbing the Peace.*

4. As William Connolly notes, in the modern state "the moment of individuality—of self as an independent agent of rights, interests, conscience and knowledge—is enabled and delimited by the institutional setting which makes it possible" (*Political Theory and Modernity* 118).

5. The street, as analyzed by geographers and architects and acted upon by performance artists, is crucial to the demonstration. See Jacobs, and also Berman, esp. 320–24. Berman gets much of the performative aspect of the demonstration exactly right, but I think he sometimes misplaces this phenomenon—and others—as distinctively modernist, because he (just barely) misses the TV camera there at the side of the street, transforming the event.

6. The actual connection between these various demonstrations (as demonstrations) may be open to some question. For my purposes in this essay, I assume a connection. Support for this position was affirmed by one of Ted Koppel's editorial producers, who wrote, "It is not too much of an exaggeration to say that the German revolution began in Tiananmen Square," and quoted a leader of the Leipzig demonstrations to support her point (Sonenshine).

7. For more on the role of speed, see Virilio. Der Derian notes: "given the obvious importance of speed in international relations—from the rapid increase

in weapon delivery speed and concomitant decrease in human response time, to the appearance of real-time representation and surveillance of the enemy—it does seem strange that Virilio's work has gone largely unnoticed in the discipline of international relations" ("The (S)pace of International Relations" 306–7). In one remarkable instance, the demonstration completely left the realm of place and became total, giddy electronic communication. In early 1990, fifteen Western magazines (including *Spy*, the *LA Weekly*, and Britain's *The Face*) printed a protest message, in Chinese, with instructions on how to FAX the message to Chinese government machines. The "FAX for Freedom" action echoed the earlier use of these machines by protesters, who communicated with Chinese expatriates throughout the world during Tiananmen ("Play a Prank for Freedom!").

8. Patterson's introductory political science text is probably a representative example. He covers the demo in four paragraphs of a large book, conceding that early civil rights legislation "can be explained only as a response by Congress to the pressure created by the civil rights movement." After a nod to diversity ("American history would be very different had not the abolitionist, labor, suffragist, and other major movements pressed their claims"), Patterson effectively dismisses protest. "The majority of the general public sides with authorities. . . . In a *Newsweek* poll, 58 percent of respondents blamed the Kent State killings on the student demonstrators, while only 11 percent blamed the guardsmen. . . . In a 1972 . . . survey, only 15 percent . . . expressed approval of the civil disobedience that accompanied the civil rights and anti-Vietnam movements. . . . Only 1 to 2 percent of the American public took to the streets in protest at any time during the 1960s and 1970s" (215–16).

9. See the Oxford English Dictionary, in which the first six meanings of *demonstration* refer to that objective dimension, before the seventh refers to a public action, on some public question. The OED cites an 1861 issue of *Saturday Review:* "Then, besides 'ovations', there are 'demonstrations', the Q.E.D. of which is not always very easy to see. We read how the students of [a] University 'made a demonstration'. This we believe means, in plain English, that the students kicked up a row." My thanks to Thomas Dumm for helping to clarify this point.

10. Lipset's work on this topic during the sixties follows a similar trajectory (Lipset and Achaflander, *Passion and Politics*). For a thorough review of demo scholarship, see Lofland.

11. Gusfield 6–7. See also Heberle; and Lofland 27–88. Note also that precisely because sociologists have understood the protest in the context of crowd sociology, some of the best historical narratives of the form can be found in that literature. See Rudé 214–34.

12. In his 1970 book, Gusfield (309–12) could still raise the question of "collective meanings" in protest movements by reference to rumor, interpretation, and symbols—but with no mention of television and its preferences, style, and pace. Twenty years later, the mix must surely be reversed. Lipset (*Passion*

and Politics xii) mentions that modern communication helps explain the vitality of 1960s movements, but he otherwise stays with functionalism. One remarkable exception stands out from the studies published in the sixties and seventies. Orrin Klapp puts protest into the context of drama, telling his story in a tone reminiscent of Machiavelli, and on the basis of that recontextualization is able to observe many of the aspects of the demonstration that I am discussing in this essay (Klapp, *Symbolic Leaders*, esp. 66–100; *Collective Search for Identity*).

13. The demonstration slogans and sign-texts used in this essay were observed at the January 1991 San Francisco demonstration against the Gulf War. My thanks to Dan Baum and Margaret Knox for recording them and sharing their notes with me.

14. The translator's note reveals that the word translated as "cheeky" is *Frechheit*, "a word whose meaning lies somewhere between cheekiness and impudence."

15. Yet a different objection might read Plato as the disobedient, the ironist in the face of liberal power. This reading informs Seery's study of the ironic tradition, which suggests that Plato was the ironist, which necessarily implies that Diogenes was the naive joker who missed the point. Still, irony is a mood that Sloterdijk could appreciate. Seery finds a contemporary exemplar at an antinuclear demonstration in Berkeley, where a woman in a wheelchair presents her obviously powerless body as ironic counterpoint to the powers that be. Although the question is beyond the scope of my essay, the ironist—even if mock serious in public performance—is clearly another moment of the demonstration, another element of the rhetorical workings of the streets. This is one of the things that Richard Rorty has missed in his discussion of irony (Seery, esp. 294–99).

16. Lewis reports that "the speech that Martin was about to give had been more carefully prepared than any he had made before, more worried over by paragraph, line, and comma. . . . During the preceding two days and even late into the last night, he had written and rewritten his text" (227).

17. Much more prominent in "dishonoring" Vietnam vets were the traditional veterans' organizations, which did not understand these vets, so many of whom immediately adopted the cultural style of the counterculture—not that of the VFW or the American Legion—when they returned. Kovic reports encounters with such vets throughout his book.

8 A Show of Defiance

Poetry as "Protest" in Contemporary America

John C. Dolan

The romantic pose of modern man:—the noble man (Byron, Victor Hugo . . .):—noble indignation . . . siding with the oppressed and under-privileged . . . altruism as the most mendacious form of egoism . . . most sentimental egoism.   —Friedrich Nietzsche, 1887

In the West, protests about cretinization are an integral part of the cretinization process itself.   —Alexandr Zinoviev, 1983

Can you face disdain? Can you face ridicule? Can you face *utter indifference?*   —Matt Groening, "How to Be a Sensitive Poet," 1986

I attended two poetry readings during the Gulf War. Both began, as I knew they would, with the reading of poems against the war. But something odd happened; both times . . . these antiwar poems infuriated me. The first time it just seemed odd—a biochemical blip maybe. Then it happened again. It puzzled me. Why should these harmless things bother me? Certainly not because of any patriotic indignation . . . or an aesthete's anger at bad verse—they were not, as I recall, really *bad* . . . no worse than most current poetry. "I too dislike it . . ." as Marianne Moore said.

So why should these poems have made me so inarticulately furious, I who have sat doggedly through so many earnest lyrics about dead relatives and sexual awakenings? Surely getting angry at a couple of antiwar poems—which were, at least, topical and comprehensible— was to swallow a camel and balk at a gnat. It made no sense. And yet there it was: this intense sublingual rage, a feeling like that underlying certain of Orwell's essays: the feeling of violent hatred for people with whom one ought to be in complete agreement. I have come to the conclusion that what is usually called "protest poetry" is particularly infuriating (because I later found that many others had felt the same guilty, confused anger at these readings) because of the peculiarly false—as opposed to simulated—scenario, in which the poet becomes a fake oracle of populist indignation, which three hundred years of literary history now force upon American poets.

Poetry has followed a bizarre path in the past three hundred years, diverging markedly from the rules governing author/reader relations characteristic of most other literary forms. The central expression or symptom of the odd relation of poet and reader is discernible in that paradigmatic meeting between them: *the poetry reading itself*—a cultural phenomenon not, so far, the subject of much theoretical attention.

Considered in terms of Lyotard's essential distinction between modern and postmodern artist/audience relations, the poetry reading, which is particularly central for socially conscious "protest" poetry, seems to suggest that lyric poetry has not attained the pagan or postmodern at all. Lyotard defines the modern situation thus: "[The work is] intended for a public, for a set of readers, for a definite cultural group. [The artist] justifies, he defends, what he has done in the name of a system of values that are the values held by this public" (Lyotard and Thébaud 9). By contrast Lyotard depicts the pagan or postmodern as an ungrounded, isolated act, like that of throwing a message in a bottle to the waves: "I believe it is important that there be no addressee. When you cast bottles to the waves, you don't know to whom they are going, and that is all to the good. That must be part of modernity, I think" (Lyotard and Thébaud, 5). In Lyotard's division, "the [pagan] artifact . . . will end up producing its own readers" (Lyotard and Thébaud). What one sees instead with poetry, especially public protest poetry like that at the Gulf War readings I attended, is a moribund simulacrum of the situation Lyotard distinguishes as modern: one in which the text is *liturgical;* in which the protest poem, its ideological bent a trivialized given, is performed before a public that knows what to expect, knows precisely what values will be invoked, and settles back to listen to this invocation of simulated shared values in smug boredom.

The poet, in such a situation, is the very opposite of Lyotard's postmodern artist; while the postmodern writer tosses her or his message to the waves, the modern protest poet wins by displaying herself or himself as a vessel of shared values. The audience of the protest poetry reading wins too, in the sense that it gets to display, at no cost, its adherence to those shared values by sitting through the performance; the text alone loses. It is dictated and dismissed in advance—just as a priest's sermon, iterating a given, familiar, trivialized agenda, is forgotten, its only purpose having been to serve as a simulated display of community solidarity.

Lyotard's distinction offers a means of discovering how protest poetry, and particularly war protest poetry, works in America—and, in the process, may help explain why the genre is so much despised and avoided by otherwise literate audiences. If a protest poem is a Lyotardian modern (or rather pseudo-modern) genre—a public liturgical occasion so tightly scripted that actual reading and listening is not necessary, any more than actual listening is necessary in any other liturgical situation—then the text itself cannot really be heard. It will become a comforting background hum; it will be the occasion for the audience to examine its fingernails, or mentally balance the checkbook.

But why should this have happened? Why should poetry, in a century in which the novel, the dominant literary form, went "pagan" with a vengeance, have remained in modernism, rehearsing public virtues? The reasons lie, naturally, not in the malign influence of this or that poet but in a tremendously long and complex generic negotiation between poet and reader over the past several centuries, a negotiation centering on the concept of "fiction" and the rival concept, "hyperrealism," identified by Umberto Eco and Jean Baudrillard as an essential characteristic of American culture.

In attempting to place author/audience relations in historical context, focusing on concepts of truthfulness or realism, Baudrillard's conception of the progressive stages of simulation can be useful. In fact, we can usefully place Baudrillard's four stages of simulation within the context of the development of English-language poetry since 1740, and by so doing explain such bizarre anomalies as the Gulf War poetry readings and, more broadly, the prevalence of "daring" poetry of "protest," which is not daring and serves no purpose of protest.

Baudrillard lists, in *Simulations*, four stages in the evolution of "the image":

—it is the reflection of a basic reality
—it masks and perverts a basic reality
—it masks the *absence* of a basic reality
—it bears no relation to any reality whatever; it is its own pure simulacrum.
(11)

If we impose this progression on the development of readers' belief in the reality of literary works, an interesting distinction between prose fiction and lyric poetry emerges. The term *fiction*, commonly accepted as the natural or universal contract between author and reader, is in fact a recent stage in the development of reader belief in literature (as Mylne, Stewart, Showalter, and Haywood have shown). *Fiction*, in its currently popular definition, developed by Coleridge, as the reader's "willing suspension of disbelief," in fact developed its present form as a result of the co-optation of novel readers—not poetry readers—in France and England during the late seventeenth and early eighteenth centuries.

The modern novel (as distinct from the lengthy, fantastical romances that preceded it) began not as fiction but as an attempt to deceive, to present an invented narrative as real (thus the proliferation of disingenuous introductions attesting that the enclosed manuscript had been found in an old trunk in an attic). As readers simultaneously grew accustomed to larger and larger doses of such narrative and became suspicious that there could have been so many manuscripts secreted in attics to be found in a timely manner by "editors" (who were, of course, actually authors), the set of relations that was to become fiction emerged as a compromise in which the addicted reader agreed to experience certain emotions associated with belief in the narrative for the duration of reading in order to get the fix that the novel provided. Fiction, then, does reproduce in some measure the progression, suggested by Baudrillard, from the real (for there were, of course, real manuscripts found in real attics, which provided the model to be copied) to the explicitly deceptive, to the hyperreal—the realm in which the novel continues today, accepted as neither true nor untrue but unreal, fictional, hyperreal.

Contrary to the general assumption, reader belief in lyric poetry has not developed in an analogous way. The naive, absolute distinction between true and false has been more basic to English-language lyric poetry than to any other artistic genre of the European repertoire. Thus poetry, unlike the novel, has not attained Baudrillard's "hyperreal" and remains devoted to forms that rely on audience belief in the literal truth of the poetic narrative. The novel was free to work out its historic compromise in hyperreality because, as a pop form, its purity was not really an issue (since it was deemed inherently impure by most French and English literary judges). The late seventeenth century, the period in which the negotiations leading to the development of fiction occurred, was as crucial in the development of norms of simulation in poetry as in the novel, but poetry had to operate, especially in England, under tremendous social pressure on the issue of reality. (Roughly speaking, the technology of realism in the novel was emerging more quickly in France, and that of the lyric poem in England, largely due to differences in the religious and moral climate). As Russell Fraser has documented in *The War Against Poetry,* the era of the English Civil War saw poetry move in a direction almost opposite to that followed by prose fiction.

Poetic invention underwent a violent constriction, from the Jacobean hyperreal in which poetry was accepted as the product of pure writerly invention (usually trellised on one of a number of acceptable familiar romantic situations, paradigmatically the male lover in a moment of unrequited love), to the late-seventeenth-century poetics of occasional poetry grounded in public, confirmable "reality."

As Fraser has demonstrated, the 1640s and 1650s produced a huge number of pamphlets, sermons, and books that shared a deep hostility to poetic invention of any sort. Calling the impetus behind these critiques of poetry Puritan might invite historical quibbles, but it is broadly true that the evangelical, Puritan, Cromwellian stratum of English society was the source of much of the hatred of poetry. This is particularly important to note because of the very profound influence that stratum had, and has, on the shape of American culture.

These numerous critiques, which, as Fraser shows, freely mixed Puritan Christian moralism with Platonic scorn for lesser orders of reality, aimed precisely at destroying the set of poetic conventions that could be called fictional or hyperreal. Poets struggled to find material that could meet the approval of an audience fixated on narrative truth and in desperation came to rely on the celebration of verifiable public occasions (paradigmatically a battle or the death of a famous person) or on the one source of narrative still regarded as legitimate (because true) by their readers: Scripture. Broadly speaking, then, the second half of the seventeenth century saw English poetry moving as decisively away from the hyperreal compromise as prose fiction was moving toward it.

The eighteenth-century English poets, best represented by Thomas Gray, responded to the constriction of literary invention by the invention of what has since become the popular idea of poetry in general: the discovery of unverifiable (hence uncontradictable) mental events as a safe, "true" source of poetic invention. The discovery and exploitation of the mental event as poetic occasion account for most of the subsequent developments in poetic technology, notably the phenomenon called Romanticism.

The true beginning of the modern era in poetry (using *modern* in a sense that does not imply Lyotard's modern) is Edward Young's publication, in 1742, of the first of nine sections of *The Complaint, or Night Thoughts*—ten thousand lines of description of the author's mental state (resembling clinical depression) with a very significant author's note at the beginning informing the reader that the "events" (mental events) to be described really happened: "As the occasion of this poem was real, not fictitious, so the method pursued in it was rather imposed by what spontaneously arose in the author's mind on that occasion, than meditated or designed" (Young, in *The Works of the English Poets from Chaucer to Cowper* 14:420). Young's brilliant discovery was that, behind the safely opaque cranial barrier, the poet could claim that tremendous and "real" battles, wars, and deaths were occurring—unseen by anyone else, but true—that is, not fictional, but autobiographically real.

The poet who regularized modern English poetics, Thomas Gray—perhaps the most important poet in the past three centuries, in terms of changing the basic rules of poetry—wrote only a few dozen poems; but each one of his most important pieces (which also date from the crucial decade, the 1740s) consists of an attempt to extend Young's innovation, either by developing a private, unverifiable occasion, as in "Sonnet: On the Death of Mr. Richard West," or by extending the funereal occasion ironically, as in "Ode: On the Death of a Favorite Cat . . .," building on the conventions of the funeral ode, as cataloged by Eric Smith in his excellent study *By Mourning Tongues*.

Gray's most famous work, and probably the most famous single poem in English, "Elegy Written in a Country Church-Yard" is actually the working-out of a single essential innovation that descends from Young: that the poet can satisfy the onerous truth requirement by the use of a container-for-contained metonymy, in which the graveyard becomes the topic itself. Thus the upper-class visitor can use the "Country Church-Yard" without having to have any relatives die. Another enormously successful poem of the 1740s, Robert Blair's "The Grave," consists of 810 relentlessly lugubrious lines exploiting, as its title suggests, the same graveyard metonymy. In poems like the "Elegy" or "The Grave," a privatization of the occasion leads to the combination of funereal and martial poetics (poetics of war and death) and Romantic isolation (war and death happening silently in the poet's head).

An almost comic high point of collision/collusion between the war/funeral public poetics and the private mental event occurs in the epochal "Castaway" by William Cowper. "The Castaway" is a late development in modern poetry, dating from the very end of the eighteenth century (1799), and displays a radically intensified hijacking of the ostensible subject—the occasion of the poem—by the true subject, the "mendacious ego" mentioned by Nietzsche. "The Castaway" is ostensibly about a true incident, a sailor washed overboard during Anson's circumnavigation of the globe, recorded in Anson's *Voyage Around the World* (1748). Indeed, "The Castaway" spends ten of its eleven stanzas very movingly describing the fate of the sailor, who struggles without hope in midocean:

> Not long beneath the whelming brine,
>   Expert to swim, he lay;
> Nor soon he felt his strength decline,
>   Or courage die away;
> But waged with death a lasting strife,
> Supported by despair of life.

But Cowper, trained by the innovations of Gray and Young, has no intention of letting the occasion be the true subject of his poem; instead, he takes this public funereal occasion and, in a stunning reversal, uses the last stanza to make an unspecified mental event occurring in the poet's head the real subject of the poem:

> No voice divine the storm allayed,
>   No light propitious shone,
> When, snatched from all effectual aid,
>   We perished, each alone:
> *But I beneath a rougher sea,*
> *And whelmed by deeper gulfs than he.*
> (emphasis mine)

"He," the drowned sailor being elegized, suddenly finds himself as it were drowned a second time, the victim of a comparison in which his sufferings are declared less than those of the poet's less visible, mental event.

The private mental event and the public funereal occasion, in various combinations, continue to dominate English-language poetry to this day. Two episodes from the annals of recent American poetry show the extent to which occasional truth, rather than fictionality, undergirds the American lyric. Diane Wakoski, a contemporary American poet, has described in an essay her worry and evasions over the poem "Justice Is Reason Enough," in which she describes being raped by her brother, who then commits suicide. Wakoski confesses that she never had a brother—but it is the fact that she must confess this that is most significant. So deeply is the truth requirement embedded in lyric poetics that Wakoski describes her tortuous lies and evasions *at poetry readings* when approached by would-be comforters who assumed the truth of the narrative in the poem: "For years, people thought this was a true story, because when anyone asked, I averted my eyes and said I didn't want to talk about it. Then later I let it be known that during that period in my life I had a mental aberration and had really thought that the whole story was true and that I had a brother" (*Toward a New Poetry* 116). As Wakoski bravely confesses, she first used a stratagem to avoid revealing the "lie"; saying, truthfully enough, that she did not want to discuss the narrative of the poem, allowing her comforters to infer that it was all too painful. Faced with the failure of this stratagem, she actually resorted to a degrading plea of insanity rather than simply admit that she had made up the story of the dead brother. Other American poets have faced the same problem; one, Robert Pack, has even written "Lyric Narration: The Chameleon Poet" as a frantic defense of his right to do what most critics still regard as natural to poetry: making things up. Pack's defense of this right was provoked, he tells us, by exactly the situation implied in Wakoski's account; he was confronted by a would-be comforter after a public reading of his poems. Pack, too, had written a poem in which his brother died; Pack, too, had no brother. Learning this, a member of the audience turned on him furiously, calling him a liar. (Pack's article itself is not as interesting as the fact that it had to be written at all; no novelists have had to write articles justifying their right to make up stories.)

The public reading of poetry, the scene of Wakoski's and Pack's bizarre humiliation, is clearly its primal scene. The reading is an ersatz community liturgy, as far from Lyotard's pagan "message in a bottle" as can be imagined. Thus the need for truth above all in a poem delivered at a public reading; thus the outrage felt by Pack's auditor; thus the queasy rationalizations detailed by Wakoski. All of this is clearly a long way from fiction, or willing suspension of disbelief. Poetry has clearly diverged from prose fiction and has not followed the stages of image production postulated by Baudrillard, but has in fact regressed to earlier stages in which audiences demand and poets supply work that, in sharp distinction to prose fiction, attempts to maintain a "relation with a basic reality."

The development of Romantic poetics, which, rather than attaining hyperreality, "mask the absence of a reality," has been a sinuous one since the time of Young and Gray, but not really very complex: poetry has evolved, as it has had to evolve, as an art form in which literal truth of narrative has been basic; and the literal truth that poets, in desperation, have turned to has been the safe, private, uncontradictable truth of the mental event, often juxtaposed for pathos with a public occasion— and of course the paradigmatic occasion for English-language poetry has always been war. It is from this that the Romantic commonplace of the poet as a man apart, a special person, has come about; and it is that reliance on the self-absorbed speaker "truthfully" telling his or her mental experiences that has alienated the larger public, which would rather make the compromise called fictionality (and thus prefers prose fiction) than trust the shaky truth of lyric narrative.

But though this line of development has been precisely one most likely to alienate "the people," it is one that necessarily leads the poet (as opposed to the novelist) to force a false (as opposed to simulated or hyperreal) identification with any others who are "set apart" or persecuted or otherwise analogous to the paradigmatic situation of the Romantic narrator. Thus it is inevitable that there should have arisen a Byron, a Lermontov, even, eventually, degraded pop epigones in the form of a Phil Levine or a Ginsberg—practitioners of late-twentieth-century lyric poetry, *the* most academic, arcane, and unappealing of literary forms—who nonetheless declare themselves, all the more fiercely in fact, to be (like Ginsberg in "Howl") one with every loser who can be included in a book-length list, from the insane to the children to the animals. And so, inevitably, we witness the spectacle of an academic poet like Phil Levine declaring himself to be the voice of the voiceless, despite the daunting fact that the voiceless, in America, almost universally hate and distrust poetry. The relation between the poets of protest and the true victims in America is one of unrequited love: poets must, as part of their inheritance of a truth-oriented, public genre, make love to "the people"; but the people (for precisely the same historical reasons, amusingly enough) despise poets and poetry.

Popular scorn for poetry is discernible everywhere; in a radio commercial I heard recently, a copywriter uses poetry to define that which is lonely, twerpy, un-fun. While fast, loud young voices party (mentioning the station's call letters as often as possible), a lugubrious male voice says, "No thanks, I'll just curl up with this volume of haiku." The twerp-poet, offered the chance to party, chooses to be alone with a particularly tiresome imported form of lyric, reenacting as comedy what originated as Romantic tragedy—the poet who walks the lakes and hills alone, "lonely as a cloud." As the commercial implies, American consumers understand the paradigmatic poet-biography created by Young and Gray and popularized by Wordsworth quite well—that is, they understand the reality it attempts to mask: the poet chooses this isolation not because of persecution but because of literary vanity, which has ceased to become tragic and has become a comic cliche.

The comic aspect of the figure of the "sensitive poet" is brilliantly sketched in a cartoon from Matt Groening's brilliant *Love Is Hell* (1984). The cartoon begins with a sort of aptitude test: "How to Tell If You Are a Sensitive Poet." The questions on the test begin with the Wordsworthian popularization of the figure of poet as lonely container of mental events: "Are you 'different'?" "Do you feel 'special'?" "Are you 'complicated'?" But the last question, the punch line, emphasizes failed ambition: "Do you enjoy 'poverty'?"

Each of the panels in Groening's cartoon works the same way: ironic dramatization of the Wordsworthian poet, ending in wry hints at the veiled, thwarted ambition underlying the enactment of this life-script. Significantly, Groening's portrait of his sensitive poet is set at a poetry reading. The "Sensitive Poet" is pictured wearing a turtleneck sweater and a lugubrious expression, reciting, "I sit in my cubbyhole, waiting, waiting," with the scribbled stage-note to himself, "Pause, look stalwart." Under "Advanced Exercises for Sensitive Poets," Groening mocks the dilemma in which American poetry finds itself, a vehicle for literary ambitions locked in a poetics of solipsism that can never find an audience: "Write a poem about a fleeting emotion unique to you, using a complex and private system of symbols that no one else can possibly understand." Here is a strikingly compact description of the poetics that I have tried to outline as defining the past three hundred years of development: reliance on uncontradictable mental events ("a fleeting emotion unique to you") as a pseudoreal (as opposed to hyperreal) narrative base, with the consequence that readers, while grudgingly conceding the possibility of truthfulness, find no appeal and turn away ("using a . . . system of symbols that no one else can possibly understand") (Groening).

What Groening has understood (far better than most academic poetry critics) is the agonizing interweaving of this self-defeating poetics with violently intense literary ambition. Groening's last two panels drive home the dilemma, emphasizing the intense yet feckless ambition underlying contemporary poets' lives: under "How to Be a Professional Sensitive Poet" he suggests, "Submit your poems to publications you don't read" and "Cultivate a sneering hatred of all other sensitive poets," and in a brilliant mockery of ambition in a hopeless cause, he ends with "and remember; when in Elkville, be sure to stop by the tomb of the unknown sensitive poet and set a spell."

Let us consider how all this tormented mixture of ambition and fecklessness works out in the crux: the actual scene of a protest poetry reading during the Persian Gulf War. The scene is a big wood-paneled auditorium on the Berkeley campus of the University of California. A well-known poet-critic is reading tonight. About two hundred people are attending—a very good crowd by poetry standards. When the poet steps to the podium, he sees a crowd almost all white, overwhelmingly academic, politely underdressed, and very pleased with itself just for being present. If he were to ask who in the crowd voted for Reagan, not one hand would be raised. That is not to say that no one in this crowd voted for Reagan, merely that no one would be so foolish as to raise a hand.

So, when he lets the applause die down and introduces his antiwar poem, the poet is relaxed. He knows the risks—or rather he knows that there is no risk. It is a great way to open the reading—get some solidarity going. This is not to say that he really believes everybody in the room opposes the war in Iraq: surely he knows that behind locked doors and drawn blinds, half of Berkeley is getting sexually excited every night watching that miserable Arab blusterer's bunkers go sky-high. But that is no problem: this is not rabble rousing, this is not politics, *this is liturgy. Poets are antiwar; poetry about war is antiwar poetry.* This is something understood even by those who could not name a single twentieth-century war poem (and in spite of the fact that Wallace Stevens, the greatest American poet, wrote many war poems, none of which is at all antiwar).

The script has by now been universally disseminated. Anyone can do it; during the time that "Desert Shield" was changing sibilants to become "Desert Storm," I asked a poetry class I was teaching at the University of San Francisco to write a poem on the buildup. Naturally, all the poems were antiwar; but what was more interesting about them was the evident cynicism with which they had been written, as if a priest had assigned a catechism class to write essays on the benefits of turning the other cheek. By this time—the tenth or eleventh generation of mass-produced bohemians—literally anyone can learn to write an antiwar poem, be a poet in struggle, a "sensitive poet," earn a feeling of political virtue—and all at very little risk.

I recall very clearly the moment at which the script was passed on to me. I can recall being literally taught to write antiwar poetry in order to foster my literary ambitions, literally to earn a prize. I was twelve. My seventh-grade teacher, a good liberal, taught us about haiku poetry and assigned us to write a haiku on "peace." I began my literary career by composing the following winning entry:

> Peace means never
> Looking up when you hear the sound
> of an airplane

Painful to recall; but useful in that even at the age of twelve I had learned to use the scripted antiwar pathos to make the grade—and without even dreaming of consulting my inner feelings about war, which, like those of many male twelve-year-olds, were extremely enthusiastic (though tempered by the vague, depressed admission that Vietnam looked pretty hot and humid and unheroic). The entire class knew instantly that the assignment called for a working of an antiwar theme into the required number of syllables; our performance of the assigned task in no way interfered with actual feelings, if any, about the war in Vietnam, which, then and later, broke down fairly simply on class lines, with the hippielike children of technocrats enacting a very public, stylized opposition and the grubbier offspring of blue-collar parents maintaining an inarticulate, sullen nationalism.

Just as the writing of scripted protest poetry was easy, done from prefab kits, so the reading of such texts was scripted, as I found two years after my haiku experience. Like millions of twerps of that era, I found in Tolkien's *Lord of the Rings* my true scripture; so, when I was asked to choose a reading for the new-model catechism class I attended each Wednesday night, I chose the passage that meant the most to me— the rapturous gore of the sally out of Minas Tirith. I practiced all evening, working on projecting the pure genocidal glory of the passage. By the time I got up to deliver it, I was in a sort of pubescent berserk state. I read the passage, shouting at times, and sat down, still quivering, half-hoping that the entire catechism class would rise and join me in any available jihad. Instead, Mrs. Reese, the well-meaning progressive who ran the class, stood up and said blandly, "Thank you, John, for that moving depiction of the horrors of war." I didn't get it for a second— horrors of war? Horrors of war? But no sarcasm showed in her voice, no sign of anything in her face at all. She had not heard a thing, any more than anybody at the Gulf War reading I attended heard anything but a piece of liturgical rectitude—what Zinoviev bitterly calls "part of the cretinization process."

This is not to say that nothing important goes on in the presentation of such poetry. Such denials are a very common delusion, based on a sort of curdled sulk at the broken promises of pure content. The fact that antiwar poetry has no effect on the American polity hardly means that it has no effect at all. Poetry does not effect political change; what, then, does poetry effect? Poetry effects the elevation of poets. Gerard Genette has emphasized the tendency of twentieth-century poetry to declare itself, above all, to be poetry, to assert itself and grab coveted space for itself on the page: "The essence of poetic motivation . . . is to be found in the attitude of reading that the poem succeeds (or, more often, does not succeed) in imposing on the reader: a motivating attitude which . . . accords to all or part of the discourse the sort of intransitive presence and absolute existence that Eluard calls "poetic evidence" (95).

Poetry, in other words, aggressively declares itself to be poetry and demands a sort of extra credit from the reader as such. This extra credit is no mere abstraction; it is the essence of the matter, the stuff of which careers are made. Beneath the apparent level of courageous political stance runs the old constant of American life, running straight from the Massachusetts Bay Colony to the present: the building of a career under cover of public rectitude.

Since the era of Byron (possibly even since Voltaire), one of the ways in which fans recognize a "true" poet is by his or her stance of daring opposition to the corrupt power structure. The truthfulness or verifiability of this paradigmatic narrative rests on real death, real misery; in its original incarnation (and more recently in other parts of the world, like Latin America or the former Soviet Union) this scenario has survived in its original form: the forbidden anthems shouted by poets were genuinely forbidden, the proof being in the fact that the poets who sang them went to prison, were tortured, or were executed. But in American culture, where poetry exists only as the most abstruse art form—where most people run from rooms at the thought that a poetry reading might break out, and poets are used in commercials as instantly identifiable boring nerds—there is not the least necessity to use state power against poetry of protest. (Indeed, a wiser CIA might have done well to fund protest-poetry centers, enhancing the fatal association of antiwar sentiments with a despised art.)

Yet the scenario survives, a continent and a couple of centuries from the environment that spawned it; a poet is an "unacknowledged legislator" who bravely takes a stand against corruption in power. It is this model, dimly remembered, that leads the poets I heard read during the Gulf War to choose their antiwar poem to read first; that tang of forbiddenness with (the best part) no real risk behind it. The audience, raised in bohemian aesthetics, has been long accustomed to the use of an entire range of adjectives in very idiomatic senses, among them *daring* (for works that require no daring at all) and *forbidden* (for poetry that no administration would ever waste time forbidding). This loss of the true sense of "forbidden" is part of the simulation of danger and bohemian revolt that is the dominant script of the current poetry scene. A quick index of the difference between this purely simulated forbiddenness and the real thing may be got in comparing reaction to these antiwar poems (applause, indulgence, boredom) and the reaction to a Stanford University lecturer who, a few months later, publicly declared that he used marijuana and that he had sometimes brought it to work with him. He was fired. No one reacted.

One of the things that current cultural critics have been least capable of grasping (precisely because of their own cooptation by bohemian/ Romantic aesthetics) is that true forbiddenness means that if you say what is forbidden, really forbidden, you get fired and nobody comes to your defense (just as true voicelessness means that nobody hears you or laments you in print or even knows you exist). The difference between real daring, as in the heroic statement by the Stanford lecturer, and pro- test poetry's ersatz daring, its simulation of nineteenth-century causes célèbres, is a difference between politics and aesthetics; *daring*, when used to describe a contemporary American poet's work, is an idiomatic term that simply means "pleasantly evocative of the Romantic-rebel archetype."

Coming to the realization that our poetic "show of defiance" is only a show has not been pleasant, especially since I find myself and my work implicated as deeply as anyone's in enacting and profiting from the display of ritualized alienation and rebellion. How long it has been going on, this safe, harmless reenactment of routines that once pos- sessed real risk! And how strange to realize that for generations our apparently spontaneous anger and rebellion have poured smoothly into the forms of the literary career.

9 "Bigger" and "Booker" and the GOP

Race and E/Racing in the Struggle for Hegemony

Stuart Alan Clarke

Introduction

In 1988, Willie Horton was the black male figure most closely associated with presidential candidate George Bush. As utilized in a television commercial focusing on the inability of Democrats to cope effectively with violent crime, the figure of Willie Horton drew on our national history of representations of black men as threat, both to civilization in general and to white womanhood in particular. Political pundits insisted that, Bush campaign protestations to the contrary, the Horton symbolism quite effectively exploited the fear (and anger) of white working- and middle-class voters.[1]

It seems likely that in 1992 Clarence Thomas, the newly appointed associate justice of the Supreme Court, will be the black male figure most closely associated with President George Bush. As presented in his confirmation hearings, Thomas-as-racial-symbol drew on our national history of representations of "rags to riches" trajectories in which hard work engineers a convergence between individual character and social success. Political pundits now argue that the Thomas symbolism may quite effectively rebut allegations of Republican insensitivity to the concerns of minorities, perhaps even provoking a trickle of black voters into the GOP ranks.

How can these two seemingly divergent traditions of racial representation—"bad niggers" like Bigger Thomas and Willie Horton on the one hand, and "good niggers" like Booker T. Washington and Clarence

Thomas on the other—converge in the symbol apparatus of the presidency? Why does this self-evident presidential hypocrisy not generate centrifugal forces sufficient to destroy Bush's credibility? How do these symbols function with respect to the larger political aims of the president?

These are complicated questions that are made more difficult because the events at issue are seldom rigorously analyzed. Indeed, we are generally treated to an "analysis by metaphor" whereby Horton and Thomas are considered contradictory examples of Bush's "playing of the race card." While Horton represented an opportunistic effort to foster racial divisions, Thomas represents a cynical attempt to soften the Republican racial image just in time for the 1992 elections.

The problem with this "analysis" is that it rests on a metaphor that discourages careful considerations of the relationships between race, representation, and political hegemony that are enacted by these symbolic episodes. Instead of contextualizing seemingly contradictory representations with reference both to broader social logics and to particular political configurations, it is presumed that contradictory representations are easily dissolved in mass amnesia and elite manipulation.

In this essay I attempt to locate these symbols with reference both to a broader logic of political hegemony and to the particular political configurations that confront George Bush and his Republican party. I understand them as part of conservative efforts to construct what Antonio Gramsci called an "organic ideology" that, by articulating "into a configuration different subjects, different identities, different projects, [and] different aspirations," attempts to "construct a 'unity' out of difference" (Hall, *The Hard Road to Renewal* 166). In other words, I contend that the Horton-Thomas presentation is an integrated symbolic tactic, rather than two successive and contradictory gestures.

The breakup of the New Deal coalition, the postwar evolution of economic and demographic forces that condition the development of black urban political regimes, the Great Society-abetted bifurcation of the black population into growing middle and "under" classes, and the ramifications of this bifurcation in the popular culture industry all contribute to a broad destabilization of racial meanings and the political accommodations that they engendered.[2] These developments provide an opportunity for Americans to renegotiate the meanings of race and the accommodations that such meanings encourage—indeed they require such a renegotiation. The terms of these renegotiations will have an important impact on political configurations for decades to come.

By "racial meanings" I refer to the social meanings whose production constitute the ideological construction of "race" as a dimension of social difference. There are (at least) two different overlapping sites where this production takes place—the site of the construction of individual and corporate political bodies and the site of the configuration of the body politic. The former involves the production of "blackness" as an ideological and material element in the everyday social experience for people of color. The latter involves the production of blackness as a moment in the processes that constitute the ongoing imagining of the national community.[3] Although analytically separate, these sites are, in practice, profoundly interactive. As a practical matter it is impossible to separate the blackness that is experienced and represented by persons of color as they confront their everyday social lives from the blackness that is the representation of persons of color to themselves and to others in the ongoing construction of social life.

By "racial accommodations" I refer to how the configurations of the body politic and the construction of individual and corporate political bodies are involved in semiotic negotiations that can clarify, obscure, valorize, and demonize interactions between race and other elements of social difference. The Horton-Thomas presentation is part of the process by which racial meanings and accommodations are renegotiated, insofar as it helps to construct parameters of public discourse about race and politics. The broader context for this discourse is the ideological effort to reestablish an American political identity in a post–cold war world. With the removal of the "Soviet threat" as a demonological enforcement mechanism for the representation of identity, it becomes that much more important for the representatives of the dominant discourse to discredit the institutional and cultural modalities through which opposition to a consensual American identity was channeled in the sixties and seventies.

The political mobilization of blacks, women, and youths in the sixties and seventies opened (in an always partial and contradictory way) social space for the articulation of different conceptions of American identity. These new articulations were both enhanced and contained by the centripetal forces of America's countersubversive movement (Rogin, *Ronald Reagan,* chap. 9). With the ongoing construction of the Soviet threat came a cold war rhetoric of American political liberty and economic happiness that encouraged the desire within aggrieved domestic populations for equitable integration into the American political economy. At the same time, red baiting in the civil rights movement provided forceful evidence of the fact that the demonology basic to the countersubversive impulse was available to contain the fires for equality once they had been lit.

With the partial removal of the Soviet threat as the principal external object of the countersubversive tradition, it is not surprising that the inclination toward demonology in American political culture should get channeled with renewed energy toward the legacy and legatees of the movements that posed a challenge to the maintenance of a consensual American identity in the sixties and seventies. In this renegotiation of American identity, race-based claims on public attention become a powerful metaphor for the generally destabilizing consequences of the politics of social difference.[4] A point that is often overlooked in discussion of the symbolism of the 1988 presidential campaign is that in its link to the Democratic party the symbol of Willie Horton signifies and stigmatizes not just racial disruption, but also the general "disorder" that results from political mobilizations explicitly grounded in subnational and transnational social identities. The road to Bush's New Domestic Order is cleared by hacking through these oppositional claims (and the claimants who articulate them). More precisely, the Horton-Thomas tactic exploits sociopolitical divisions developed and exacerbated over time by the mobilization strategies of the Democratic party, framing a discourse within which Republicans can easily present themselves as the "solution" to the Democratic party-generated "problem" that social difference (most strikingly, race) poses in the American polity.

This discourse is of immediate tactical advantage to Republicans, who can quite easily associate political expressions of social difference with the Democratic party. However, Adolph Reed, Jr., and Julian Bond argue persuasively that this tactic is also used, paradoxically, by Democrats as well, when such Democrats present the argument that "Liberal and progressive forces have fallen onto hard times in American politics because they have become too closely identified with the excessive demands of blacks, feminists, etc. and have failed to give proper weight to the concerns of the beleaguered white working and middle classes." This discursive claim has "congealed" into an "unexamined orthodoxy" in the writings of such self-proclaimed liberals and leftists as Theda Skocpol, William Julius Wilson, Thomas Byrne Edsall, and Mary Edsall (Reed and Bond 733). The fact that both self-identified liberals and leftists on the one hand, and rightist politicians and strategists on the other, can occupy this same ground represents a striking victory for the right wing in the ideological war for position. Indeed, this capacity to define the terms of debate signals the hegemonic power of the Reagan-Bush bloc in contemporary American politics.

Reed and Bond insist that an important consequence of this narrative of the racially induced fall of the Democratic party is that it deflects attention away from resuscitating "the project of confronting racism in the white electorate for what it is and struggling with whites to overcome their commitments to racial privilege" (737). They are surely correct. But it is equally important to recognize (as I am sure Reed and Bond do) that the political significance of constructions of race (and the narrative instruments that effect these constructions) is not limited to their capacity to produce (or obscure) racism.

I point this out because it is easy, if we just attend to the symbolism of Willie Horton, to assume that the Bush administration simply marshals racism to delegitimize minority claims to participate in and contest state and culturally defined American political identities. But this analysis is short-sighted; it misses the important fact that a symbolic *re-negotiation* is called for to *restabilize* racial meanings and accommodations in a manner that will support new political alignments. In this project, Clarence Thomas is necessary to complete the story that Willie Horton begins.

In this context the important interpretive concept is not racism, but *e/racing.* As an integrated symbolic tactic, the Horton-Thomas "race card" is a wild card that e/races. That is to say, it draws attention to the fact of race *in order to deny its significance,* allowing Americans to "have their race conflict and digest it too" (Rogin, "Make My Day!" 104). The Horton-Thomas representation offers a condensation of a narrative about the post–Great Society trajectory of identity politics. From Democratic party politics as cause and consequence of black social disruption to the nondisruptive incorporation of race into the conservative governing regime of the Republican party, this is, in the first instance, a narrative of the political transcendence of race. Through Horton, race provides violent signification of the failures of the old (liberal Democratic) American order. Through Thomas, race provides poignant signification of the triumph of a new (conservative Republican) American order.

In this way, the narrative of political transcendence is both resolved and replicated in the figure of Clarence Thomas. Because he represents the Republican liberation of the country from the disruptive racial meanings and accommodations that were generated by the policies and practices of the Democratic party, Thomas symbolizes the resolution of the narrative of the political transcendence of race. At the same time, Thomas's own biography replicates that transcendence, with Republican senator John Danforth liberating Thomas from the dangerously liberal potentialities of the Yale Law School.

In this story, concerns about racism, although obviously important, are nonetheless somewhat beside the point. Like "playing the race card," "racism" too often substitutes moral indignation for political analysis, obscuring the *political particularity* of the manipulation of racial meanings. In the present context the tactical limitations of liberal accusations of racism are obvious—a narrow focus on the racial significance of symbolic gestures is a sucker bet when Clarence Thomas is your conservative opponent's hole card.

There are critical strategic limitations to accusations of racism as well. It is more important to be clear about the functioning of race in specific political contexts than it is to lament the moral or ethical lapses of particular public figures. In this regard, charges of racism can detract attention from the larger politico-ideological effort to reconstitute American nationalism in an ostensibly inclusive manner. The Horton-Thomas presentation offers a narrative—in the first instance—of the political transcendence of race. But its metanarrative involves a reconstitution of American political identity in which race, class, gender, sexuality, and ethnicity are collapsed back into liberal individualism. In other words, the political transcendence of race is a model for the political transcendence of *all social difference:* Clarence Thomas is symbol for the political transcendence of difference as surely as Willie Horton is symbol of the socially disruptive character of untranscended difference. Consequently, attempting to contest the Horton-Thomas representation with charges of racism is like bringing a knife to a gunfight.

In the rest of this essay I will situate the Horton-Thomas tactic with reference to a logic of political hegemony. In order to do this I will sketch both an analytical framework for "thinking" the relationship between cultural symbols and political power in the struggle for hegemony, and a cartography of the political terrain upon which that struggle takes place. The Horton-Thomas representation can then be situated upon this terrain.

Hegemony and Cultural Politics

Most people accept the idea that Americans live in a representative democracy. Making good on these claims requires a serious confrontation with *the problem of cultural empowerment as a precondition for the exercise of democratic citizenship.* The term *representation* presents an instructive ambiguity that gestures at this relationship between cultural empowerment and political agency. Representation often refers to the practices and institutions of our governmental system. The term can also refer to the products of mass and elite culture, like the images of blacks that are produced in Hollywood or on the evening news. In other words, representation can refer both to delegation and to depiction. *Indeed, one useful way to think about cultural politics is in terms of a dialectic between representation as delegation and representation as depiction—between cultural representations and political representation.*

What is crucial in this regard is being able to articulate the relationships *between* developments on the terrain of political representation and developments on the terrain of cultural representations. Indeed, it is difficult to overestimate the importance of this articulation. As an intellectual matter, inattention to these relationships lends an air of unreality to too much academic political and cultural analysis; as a political matter an abdication of the responsibility to manage these relationships characterizes the recent dismal performances of both the Democratic party in the United States and the Labor party in Great Britain. (See Kuttner; Hall, *Hard Road* 161–73.)

An important hinge between political representation and cultural representation is "narrative," the stories and myths that help to configure our political world. On the one hand, cultural representations—especially fictional characterizations or iconographical extensions of historical figures—often embody narratives about important categories of social existence. On the other hand, decisions on public policy measures inevitably rest on stories that fill in where our always quite limited information leaves off.

Robert Reich (among others) has written of the important role that these "public myths" play in political decision making:

> In modern America, the vehicles of public myth include the biographies of famous citizens, popular fiction and music, movies, feature stories on the evening news, and gossip. . . . In whatever form, they are transmitted constantly, and all around us—in our schoolrooms, dining rooms, poolrooms, and newsrooms. They shape our collective judgements. They anchor our political understandings. (7)

What Reich is describing is the role of public myth in the development of political hegemony: the forming and reforming of the "common sense" that "anchors our political understandings." In this context, the narrative hinge is the site at which the relationship between cultural representations and political representation becomes part of the struggle for hegemony. The Bush administration can constitute an ideological unity out of the different symbolic traditions represented by Thomas and Horton to the extent that they can develop a narrative that both consolidates these symbols and resonates with the experiences of important segments of the electorate.

Democratic Growth Politics

A full understanding of the struggle for hegemony requires an understanding of the relationship between ideological struggle and politically and economically determined patterns of social conflict. More particularly, the racial component of the struggle for hegemony is both informed by and intended for intervention in historical partisan patternings of racial and ethnic conflict.

The political terrain on which the struggle for hegemony takes place is defined by the breakup of the New Deal Coalition of the Democratic party. This dealignment has not resolved into an electoral realignment, but rather into the establishment of conditions that allow for a more competitive contest for national political power. Notwithstanding the notable presidential success of Republicans, the overall balance of power between the two parties is now relatively even.

The character of the partisan competition that results has been described by political reporter Thomas Edsall in notably Gramscian terms. The inability of either party to provoke decisive shifts in political allegiance makes for a political competition that "occurs along an extended battlefront, with the resources of each side spread thinly along the entire line of conflict" (Edsall 6). Edsall's description of incremental struggle in which each party "chips away at the other, seeking to make incursions and to hold ground at every point along the battle line" gestures (if unselfconsciously) toward Gramsci's notion of a war of maneuver.

Edsall persuasively suggests that a critical tactic for victory in this war of maneuver has become "the development of 'wedges' designed to break up the opposition's core of support, as in the case of Republican tactics designed to encourage tensions between black and white urban voters, or Democratic maneuvers accentuating the splits between Christian activists and Republican Party regulars" (6–7). It is only natural that a critical—perhaps *the* critical—component in the Republican "wedge" tactic would be race. This is not because race is a "natural" line of social division in any essential or essentialist sense. It is, rather, that as a matter of political history race is prominent among the fault lines that have been structured into Democratic party politics at least since the New Deal. The racial component of the political struggle for hegemony operates on terrain that is defined both by these fault lines and by political efforts to exploit them.

In *The Contested City*, an excellent work on the politics of federal urban policy, John Mollenkopf has written, "Beginning with Roosevelt's invention of national urban policy during the New Deal, federal urban programs have provided a principal method—perhaps the key method—by which national Democratic political entrepreneurs have attempted to widen and organize their political support" (48). Mollenkopf persuasively argues that the New Deal established the practice of using federal urban policy to organize political constituencies and generate political power. Succeeding rounds of federal policy making—principally Harry Truman's Fair Deal and Lyndon Johnson's Great Society—adapted this model to changing political circumstances. In important respects these efforts proved quite successful in interpellating new claimants on the political system as constituents of the Democratic party. Nevertheless the programs associated with these episodes of "reform" also generated new types of urban political conflict that the Democrats demonstrated a limited ability to manage. These conflicts and the unsuccessful efforts of the Democratic party to manage them sowed the seed for the "Reagan revolution" and constitute an important part of the resources with which George Bush intends to construct his New Domestic Order.

Mollenkopf argues that the fundamental political achievement of the New Deal was to introduce a new Democratic model of political mobilization centering on the development and implementation of urban policy. He points out that the components of the New Deal coalition— liberal reformers, labor, working-class ethnics and minorities—"were brought together in particular places (cities) around particular programs (the New Deal 'urban policy')" (Mollenkopf 55). Through programs like the WPA, the Roosevelt administration was able to reconcile previously unrepresented urban constituencies with traditional participants in the political process and mold the combination into a durable and dominant electoral coalition.

Successive rounds of urban policy making can be understood as, in part, efforts to modernize political alignments in order to cope with socioeconomic change. For example, from 1939 to 1959 real median family income doubled, provoking fundamental transformations in the urban ethnic, blue-collar social base of the New Deal Democratic party. The suburbanization of an expanding white middle class (composed of unionized workers and the burgeoning professional/managerial strata) combined with the considerable black migration to central cities (to heavily nonunionized jobs) to emphasize class and racial tensions within the New Deal coalition (Mollenkopf 72–74).

In order to cope with these new political realities Truman adopted a strategy of "growth politics": rather than a painful negotiation of different political interests, economic growth would be used as the glue to hold the Democratic coalition together. Growth politics had a simple logic: sacrifice control over the economy for the sake of its expansion, on the assumption that everyone will get a bigger piece of a bigger pie. Of course, this commitment to the overall size of the pie was also a commitment to de-emphasize questions about who gets to cut it, how big the different slices are, and who gets to eat them.

This was an extremely important strategic decision. "Since," as Alan Wolfe writes, "growth can only be obtained by offering concessions to businessmen in order to induce them to invest . . . (the Democrat's) popular electoral base could be held together only by following policies advantageous to big business. Domestic policy under the Democrats in the post war years would become a search for the proper way to win business confidence" (22).

In this context, the Taft-Ellender-Wagner Housing Act of 1949 was perhaps the critically important piece of legislation of the Fair Deal. The 1949 housing act graphically illustrated the way in which the nascent New Deal concern for social equality became subordinated to a concern for economic growth. The act also prefigured the consequences that this would have for the Democratic party in terms of organizing new constituencies and generating new political conflicts.

The bill was a compromise between the real estate lobby, the powerful conservative bloc in Congress, and progressive reformers. The terms of the compromise are apparent in the structure of the bill. Title 1 of the bill, which provided for the creation of local redevelopment agencies and a $1.5 billion federal write-down of land acquisition and clearance costs, became the basis of massive urban renewal programs. Title 2 put the public housing program on a permanent footing, mandating the construction of 810,000 housing units over six years. Public housing activists were skeptical of the urban renewal provisions but felt that an omnibus bill was the only possible way to ensure the continued provision of public housing. Although initially reluctant, many in the real estate industry eventually began to realize that a federal commitment to urban renewal would mean great profits for the industry (Wolfe 80–88). In its implementation the 1949 housing act was clearly and forcefully tilted toward private enterprise. By 1952 only 85,000 units were under construction, and Congress reduced public housing authorizations to 50,000 for fiscal year 1951 and 35,000 for fiscal year 1952. By the end of the Truman administration only 60,000 had been built. By 1964 only 325,203 had been built (Mollenkopf 79; Wolfe 86).

On the other hand, Title 1 became a powerful instrument for reconstructing both the urban landscape and the Democratic party. Urban renewal became "Negro removal," as powerful figures like Robert Moses used Title 1 to gain control of valuable commercial land. In 1951, for example, Moses built an exhibition center, a parking structure, and luxury housing on Broadway and 57th Street in Manhattan with $26 million in federal assistance by including a "few rundown tenements sheltering less than three hundred people" (allowing him to gain control of more than two square blocks of commercial land) (Mollenkopf 80). Instead of being used to address the housing needs of the poor, the 1949 act was used to promote and consolidate the development agenda of the newly dominant institutions of the postindustrial central city economy (Mollenkopf 80–81). As Wolfe writes:

> It [the housing act of 1949] did very little for the homes of poor people except to tear them down; indeed, the poor would have been better off if the law had never passed. . . . The Housing Act of 1949 . . . financed the destruction of America's cities, while sustaining a rebuilding machine that united politicians, bankers, and developers into a powerful coalition that took over the Democratic Party. (Wolfe 88)

The massive urban renewal underwritten by the act had crucial consequences for the future of the Democratic coalition. While the urban liberalism of the Democrats promised an improvement in the lives of the poor as well as the rich, its instruments—freeway and hospital construction, slum clearance, and commercial development—had destructive effects on the poorer and blacker sections of central cities. By 1964 poor people, most of them black, went to the streets in protest against, among other things, these disruptive effects.

This is the context in which Johnson's Great Society can be understood as part of the ongoing effort to modernize and adapt political alignments. In the face of a booming economy, black urban unrest, and large congressional majorities, the Great Society was an effort to address the conflicts engendered by the inequitable functioning of urban liberalism as well as to integrate a new black urban constituency into the Democratic party.

In the housing acts of 1961 and 1964, and the housing and urban development acts of 1965 and 1968, the Great Society reinvigorated federal housing programs, shifting the emphasis of urban renewal to rehabilitation from clearance. With the Community Action Agencies of the CAP, the Great Society was concerned to shape directly the character of neighborhood leadership, constructing instruments with and through which new black urbanites could be mobilized for the Democratic party.

Johnson's War on Poverty served both important functions of the Democratic strategy. Notwithstanding the claims of its most recent detractors, programs like food stamps, SSI, AFDC, Medicaid, Head Start, and Manpower Training did serve to ameliorate some of the harsher effects of the new urban economy. To this extent, these programs augmented the Community Action Program in constructing new black political subjects (service providers and service beneficiaries) umbilically linked to the Democratic party.

The Great Society was, of course, part and parcel of the Democratic growth politics strategy, a strategy heavily reliant on an expanding economy. This strategy turned particularly sour in the stagflating seventies, when it became painfully evident that the white working class bore a disproportionate share of the burdens of the Great Society welfare programs. In the absence of serious political and ideological efforts to force a restructuring of social burdens—efforts difficult to imagine in the face of the demobilization of sixties activism, class and sectoral shifts in power within the Democratic party, and a general unwillingness to work toward an expanded electorate—it was inevitable that the Democrat's white working-class constituency would rebel. Writers like Jonathan Reider and Jim Sleeper have told the story of that rebellion.

Republican Racial Politics

The adoption on the part of the Democratic party of a growth politics strategy to maintain its electoral strength meant that fundamental conflicts of class, race, and political culture were papered over. Democrats used what was often Republican-generated money to buy time, allowing them to defer a serious consideration of the relationships between class, race, and the American political culture of liberal individualism.

In a very real sense, the future of the party and its less well-off constituencies—the black and white working class—depended upon a successful political, social, and cultural renegotiation of these relationships. In this crucial task, the Democrats simply failed, and when the money ran out, the Republicans began to repossess a constituency that had been mortgaged to them back in the 1940s.

The Republicans, of course, have their own class problem: hence Reagan's limited success as "Repo Man." The Democratic disability involves the party's unsuccessful efforts to represent diverse constituencies whose interests are perceived to be in conflict. Of course the fact that this effort must even be made indicates why the Democrats are the nation's "natural" majority party. Conversely, the Republicans are the "natural" minority party becuase they so clearly represent the interests of a small, well-fed minority of the American people. Consequently, subtracting votes from the Democratic coalition is no easy matter and requires, at a minimum, a mechanism to redirect class resentment from its traditional targets in the Republican column.

In practice this is also a question of negotiating relationships between and amongst race, class, and traditions of American liberal individualism. The genius of the Reagan administration was in recognizing that this renegotiation is not, in the first or most important instance, a matter of backroom bargaining between leaders of the NAACP and the UAW. Instead, this renegotiation takes place, in the most important instance, in the sphere of symbols and ideology.

Durable electoral success for the Democrats now would seem to require the forging of new relationships between race, class, gender, and American traditions of individualism. The problem is that, as a party, they have neither the inclination nor the resources to develop the political vision that would accommodate these new relationships. Indeed, such a vision would necessarily be a problematic articulation of some of the more radical traditions of our past with a clear analysis of the problems of our present and a compelling story about the possibilities of our future. In the present ideological climate, each of these elements is difficult to come by.

The Republican renegotiation is simpler, because race, class, and liberal individualism each has prevalent social meanings that are easily mobilized into a useful formula for the Republicans. Throughout most of our history, dominant political and cultural rhetorics have presented liberal individualism as a solvent of class. It is not difficult, and yet very effective, for Republicans to present race as a pernicious interruption of this process. In this context Bush's quota baiting is a perverse inversion

of the late nineteenth- and early twentieth-century antilabor insistence
that blacks kept whites out of jobs by driving wages down. Indeed, the
fact that in the face of the incredible, state-generated concentration of
wealth of the Reagan years race can be effectively presented as the
fundamental bar to equal opportunity in America is evidence both of
the power of the symbolic meanings at the disposal of the Republicans
and of the dismal abdication of cultural and ideological responsibility
on the part of the Democrats.

So, the Republicans enter this struggle for hegemony with the weight
of American cultural traditions on their side. This advantage is enhanced by the historical mistakes of the Democrats. As I have suggested, part of the ideological and political failure of the Democratic
party has been an inability to integrate race and class (and increasingly
gender) into a larger political vision. The space between classical liberalism and this absent political vision is filled by an interest-group
liberalism in which political constituencies often have little incentive
or ability to reign in their claims on the state and on one another. This
situation provides the empirical base for claims that the politicization
of race (and class) are socially disruptive.

Republicans reinforce this situation and then take advantage of its
existence. More precisely, in political, economic, and symbolic ways,
they reinforce the social notion that race is disruptive, and then take
advantage of the ways in which this disruptiveness is associated with
the Democrats. The larger strategy involves the creation of a bipolar
representation of race and politics in which the poles—race as politically disruptive on one end, and race as politically irrelevant on the
other—are associated with the Democratic and Republican parties re-
spectively. To the extent that the GOP is successful in this construction, they set for themselves a win-win proposition that obscures their
class agenda: race is the critical social problem to which they are the
undeniable political answer. In a very real sense they play both (racial)
ends against the middle (class).

Little need be said here about the quota baiting of the Bush administration during the legislative debates over the Civil Rights Bill of
1991. The important point is that one clear consequence of quota baiting is to delegitimate race-based claims on the state, with broad and
immediate consequences for the party—the Democrats—traditionally
associated with such claims. The implicit claim is that race should be
irrelevant socially, and that the claims for its social relevance are un-
wise and misguided.

It is less frequently noted, however, that Republicans in general and the Bush administration in particular are also working to buttress the specific mechanisms by which these claims are made. In several ways, Republicans have worked to enhance the efforts of blacks and Hispanics to achieve "safe" minority districts in the legislative redistricting following the 1990 census. In addition, the Republican party has offered technical support to aid the efforts of black state legislators to construct "safe" minority districts.

There are three purposes served by these Republican tactics. First, they assist in the racial and ethnic balkanization of our polity. Political spectacles like the recent council redistricting in New York City can only serve to reinforce political rivalries and resentments along racial and ethnic lines. In this instance political competition is quite clearly and forcefully represented as a zero-sum game in which one racial or ethnic group's gain is another group's loss.

Second, these tactics have a direct impact on Republican electoral chances. "Safe" minority districts are often created by siphoning off black voters from surrounding districts. These voters are overwhelmingly Democratic. In the process of creating safe minority districts, safe Republican districts are often created as well. Third, these redistricting practices have the ultimate result of electing more black Democrats, reinforcing the problematic public perception of the Democratic party as the "black" party. In this manner Republicans can be seen to participate in constructing the problem—a disruptive politicization of race—for which they present themselves as the solution.

A similar dynamic is at work in the economic policy of the Republicans. Global and specific defunding of the traditional instruments of Democratic party mobilization exposes the economic and cultural tensions between race and class that the Democrats had used these instruments to obscure. First of all, the huge budget deficits of the Reagan regime effectively preclude restoration of the kind of government spending that Democrats have historically used to develop and sustain their constituencies. Similarly, Republicans have also defunded state and municipal governments, exacerbating tensions between outgroups who have or appear to each other to have differential access to social resources and governmental attention. This latter point is especially important. Federal policies have exacerbated the growing inability of municipal governments to deliver services efficiently and effectively, fight crime, and encourage balanced economic development. Coupled with the secession of more well-off residents to the suburbs, this constructs urban areas as a terrain that is ripe for the kinds of ethnic tensions most recently and chillingly manifest in the Brooklyn neighborhoods of Canarsie, Bensonhurst, and Crown Heights.

Inasmuch as these incidents provoke predictable responses from black activists like Al Sharpton, they contribute to a mass-mediated representation of a politicization of race that leads to social decay and disorder. Here again, the Republicans help to construct the problem for which they present themselves as a solution.

This win-win tactic of racial politics is replicated in the recent racial symbolism of the presidency. The movement from Willie Horton to Judge Clarence Thomas as the black male most closely associated with George Bush signifies a movement from a powerful but unstable symbol of racial difference to a more stable but no less powerful symbol of racial indifference. This movement can be understood as an important component of the attempt to consolidate the electoral gains associated with the elections of Ronald Reagan and George Bush. Thomas and Horton are part of the symbolic component of the "wedge" tactic, as race becomes a privileged marker in efforts to reconsolidate a post–cold war American nationalism.

Because of its volatility, the symbol of "Willie Horton" was a problematic tactic in this larger strategy. "Willie Horton" graphically insisted on the proposition that *race matters*, particularly in its negative social and political significance. This proposition could obviously be used to mobilize voters, but it also had important backlash effects, subjecting Bush and the Republicans to forceful charges of racism. By contrast, the political efficacy of a symbol like Thomas lies in its structured ambiguity—*Thomas focuses the significance of race in his insistence on its transcendence.* In acquiescing in Bush's ludicrous protests that color played no role in his nomination to the Supreme Court, Judge Thomas loudly and proudly e/raced himself.

Foregrounding Thomas contributes to the construction of parameters within which political understandings of race can be situated. Thomas allows Republicans to associate themselves with the idea that race has social relevance, but no particular political valence. This idea helps to delegitimize race-based claims on the state and the instruments—principally the Democratic party and the Great Society welfare programs—traditionally associated with those claims.

Several of the narratives by and through which Thomas is represented converge on the notion of a depoliticization of race. First of all, Bush has placed Thomas in a position such that he symbolizes the political and social ascendancy of race. This underlines the notion of a racial progress that implies that the need for race-specific governmental measures is exhausted. This, in turn, stokes resentment at forceful campaigns for those measures. If affirmative action played no significant role in his movement from Pin Point, Georgia, to the Supreme Court, then Thomas is a forceful example of the progress that this country has made in solving its "race" problem. The distance that Thomas traveled on his own indicates that that progress is sufficient to render race-based governmental measures unnecessary.

Second, Thomas's own narrative of his move from Pin Point to the Supreme Court, combined with his conservative political views, places him squarely in the rags-to-riches tradition of a Booker T. Washington. In this context Thomas situates himself as a symbol of a racially credible depoliticization; that is to say, he legitimizes a depoliticization of race by representing its roots in the history of African-American leadership. This is a representation that is buttressed by the promotion of black conservative voices like Shelby Steele and Robert Woodson.

There is a narrative that might be expected to subvert the two that I have mentioned. This might be characterized as "the journalistic savvy-talk metanarrative." This narrative suggests that not only is the nomination a sharp example of racial politics, but also that Bush is using Thomas to fulfill a quota, and that he has passed over more qualified white (potential) applicants to do so. However, even this narrative sends a certain message about the depoliticization of race. This is so inasmuch as race is, in the political context, an empty signifier. Indeed, this is what allows for its nondisruptive incorporation into a conservative governing regime.

The movement from Willie Horton as symbol of the disruptive, destabilizing political significance of race to Clarence Thomas as symbol of the nondisruptive incorporation of race into the state apparatus does not, of course, remove race from politics. Willie Horton is gone, but hardly forgotten. Indeed, he is the silent subtext of the Thomas narrative, forcefully gestured at with each evocation of Thomas's unique racial autobiography. And, of course, the ongoing tradition of racial representation of which "Willie Horton" is a part—black males as primary source of social disruption—is constantly manifest in American popular culture. In this regard, Willie Horton is always already present in political discussions. Adept manipulation of symbols like Willie Horton and Clarence Thomas allows for a replication of the Republican win-win racial strategy in the symbolic realm. Whereas Horton stands as a representation of the role of race (social difference, politically assertive) in a Democratic Order, Thomas represents the

nondisruptive presence of race (social difference, politically transcendent) in Bush's New Domestic Order.

The ability to contest successfully this "New Domestic Order" ultimately rests on the possibilities for coordinating cultural struggle
with the political and economic patterning of social conflict in such a
way as to facilitate a progressive renegotiation of race, class, gender, and
traditions of liberal individualism. Needless to say this is an enormous
task with various complicated components. One important element of
this task involves beginning to substitute a keen awareness of the
political particularity of racial meanings for passionate accusations of
"racism!" or casual references to "playing the race card." This essay has
been an effort in that direction.

Notes

1. For an example of this debate see Kunkel 113–29.

2. On the economic bifurcation of the black population see Wilson Julius
Wilson, *The Truly Disadvantaged*. There has not been nearly enough careful
consideration of the ramifications of these economic and demographic changes
for the representation of race in the popular culture industry.

3. On processes of racial formation in the United States see Barbara Fields,
"Ideology and Race in American History," and Michael Omi and Howard Wi-
nant, *Racial Formation in the United States from the 1960s to the 1980s*. Also
see Stuart Hall, "Ethnicity: Identity and Difference." For a general discussion of
the "imagining of national communities" see Benedict Anderson, *Imagined
Communities: Reflections on the Origin and Spread of Nationalism*. Useful
discussions of the historical relationship between race and the construction
of American identity include Ronald Takaki, *Iron Cages: Race and Culture
in Nineteenth-Century America*, Alexander Saxton, *The Rise and Fall of
the White Republic: Class Politics and Mass Culture in Nineteenth-Century
America*, David Roediger, *The Wages of Whiteness: Race and the Making of the
American Working Class*, Michael Rogin, *Ronald Reagan, the Movie and Other
Episodes in American Political Demonology* (esp. chapters 7 and 9), Mike
Davis, *Prisoners of the American Dream* (chapter 1), and Michael Goldfield,
"The Color of Politics in the United States: White Supremacy as the Main
Explanation for the Peculiarities of American Politics from Colonial Times to
the Present."

4. For a fuller presentation of this point see my "Fear of a Black Planet: Race,
Identity Politics, and Common Sense."

Part Three **Democratic Vistas**

The essays gathered in this section address some of the problems encountered by those who would seek to negotiate a way through our rhetorical republic. Bonnie Honig asks how the construction of political authority is possible in a polity conspicuously lacking the foundational myths and appeals that premodern politics relied upon. Taking as her point of departure Hannah Arendt's and Jacques Derrida's explorations of the paradoxical and parasitical logic of founding, Honig discusses how the speech acts that guarantee the authority of fellow-promisers in the liberal polity rely upon both the performative and the constative characteristics of utterances. She shows how a gap exists in every founding that can be filled only by a promise, and how the act of constitution is always a *fabulous* act that conjures into existence that which is already in existence. If the Declaration of Independence is to serve as an inspiration for contemporary political thinkers, Honig suggests, it should be as a past from which to spring rather than a model from which to derive the present.

Dana R. Villa addresses postmodern skepticism about the very idea of the political in relation to parallel concerns about the recovery of the political enunciated by Hannah Arendt and others. Taking issue with Jurgen Habermas's appropriation of Arendt for his theory of communicative rationality, and cautiously linking Arendt's concern for plurality, agonism, appearance, and theatricality to the political projects of Jean Baudrillard, Gilles Deleuze, Michel Foucault, and François Lyotard, Villa analyzes the postmodern critique of public sphere theory at the levels of power, epistemology, and ontology. Arguing that, in the case of Arendt, most such criticisms misconstrue their object, he shows how Arendt's understanding of political action might clarify some of the confusions, hesitations, and obscurities marking the political thought of these figures. Villa concludes that Arendt's theory, properly understood, leads to an appreciation of the values of preserving public spheres (i.e., spaces of plurality and theatricality) wherever they have been constructed, rather than to an attempt to impose upon citizens (or theorists) a common understanding of what politics is or where it must "properly" be located.

Questioning the idea that politics has a "proper" location is a good statement of William E. Connolly's point of departure. Warning that political theory is animated by a dangerously ambiguous "politics of place" (the ideal convergence, in one sovereign territory, of the various elements of democratic sovereignty), Connolly seeks to articulate the possible conditions of democratic practices in a world in which territoriality operates to intensify the desire for a stable identity while simultaneously disabling the realization. Focusing on the metaphors of containment and contamination in thinkers from Jean-Jacques Rousseau and Paul Ricoeur to Michael Walzer and Joseph Schumpeter, Connolly suggests how the overly tight bonds of territoriality might be loosened to permit the emergence of democratic cultures whose commitment to democracy need not depend on deeply shared understandings, and which would be better positioned to respond to pressures, all too evident today, that threaten to shatter identities whose constitutional requirements include rigid "final markers." The development of such identities is impeded by the assumption that democracy can occur only in a state-secured territory. A major task for political theory will therefore be to articulate what might be called "atopical" democratic allegiances.

10 Declarations of Independence

Arendt and Derrida on the Problem of Founding a Republic

Bonnie Honig

The men who create power make an indispensable contribution to the Nation's greatness, but the men who question power make a contribution just as indispensable, especially when that questioning is disinterested, for they determine whether we use power or power uses us.
—John F. Kennedy

For Hannah Arendt, there was something unique about America: its early practices of compact making and local town meetings, and its (consequent) success in bringing its revolution to culmination in the founding and constitution of a new and stable regime, its institutional separation of powers, and its (not unrelated) tradition of civil disobedience. These moments are all awarded a central place in Arendt's narrative of American political culture and practice. But the most central place in her account is reserved for the uniquely modern practice of authority that undergirds and safeguards these moments, a practice that she identifies specifically with the United States and celebrates as the solution for the problem of politics in modernity.

Arendt saw traditional political authority as a casualty of the rise of secularism, which leaves the modern world bereft of authority's traditional resources—tradition, religion, and authority—the very things that secured the foundation and longevity of the Roman republic (Arendt, *On Revolution* 117–18). Because Arendt identifies traditional political authority so strongly with Rome and because she mourns its loss, many of her readers assume that she is a nostalgic or essentialist theorist for whom political authority is (or was) a uniquely ancient and Roman experience.[1] But Arendt is no mere nostalgist. She also celebrates the modern disappearance of traditional political authority: it marks the restoration of the world to humanity, the recovery of human worldliness, and new possibilities of innovative political action, revolution, and foundation. The problem is that these possibilities cannot be realized without the reappearance of the traditional resources of authority, whose disappearance gave rise to them. Without the resources of authority, it seems as if the task of founding and maintaining lasting institutions is impossible. Arendt poses the problem, quoting Rousseau:

> "The great problem of politics, which I compare to the problem of squaring the circle in geometry . . . [is]: How to find a form of government which puts the law above man." Theoretically [Arendt adds], Rousseau's problem closely resembles Sièyes's vicious circle: Those who get together to constitute a new government are themselves unconstitutional, that is, they have no authority to do what they set out to achieve. The vicious circle in legitimating is present not in ordinary lawmaking, but in laying down the fundamental law. . . . The trouble was—to quote Rousseau once more—that to put the law above man and thus to establish the validity of man-made laws, *il faudrait des dieux,* "one would actually need gods." (*On Revolution* 183–84)[2]

For Arendt, then, the problem of politics in modernity is, How do we establish lasting foundations without appealing to "gods," a foundationalist ground, or an "absolute"? Can we conceive of institutions possessed of authority without deriving that authority from some law of laws, from some extrapolitical source? In short, is it possible to have a politics of foundation in a world devoid of traditional (foundational) guarantees of stability, legitimacy, and authority? Arendt answers yes, and she turns to the American Revolution and founding as a model of this possibility. In that setting, she discerns and constructs a practice of authority for a nonfoundational politics.

The American Model

1. The quest for examples. Arendt glorifies the American revolutionaries and founders of the American republic for their great innovations, their courage, their vision. But she faults them for being inadequately conscious of themselves as innovators. Their revolution took them by surprise (*On Revolution* 44). Somewhat frightened, they sought to mitigate the radical contingency of the revolution by speaking the language of restoration, which was indeed true to their original intentions in rebellion. Ultimately, though, it became clear to them that restoration was not the whole goal. Their experience of public freedom in the revolutionary process made them value political action and participation, the act of coming together in deliberation, debate, and decision. Free political action is seductive (*On Revolution* 33).

Thus, they were moved to complete their revolutionary task, seeking in the end not just liberation but the reconstitution of the political realm in order to enable the citizenry of the new republic to experience the happiness of public freedom and political action. Now conscious that this new goal that they had not deliberately chosen was radically new, they both reveled in their good fortune to be a part of this world-historical event and sought comfort from its weightiness. They turned to theory—to the science of politics—for aid in their "task, the creation of new power." And they turned to history, pedantically documenting republican constitutions of all sorts, driven, Arendt argues, not by the need to learn how to "safeguard . . . civil liberties—a subject on which they certainly knew more than any previous republic," but by the need to learn about "the constitution of power" (*On Revolution* 149–50).

2. *The quest for an absolute.* The turn to antiquity, however, constituted not only a search for pedagogic examples; it was also a search for a beginning to anchor the newly constituted republic. "Politically speaking," the men of the American Revolution were right, Arendt argues, to believe that they had to derive "the stability and authority of any given body politic from its beginning." The problem was that "they could not conceive of a beginning except as something which must have occurred in a distant past" (*On Revolution* 198). In this respect, then, the turn to antiquity was in quest of reassurance that the innovation of the revolution was not radical but derivative. But the reassurance was false for their action *was* unprecedented. Hence its greatness.

The quest for reassurance marked a lack of faith on the part of the revolutionaries in their own action. This lack of faith led them also to attempt to ground their reconstitution of the political realm in an absolute, a law of laws that they trusted to serve as "the source of validity of their laws and the fountain of legitimacy for the new government" (*On Revolution* 199). The result was a paradox: "It was precisely the revolutions . . . which drove the very 'enlightened' men of the eighteenth century to plead for some religious sanction at the very moment when they were about to emancipate the secular realm from the influences of the churches and to separate politics and religion once and for all" (*On Revolution* 185–86).

This quest for an absolute in which to ground and legitimate the reconstitution of the political realm is, according to Arendt, deeply misguided. The positing of an absolute undermines the contingency that is the quintessential feature of the public realm, the feature in virtue of which political freedom and human innovation are possible (*The Human Condition* 179–240; *On Revolution* 184–85). Moreover, it deprivileges the very human achievement of reconstitution and founding, making it dependent on something external to the human world. And that external something is untenable in the modern era whether it be god, natural law, or self-evident truth. Natural law needs "divine sanction to become binding for men" and "the authority of self-evident truth . . . still bears clear signs of divine origin," while in modernity "the loss of religious sanction for the political realm is a matter of accomplished fact" (*On Revolution* 190, 194, 196).

But there is a more fundamental issue at stake here. Even if appeals to an absolute could still bind us, even if religious sanction was still viable for the political realm, appeals to an absolute as a ground of politics, in Arendt's view, would be illicit. For an absolute is

> a truth that needs no agreement since, because of its self-evidence, it compels without argumentative demonstration or political persuasion. By virtue of being self-evident, these truths are pre-rational—they inform reason but are not its product—and since their self-evidence puts them beyond disclosure and argument, they are in a sense no less compelling than "despotic power" and no less absolute than the revealed truths of religion or the axiomatic verities of mathematics. (*On Revolution* 192)

In politics, the appeal to an absolute is illicit because of its constative character. The uniquely political action, on Arendt's account, is not the constative but the performative utterance, a speech act that in itself brings "something into being which did not exist before" (*Between Past and Future* 151).[3] Thus, the "grandeur" of the Declaration of Independence, according to Arendt, consists "[not] so much in its being 'an argument in support of an action' as in its being *the perfect way for an action to appear in words*. . . . And since we deal here with the written, and not the spoken word, we are confronted with one of the rare moments in history when the power of action is great enough to erect its own monument" (*On Revolution* 130; emphasis mine).[4]

3. The ambiguity of the American declaration. In spite of Arendt's celebratory tone, she is forced to admit that the Declaration of Independence does not consistently maintain the performative posture she so admires. The preamble to the declaration contains two appeals to a "transcendent source of authority for the laws of the new body politic": an appeal to " 'nature's god' " and an appeal to self-evident truths. What is interesting, though, about the appeal to self-evident truths is that the sentence—"We hold these truths to be self-evident"—is partly performative in character. These famous words, Arendt argues, "combine in a historically unique manner the basis of agreement [*we hold*] between those who have embarked upon revolution, an agreement necessarily relative because related to those who enter it, with an absolute [*self-evident*]" that signals not agreement but compulsion (*On Revolution* 192).

The statement's performative quality Arendt attributes to Jefferson's dim awareness that it was a "fallacy" that irresistible laws were "of the same nature as the laws of a community." Were it not for this dim awareness, Jefferson "would not have indulged in the somewhat incongruous phrase 'We hold these truths to be self-evident' but would have said: These truths are self-evident, namely, they possess a power to compel which is as irresistible as despotic power, they are not held by us, we are held by them; They stand in no need of agreement" (*On Revolution* 193). Jefferson's awareness of the fallacy could be no more than dim because he was caught in a period of transition. The new political developments of his time were "nowhere matched by an adequate development of new thought." In particular, "there was no avoiding the problem of the absolute . . . because it proved to be inherent in the traditional concept of law. If the essence of secular law was a command, then a divinity, not nature but 'nature's god,' not reason but a divinely informed reason, was needed to bestow validity on it" (*On Revolution* 195).

Fortunately for the American Republic, this problem was a theoretical one. This "bondage" to the "conceptual and intellectual framework of the European tradition" did not, Arendt argues, determine "the actual destinies of the American republic to the same extent as it compelled the minds of the theorists." For if it had, she speculates (somewhat naively), "the authority of this new body politic in actual fact might have crumbled under the onslaught of modernity—where the loss of religious sanction for the political realm is an accomplished fact— . . . what saved the American revolution from this fate was neither 'nature's god' nor self-evident truth, but the act of foundation itself" (*On Revolution* 195–96). In short, Arendt believes that in practice, the *We hold*—the performative part of Jefferson's "incongruous phrase"—won out over the constative part, the reference to "self-evident" truths. This saved the American Revolution because the "We hold" constitutes the only sort of power that is "real" and "legitimate," the sort of power that "rest[s] on reciprocity and mutuality," and comes into being only "when men join themselves together for the purpose of action" by binding "themselves through promises, covenants, and mutual pledges" (*On Revolution* 181, 175).

The appeal to self-evidence stands in opposition to the *We hold*. It expresses not a free coming together but an isolated acquiescence to compulsion and necessity. The appeal, therefore, coerces and disempowers. It violates the integrity of politics and denatures and disables its practice. This is a crucial point for Arendt who, throughout her work, insists on the autonomy of the political realm and on the *sui generis* character of politics. In *The Human Condition* she argues that politics should not be held to standards external to it, that it has two precepts of its own—forgiving and promising—precepts that "are not applied to action from the outside [but] arise directly out of the will to live together with others in the mode of acting and speaking" (*The Human Condition* 245–46). It is now clear that what is unique about these precepts is that they are both performatives; indeed, it is that feature that makes these two practices—ordinarily thought of as the subject of ethics—profoundly political in an Arendtian schema. As performatives, they are marked by all the features characteristic of action as Arendt describes it: they cannot be judged true or false, right or wrong (*The Human Condition* 205). And they cannot make sense in isolation: performative utterances necessarily take place "in concert" and require for their success the presence of spectators in order to achieve their purpose, which is to bring something into being that did not exist before. In my view, Arendt wants to celebrate the American Declaration of Independence as a purely performative speech act; but in order to do so she must disambiguate it. She dismisses its constative moments and holds up the declaration as an example of a uniquely political act, an act available uniquely to human beings, an authoritative exemplification of human power and worldliness.

The Power of Performatives

The performative *We hold*, on Arendt's account, empowers an existing community inasmuch as it constitutes a free coming together and publicly expresses a shared agreement to abide by certain rules in the community's subsequent being together. The *We hold* is a promise and a declaration; it signals the existence of a singularly human capacity: that of "world-building" (*On Revolution* 175).

The source of power in this world-building act of foundation is the speech act itself, the declaration of the "We hold." And the act of foundation is the source of its own authority as well. In short, power and authority are interdependent, on Arendt's account (*On Violence* 47). The authority of the world built by power derives from all that is implied by the fact that that world is the product of power, rather than strength or violence. (What is implied, of course, is that it is the product of free action by equals who act in concert, bound together by mutual promises and reciprocity for the sake of bringing something new into being.) Properly understood and performed, the act of foundation requires no appeal to a source of authority beyond itself: "It was the authority which the act of foundation carried within itself, rather than the belief in an immortal Legislator, or the promises of reward and threats of punishment in a 'future state,' or even the doubtful self-evidence of the truths enumerated in the preamble to the Declaration of Independence, that assured stability for the new republic" (*On Revolution* 199). Thus, Arendt squares Sièyes's circle by finding the source of authority in the act of foundation, thereby making appeals to an absolute, transcendent source of authority not merely illicit, but redundant and unnecessary. Arendt's political performative does not require the blessing of a constative in order to work. Nor, Arendt claims, did the U.S. Constitution: the preamble to the declaration, she argues, "provides the sole source of authority from which the Constitution, not as an act of constituting government but as the law of the land, derives its own legitimacy" (*On Revolution* 193).

Arendt thereby seems to have found for the new world the new thought it needed, the thought that enables it to conceive of a founding that secures law for communities without appealing to a law of laws and without lapsing into foundationalism, the thought that salvages political authority for an age unable or unwilling to support the authority of tradition and religion. One might say that Arendt's project is to save authority—to find a way to sustain it—because she realizes that without it there can be no politics. In a world devoid of authority, we are denied the opportunity to exercise our "human capacity for building, preserving, and caring for a world that can survive us and remain a place fit to live in for those who come after us" (*Between Past and Future* 95).

This reading of Arendt may appear implausible because of what Richard Flathman calls the essentialist character of her account of authority. Flathman notes that Arendt asserts "a necessary connection between *in* authority and a quite definite and complex constellation of values and beliefs about tradition and religion," meaning that of ancient Rome. According to Flathman, it follows from Arendt's argument that once "this particular constellation of values and beliefs has disappeared, *in* authority has *thereby* disappeared as well" (*Authority and the Authoritative: The Practice of Political Authority,* 71). Furthermore, Flathman argues, given Arendt's insistence that power and authority are interdependent, it is curious that she both claims that authority has disappeared from the modern world and yet insists that power has not (263, n.6). On my reading, however, the problem disappears, for Arendt is understood to be claiming that a certain kind of authority, the kind that sustained the Roman republic together with tradition and religion, has disappeared in modernity. This is not, as Arendt herself says, " 'authority in general,' but rather a very specific form which had been valid throughout the Western World over a long period of time" (*Between Past and Future* 92). And it is this specific form of authority—"authority as we once knew it, which grew out of the Roman experience of foundation and was understood in the light of Greek political philosophy"— that, in Arendt's view, "has nowhere been re-established" (*Between Past and Future* 141).

In *On Revolution,* Arendt gives an account of an alternative form of authority, the authority inherent in the performative Declaration of Independence and in the practice of constitution making that "preceded, accompanied, and followed" it "in all thirteen colonies." Both, she argues, "revealed all of a sudden to what an extent *an entirely new concept of power and authority,* an entirely novel idea of what was of prime importance in the political realm had already developed in the New World, even though the inhabitants of this world spoke and thought in the terms of the Old World" (*On Revolution* 166; emphasis mine). Arendt understands that we cannot recover the lost form of authority that sustained Rome for so long; it is untenable in modernity. But neither can we exercise our world-building capacities in a world without authority. If we love the world, if we are committed to world-building—to politics—we must find another form of authority, one that can be sustained in modernity. Only then will we experience the privilege of political action that is not just revolutionary (*On Revolution* 171, 238).

Revolutions are frequent in the modern age (and peculiar to it) because of the failure of traditional authority. But most revolutions themselves fail for the same reason. They seek to ground their reconstitution of the political realm in the same sort of traditional authority whose very untenability made their own revolution possible. Arendt tries to get out of this vicious circle by offering an alternative conception of authority, one that inheres not in an untenable absolute, nor in a law of laws, but in the power of reconstitution itself.[5]

Only the modern conception of authority is viable for modernity because it requires for its sustenance not a shared belief in particular deities or myths but a common subscription to the authoritative linguistic practice of promising. Consequently, it assumes a preexisting community, but not in the strong sense of "homogeneity of past and origin," which is the "decisive principle of the nation state" (*On Revolution* 174). This is a community in a weaker sense, bound together by common linguistic practices, not even necessarily by a single, common, inherited first language. This is a community whose members understand and subscribe to performative practices. Such a community should be able to sustain this new kind of authority, in Arendt's view— assuming, that is, that it can overcome its nihilistic craving for a law of laws, for a source of authority that is transcendent or self-evident, assuming that it can see and be satisfied with the power and authority inherent in its own performatives.

Conversely, one might say not that Arendt seeks to salvage authority for the sake of politics but that she seeks to salvage politics for the sake of authority. To see Arendt's politics as a response to modern nihilism is to make sense of her claim that we need politics for the sake of the world. We cannot live without standards or some stability and yet our traditional sources of stability are no longer viable. Consequently, we are left to the devices of politics and action. Politics is more important than ever because it is the only alternative to violent domination, the only source in modernity of legitimate rules possessed of authority and capable of addressing "the elementary problem of human living-together" (*Between Past and Future* 141). Arendt's description of the signing of the Mayflower Compact is enlightening in this context. The parties to the compact

> obviously feared the so-called state of nature, the untrod wilderness, un-
> limited by any boundary, as well as the unlimited initiative of men
> bound by no law. This fear is not surprising; it is the justified fear of men
> who have decided to leave civilization behind them and strike out on
> their own. The really astounding fact in the whole story is that their ob-
> vious fear of one another was accompanied by the no less obvious confi-
> dence they had in their own power, granted and confirmed by no one and
> as yet unsupported by any means of violence, to combine themselves to-
> gether into a "civil Body Politick" which, held together solely by the
> strength of mutual promises "in the Presence of God and one another,"

supposedly was powerful enough to "enact, constitute, and frame" all necessary laws and instruments of government. (*On Revolution* 167)[6]

Like the parties to the compact, the founders of the American Republic built small "islands of security" in an "ocean of contingency" (*The Human Condition* 237) through joint action, promising, and constitution making, all performatives that are not solipsistic because they presuppose a plurality of participants who subscribe to a shared authoritative practice of promising, and not nihilistic because, by virtue of their power, they are the guarantors of their own authority. Arendt can do no better than this; she refuses to, in fact, because of her conviction that the "realm of human affairs" is "relative by definition" (*On Revolution* 213). Political action has no anchor: a "beginning," it "has, as it were, nothing to hold on to; it is as though it came out of nowhere in either time or space" (*On Revolution* 206).[7]

The Postulates of Promising

Arendt's characterization of action as a "beginning" with "nothing to hold on to" is somewhat misleading. In Arendt's own account, a beginning does have something to hold on to—the public subscription to an authoritative discursive practice in which performative utterances are understood to possess their own authority as long as they meet the conditions necessary for them to function. Arendt's performative politics presupposes a community of promisers, a preexisting community composed of people who may hold different values and beliefs but who, nonetheless, have shared understandings of what a promise is, what it means to make a promise, and what one must do in order for one's performance to be recognizable as a promise. In short, promising, even on Arendt's account, is a practice.[8]

Yet Arendt gives no account of the conditions of the practice. She only tells us why the practice of promising is of paramount importance to those committed to the activity of politics in modernity. But if the practice of promising is to be the source of legitimacy in an Arendtian politics, the question of the legitimacy of the practice and of its own techniques of self-legitimation must be addressed. Indeed, Friedrich Nietzsche addresses the problem directly: "To breed an animal with the right to make promises—is not this the paradoxical task that nature has set itself in the case of man? Is it not the real problem regarding man?" (*On the Genealogy of Morals*, 2:i).

The process by which this "problem" has been resolved historically is the object of Nietzsche's scathing criticism in the second essay of *On the Genealogy of Morals.* Arendt never addresses these questions, however, perhaps because she does not share Nietzsche's ambivalence toward the construction of promisers and the practice of promising. Promising is the "highest human faculty." Indeed, Arendt denies Nietzsche's own ambivalence, claiming with approval that "he saw in the faculty of promises . . . the very distinction which marks off human from animal life" (*The Human Condition* 245), ignoring the fact that in the phrase to which she refers Nietzsche says the problem is how "to breed an *animal* with the right to make promises."

Moreover, Arendt's practice of promising, if it is to do the work she expects of it, must be highly sophisticated, even ritualized.[9] As such, it would belie the moment of contingency that, on her account, characterizes the moment of politics. Indeed, there is an apparent paradox here. Action, which for Arendt consists partly in the activity of promising, is terribly risky because it takes place in a contingent world where its meaning and consequences are always underdetermined if not indeterminate. Yet Arendt also claims that promising serves as a "control mechanism," that it "counters the enormous risks of action" by establishing little islands of stability in the radical contingency of the public realm (*The Human Condition* 245–46). The problem is that if promising is to be a source of reassurance and stability, the operation of the practice of promising and the meaning of particular promises must be relatively unproblematic. In that case, action as promising cannot occur *ex nihilo*, and it will not be as risky—as contingent and unpredictable— as Arendt says it is.[10] On the other hand, if action is as contingent as that, promising will not by itself be able to provide the stability Arendt expects it to: the stability is coming from somewhere else, possibly from something external to action's purely performative speech act. And this is precisely the observation made by Jacques Derrida in his own reading of (Jefferson's draft of) the American Declaration of Independence, a reading that, like Arendt's, focuses on the document's curious structural combination of constative and performative utterance.

The Inadequacy of Performatives

Since Arendt dismisses the constative moments of the declaration and insists that the power of its performative *We hold* is the sole source of authority for the American Republic and its constitution, it seems likely that the *We* of the declaration (and of all political action) is the source of stability in Arendt's account. Yet, if we take seriously Arendt's claim that action is a "beginning" that occurs *ex nihilo*, if we are persuaded by her that the "We" (the people) does not exist as such prior to the declaration,[11] then the question emerges, How can the "We" stand as the guarantor of its own performance? How can it function as the sole source of stability for the Republic?

The problem is posed by Jacques Derrida in his "Declarations of Independence":

> The "we" of the declaration speaks "in the name of the people." But this people does not yet exist. They do *not* exist as an entity, it does *not* exist, *before* this declaration, not *as such*. If it gives birth to itself, as free and independent subject, as possible signer [of the declaration], this can hold only in the act of the signature. The signature invents the signer. This signer can only authorize him- or herself to sign once he or she has come to the end, if one can say this, or his or her own signature, in a sort of fabulous retroactivity. (10)

On Derrida's account, the signers are stuck in Sièyes's vicious circle. They lack the authority to sign until they have already signed. The American founders' invocation of "the name of the laws of nature and the name of God" manifests this predicament. They appealed to a constative, according to Derrida, not (as Arendt would have it) because of a failure of nerve nor because they underestimated the power of their own performative, but because they did not overestimate its power. In order to guarantee that power and secure their innovation, they had to combine their performative with a constative utterance. They needed "another 'subjectivity' . . . to sign, in order to guarantee it, this production of signature," for "in this process," Derrida argues, "there are only countersignatures":[12]

> It is still "in the name of" that the "good people" of America call *themselves* and declare *themselves* independent, at the instant in which they invent for themselves a signing identity. They sign in the name of the laws of nature and in the name of God. They *pose* or *posit* their institutional laws on the foundation of natural laws and by the same *coup* (the interpretive *coup* of force) in the name of God, creator of nature. He comes, in effect, to guarantee the rectitude of popular intentions, the unity and goodness of the people. *He founds natural laws and thus the whole game which tends to present performative utterances as constative utterances.* ("Declarations of Independence" 11; emphasis mine)

Founding, promising, or signing, cannot occur *ex nihilo:* "For this Declaration to have a meaning *and* an effect there must be a last instance. God is the name, the best one, for this last instance and this ultimate signature"; that is, *God* is the name Derrida gives to whatever is used to hold the place of the last instance, the place that is the inevitable *aporia* of founding (or signing or promising) ("Declarations of Independence" 12). In short, Derrida, like Rousseau (and yet quite unlike Rousseau), sees that in order to break Sièyes's vicious circle, in order to posit the law of institutional laws, "*il faudrait [bien sûr] des dieux.*"

The moral of Derrida's story is that no act of founding (or signing, or promising) is free of this *aporia*—this gap that needs to be anchored—and this is a structural feature of language. This gap that marks *all* forms of utterance is always filled (whether or not we acknowledge it) by a *deus ex machina,* if not by God himself, then by nature, the subject, language, or tradition. Arendt sees that this *aporia* is a structural feature of all *performatives.*[13] But she insists that the *aporia,* the gap that marks all performatives, can and should be held open. She understands that a human need is often felt to fill this gap but she does not see it as a systemic, conceptual, or linguistic need. Quite the contrary. The difference between her position and Derrida's on this point is made clear by their different assessments of the American declaration's combined performative and constative structure.

The Ambiguity of the Declaration, Reconsidered

Unlike Arendt, Derrida does not see the declaration's structural combination of performative and constative utterance as incongruous. It is not a question "of an obscurity or of a difficulty of interpretation, of a problematic on the way to its (re)solution," because "this obscurity, this undecidability between, let's say, a performative and a constative structure, is *required* in order to produce the sought after effect" ("Declarations of Independence" 9). The insecure performative is not always and necessarily anchored by another utterance. The *We hold,* on Derrida's account, is capable of anchoring itself not because of its powerful purity as a performative, but because it is in fact both a constative and a performative. It is unclear whether "independence is stated or produced by this utterance." And its rhetorical force derives in large measure from this unclarity, from the fact that "one cannot decide" which sort of utterance it is: constative or performative ("Declarations of Independence" 9)?[14]

For Derrida, the combined constative and performative structure of the document and its *We hold* illustrate beautifully a structural feature of all language: that no signature, promise, or performative—no act of foundation—possesses resources adequate to guarantee itself, that each and every one necessarily needs some external, systemically illegitimate guarantee to work. This need marks the Declaration of Independence just as it marks utterances that are more quotidian. "This happens every day," Derrida says (indeed, "every signature finds itself thus affected"), "but it is fabulous" ("Declarations of Independence" 10).

For Arendt, however, the declaration's constative moments are marks of impurity, tainting what is really, and ought to have been, a purely performative act. She does not see that her cherished performative *We hold* is *also* a constative utterance. And so there is no undecidability here for her. The other constative moments of the declaration are unfortunate errors or lapses, marring but not obviating modernity's greatest moment, the moment when a new revolution splendidly completed its course in the founding of a republic whose authority rested exclusively in the power of the purely performative *We hold*. The power of this utterance as a performative is sufficient to produce the sought-after effect. Acts of founding are not aided, but compromised, by the unnecessary and illicit intrusion of a constative.

As evidence for her claim that the declaration (and its performative *We hold*) is the sole source of authority for the Constitution, Arendt notes that "the Constitution itself, in its preamble as well as in its amendments which form the Bill of Rights, is singularly silent on this question of ultimate authority" (*On Revolution* 193–94). But there are two ways to read this silence. The alternative sees this same silence as evidence that the constative structure of the declaration *is* a guarantor of constitutional authority. Recall that Arendt identifies speech with power and characterizes violence as mute ("Understanding and Politics" 378). Recall, too, that in her view, constatives are violent, despotic, and disempowering: They are not the products of shared public agreement, they demand an isolated acquiescence to a truth. They are not held by us, we are held by them. In short, they silence us—hence Arendt's insistence that they are illicit in the realm of action, which is the realm of speech. Consequently, the fact that the Constitution is "silent" on this question of ultimate authority is not overwhelming evidence that the authority of the Republic inheres in the performative *We hold*. That silence can be read equally well as evidence that the constative moments of the declaration contribute importantly to the establishment of ultimate authority in the new republic. The silence can do no more than confirm the undecidability that Arendt resists.

Arendt resists this undecidability because she seeks in the American declaration and founding a moment of perfect legitimacy. Insofar as the authority of the founding derives from a constative, it is rooted not in power but in violence. This undecidability, then, delegitimates the Republic; and so, for the sake of her moment of pure legitimacy, Arendt must do away with it. What Arendt does not see is that the American declaration and founding are paradigmatic instances of politics (however impure) because of this undecidability, not in spite of it. Derrida's point, like Nietzsche's, is that in every system (every practice), whether linguistic, cultural, or political, there is a moment or place that the system cannot account for. Every system is secured by placeholders that are irrevocably, structurally, arbitrary and prelegitimate. They enable the system but are illegitimate from its vantage point. The question, then, for Arendt, is What placeholder fills this place, the place of the last instance, in her account?

The Place of Fables

Arendt fills the place of the last instance with a fable; her fable of the American Revolution and founding stabilizes the declaration and the Constitution; it decides the undecidable. From a Derridean perspective, it is appropriate that she turns to a fable to hold the place; for all placeholders, according to Derrida, including those that are constative in structure, are fables. Recall Derrida's claim that the signer's authorizing himself to sign by signing is a "fabulous retroactivity." By the word *fabulous*, Derrida signals that this retroactivity is enabled by a fable: "There was no signer, by right, before the text of the Declaration which itself remains the producer and guarantor of its own signature. By this fabulous event, by this fable which implies the structure of the trace and is only in truth possible thanks to the inadequation to itself of a present, a signature gives itself a name" ("Declarations of Independence" 10). Arendt herself recognizes this "inadequation to itself of a present"; her own "historical" fable is an acknowledgment of it and a response to it. Thus, her criticism of the American founders for their inability to conceive of a beginning that was not rooted in the past must be in the service of her fable for she, too, proves to be unable to conceive of such a totally present event.

Arendt turns to the declaration in the hope that it will provide her with the resources she needs to fill the gap in her own theorization of a politics of founding. The historical event is the inspiration of the fable, but it does not bind it. Arendt dismisses, among other things, the constative structure of the Declaration of Independence and insists that the pure performative of the declaration was a sufficient guarantor of the authority of the new republic—in order to fill the place with a fabulous faith, the faith that the American founding fathers did not need *gods* in order to found a legitimate republican politics; and hence neither do we. This fable of founding is meant to inspire us, just as "the classical examples shining through the centuries" emboldened the American revolutionaries "for what then turned out to be an unprecedented action" (*On Revolution* 196).

Arendt's fable, like all of her spectators' stories, is meant to define and enable new horizons of possibility. It presents itself as a recovery of the origins and heroes of the republic, as an act of memory and de-reification meant to recapture and thereby reenable the revolutionary spirit that is the vitality of republican politics. The fable must take the place of the constative in order for Arendt to theorize a viable politics for modernity, a politics born not of violence but of power, a nonfoundational politics possessed of legitimacy, authority, stability, and durability.

Arendt claims that this fable is the product of her commitment to memory, to the recovery of the American revolutionary spirit; but it invents that spirit. It claims to be a de-reification, a recovery of origins; but it erases the violence and the ambiguity that marked the original act of founding. And the effect of Arendt's fable is the same as that of all legitimating fables: to prohibit further inquiry into the origins of the system and protect its center of illegitimacy from the scrutiny of prying eyes.

Arendt seems to recognize this. At the end of *Willing*, she acknowledges that she has come to an "impasse." Her account of freedom, natality, and the will "seems to tell us no more than that we are *doomed* to be free by virtue of being born, no matter whether we like freedom or abhor its arbitrariness." The only way out of this impasse, Arendt suggests, is through "an appeal to another mental faculty," that of judgment (*Willing*, vol. 2:217 of *The Life of the Mind*). Judgment is the faculty used by the spectators who turn actions into stories. It is the faculty used by Arendt as a spectator of the American Revolution and founding. Her fabulist rendering of those events is meant to bridge the impasse of freedom, the abyss that afflicts all performative utterance, all declarations of independence, all acts of founding.

Intervention, Augmentation, and Resistibility:
Arendt's Practice of Political Authority

In spite of their apparent irreconcilability, I believe that it may be possible to bridge—or at least to negotiate—the impasse between Derrida and Arendt. If instead of dismissing, as Arendt does, the constative moment of founding, we treat that moment, as Derrida does, as an invitation for intervention, we could respect Arendt's prohibition against anchoring political institutions in an absolute while at the same time acknowledging that *all* acts of founding are (as Derrida claims) necessarily secured by a constative. By this strategy of intervention, we do not deny the constative moment of founding, but neither do we succumb to its claim to irresistibility. We resist it. Our intervention testifies to the resistibility of this (allegedly irresistible) constative anchor; and it posts our opposition to the attempt to "put the law *above* man," to secure the law of laws from all (political) intervention.

This notion of resistibility is at the center of Arendt's new conception of authority for modernity. Recall that for Arendt, an absolute is illicit in politics because it is irresistible. God, self-evident truths, natural law, are all despotic in character because they are irresistible. It is their irresistibility that marks them as antipolitical. (They do not persuade to agreement, they command acquiescence.) Resistibility is the sine qua non of Arendt's politics.[15]

On Arendt's account, it is this feature of resistibility that distinguishes secular law from divine command, political authority from religious devotion. The American founders invoked God (and a whole series of constative anchors) because they (mistakenly) believed that the "essence of secular law was a command." Their political development, Arendt argues, "was nowhere matched by an adequate development of new thought"; and this is why "there was no avoiding the problem of the absolute" (*On Revolution* 195). It was the New World's failure to distinguish secular law from divine command that left it unable to comprehend the fact that "power under the condition of human plurality can never amount to omnipotence, and laws residing in human power can never be absolute" (*On Revolution* 39).

Jacques Derrida recognizes this fact. Indeed, his deconstruction of the American declaration is in the service of this recognition. He exposes "the whole game which tends to present performative utterances as constative utterances." But he knows that this exposure cannot bring the game to an end. The game proceeds; and Derrida, by his very intervention, by his adoption of a posture of intervention, declares himself a player. In so doing, he joins Arendt in proclaiming his commitment to resistibility. Like her, he refuses to allow the law of laws to be put, unproblematically, *above* man; but he recognizes, more deeply than does Arendt, that the law will always resist his resistance ("Devant la loi," passim). His unwillingness to accept that passively is a commitment to politicization, resistibility, and intervention. And his strategy of intervention is not only consistent with Arendt's own account of the practice of political authority (as I read it); it is required by it.

Arendt's theorization of authority builds on the close connection in Roman thought and practice between the concept of authority and a practice of *augmentation:*

> The very concept of Roman authority suggests that the act of foundation inevitably develops its own stability and permanence, and authority in this context is nothing more or less than a kind of necessary "augmentation" by virtue of which all innovations and changes remained tied back to the foundation which, at the same time, they augment and increase. Thus the amendments to the Constitution augment and increase the original foundations of the American republic . . . the very authority of the American Constitution resides in its inherent capacity to be amended and augmented. This notion of a coincidence of foundation and preservation by virtue of augmentation . . . was deeply rooted in the Roman spirit. (*On Revolution* 202; cf. *Between Past and Future* 123)[16]

Since republics do not rest on one world-building act of foundation but are manifestly committed to augmentation, to the continual preservation and amendment of their foundation, they are uniquely endowed with political vigor. Not so the American Republic, however. In it "there was no space reserved, no room left for the exercise of precisely those qualities which had been instrumental in building it." This was, Arendt argues, "no mere oversight"; the American founders, intent on "starting something permanent and enduring," succumbed to the charms of the irresistible absolute. As a result, the experience of free political action remained "the privilege of the generation of the founders." That privileging, Jefferson felt, was an injustice. No constitution, in his view, was perfect, and none should be treated with " 'sanctimonious reverence.' " Consequently, he greeted the news of Shay's rebellion "with enthusiasm: 'God forbid we should ever be twenty years without such a rebellion,' " he said (*On Revolution* 233), expressing a sentiment reminiscent of Machiavelli's advice to princes to reinvigorate their rule with a repetition of the violence of their founding about every ten years.

Arendt does not endorse this reliance on violence as a way to reinvigorate the republic. But she does admire Jefferson's later idea of a ward
system, a system that he came to see as "the only possible non-violent
alternative to his earlier notions about the desirability of recurring
revolutions" (*On Revolution* 250). The ward system, Arendt says, could
correct the fatal flaw of the Constitution (which "had given all power to
the citizens, without giving them the opportunity of *being* republican
and of *acting* as citizens" [*On Revolution* 253]) by subdividing counties
into small republics in which every citizen would have an opportunity
to participate in the activity of politics.

This republican commitment to political action is important to
Arendt for two distinct but related reasons. The first is connected to her
motif of self-realization. In Arendt's view, human beings denied the
opportunity to exercise their world-building capacities live an impover-
ished life, a life that is somehow less than human, a life without
freedom, without happiness (*On Revolution* 255).

The second reason is connected to the character of Arendt's new
conception of authority for modernity. Where other theorists of authority, like Rousseau, believe that the problem of authority is how to put
the law *above* man, that is, how to *make* the law of laws irresistible,
Arendt believes the problem is how to *prevent* the law of laws from
becoming irresistible: she rejects the command model of authority as
inappropriate for the human condition of living together in a secular
and political world. A practice of authority centered on an irresistible
law of laws is inappropriate for the postfoundational age for which
Arendt theorizes a politics, and it is also deeply antipolitical. It pro-
hibits the practices of augmentation and amendment that she valorizes,
and it encourages a withdrawal from active politics; it deactivates politics. Arendt's account is aptly summarized by Hanna Pitkin's description of Machiavelli's view, in which "republican authority must be
exercised in a way that further politicizes the people rather than rendering them quiescent. Its function is precisely to keep a political movement or action that the people have initiated . . . from disintegrating
into riot, apathy, or privatization" (88).

Recall Arendt's claim that the American founders correctly perceived
that the authority of any body politic derives from its beginning, but
mistakenly believed that a beginning was "something which must have
occurred in a distant past." The "great good fortune" of the American
Republic was that this mistaken belief lost out. The success of the
revolution "was decided the very moment when the Constitution began
to be worshipped"; for that constitution worship, Arendt argues, evi-

denced the fact that the Republic was built on a beginning that was very present: "If their attitude towards Revolution and Constitution can be called religious at all, then the word 'religion' must be understood in its original Roman sense, and their piety would then consist in *religare*, in binding themselves back to a beginning" (*On Revolution* 198). This constitution worship has always been "ambiguous," its object being "at least as much the constituting act as it was the written document itself." Consequently, Arendt can say both that the "American remembrance of the event" of constitution is what keeps the authority of the republic "safe and intact" and that the "very authority of the American Constitution resides in its inherent capacity to be amended and augmented" (*On Revolution* 204, 202). For Arendt, this commitment to augmentation maintains a republic and its revolutionary spirit by, in a curious sense, keeping its beginning always present.

Derrida identifies this same structure of maintenance and calls it *survivance*, by which he, too, means a kind of preservation through augmentation. Here, as with Arendt, survival is not produced by the maintenance of a present into a future in the way that a fixed monument seeks to preserve the presence of what is past. For Derrida, this maintenance is an agumentation that takes place by way of translation, by way of a translation that is called for and "heard in" the original text. Just as, on Arendt's account, the Constitution calls out to be amended, so Derrida's text calls out to be translated: It is not present *yet*. This is not translation in the ordinary sense: just as Arendt's performative founding could never be content merely to transmit a sense of obligation or produce obedient subjects, neither can Derrida's act of translation be "content merely to transport a content into another language, nor just to communicate or to transmit something," merely to produce comprehension. Translation augments, necessarily. It does not merely copy or reproduce; it is a new linguistic event, it produces "new textual bodies." It does not simply preserve an original in a practice of mere repetition, it dislodges the constative yearnings of the original and finds there the point of departure for "a new way of life"—hence Derrida's claim that this is not *survivance* "in the sense of posterity . . . but of 'more living' "; in the sense of *"plus de vie* and *plus que vie"* ("Deconstruction in America" 24–25). This "augmentation," says Derrida, "that's what survival is." And this augmentation is, in one sense, arguably like Arendt's practice of authority, which responds to the text or document that seeks to preserve and refer to the past moment of founding by augmenting it with another event, another speech act, or, as in this case, by an act of translation.

Finally, Machiavelli, too, explores this structure of maintenance. He sees the importance of maintaining the act of foundation, understands that human institutions need frequent revitalization, and seeks that revitalization in the "return to beginnings," a kind of invitation to augmentation. As Pitkin points out, this return to beginnings may be read as a way of "frightening" the population "back into obedience," but there is also another way to think about it. "Perhaps," she suggests, "one should construe the forgetfulness that gradually corrupts a composite body as reification: a coming to take for granted as 'given' and inevitable what in fact is the product of human action." This reification distances citizens from their political institutions. From this perspective, Pitkin argues, the return to origins does not signal the recurrence of violence but a return "to the spirit of origins, the human capacity to originate." If we assume here that "In the beginning lies not chaos but human capacity" (275–79),[17] then we can see that Machiavelli's return to beginnings, like Nietzsche's genealogies and Derrida's deconstructions, is a de-reification and a political intervention.

Arendt, like Machiavelli, sees that a beginning too firmly rooted in the past is in danger of becoming reified and foundational. Our commitment to augmentation and amendment may derive from our reverence for a beginning that is in the past; but our practices of augmentation and amendment make that beginning our own—not merely our legacy but our own construction and performative. The commitment to augmentation protects that which was glorious because it was a performative from being sanctified and turned into a law of laws, an absolute whose irresistibility would ultimately and necessarily destroy the uniquely political character of the republic.[18] On this reading of Arendt, augmentation is both a necessary condition of politics and constitutive of one form of the activity of politics itself. What Leo Strauss says of Machiavelli applies equally to Arendt: "Foundation is, as it were, continuous foundation" (44).

Since, on Arendt's account, the practice of authority consists largely in this commitment to resistibility, the practice of authority turns out to be, paradoxically enough, a practice of deauthorization. On this account, then, Derrida's own project of deauthorization—his adoption of a posture of intervention—becomes *part* of a practice of authority, and not simply an unauthorized assault on the institutions of authority from some "outside." This inclusion is the genius of Arendt's account.

It is noteworthy that, both for Derrida and for Arendt, the moment of intervention is the moment of politics. But for Derrida, politics *begins* with the entry of the irresistible absolute; it is the impossible superimposition of constative on performative utterance that occasions the Derridean intervention, an intervention that is political. For Arendt, however, politics *ends* with the entry of the *anti*political (because irresistible) absolute. Arendt's intervention consists in her insistence that acts of founding can and should resist the urge to anchor themselves in an absolute. But Arendt's account of authority as a practice of augmentation and amendment does not, in my view, commit her to this insistence. It commits her only to the insistence that we treat the absolute as an invitation for intervention, that we declare ourselves resistant to it, that we refuse its claim to irresistibility by de-authorizing it. And this, in effect, is what Arendt herself tries to do in her own interventionist critique of the constative structure of the American Declaration of Independence.

The impasse between Arendt and Derrida is not easy to bridge, but neither is it nonnegotiable. If it is at all possible to negotiate it, it is in all likelihood because both these thinkers—Derrida through his strategy of intervention. Arendt through her fable of the American Revolution—seem to be inspired by Nietzsche's counsel to seek "a past from which we may spring rather than that from which we seem to have derived" (*The Use and Abuse of History* 23). And where better than in America, the mythic land of new beginnings, to seek such a past, to resist the mundane fate of derivation in the name of new, seductive (and, in that sense, irresistible) possibilities?

Notes

Thanks to Richard Flathman, William Connolly, Peter Digeser, David Mapel, Tom Keenan, Tom Eagles, Judith Butler, Jeff Isaac, and George Kateb. This article is a very slightly revised version of a paper that appeared in the *American Political Science Review*, March 1991.

Kennedy's remarks were made at Amherst College, Massachusetts, on 26 October 1963.

1. This view, that Arendt's account of authority is antimodernist, is the standard interpretation. See, for example, Richard Flathman, *Authority and the Authoritative: The Practice of Political Authority*, whose account of Arendt I discuss briefly below, and Richard Friedman ("On the Concept of Authority in Political Philosophy" 122), who cites Arendt's account as an instance of the "peculiar but interesting and important claim that the very concept of authority has been corrupted or even lost in the modern world, and that it is this loss of

understanding that lies behind the confusion over authority prevailing in contemporary thought."

2. Arendt is quoting Rousseau's *Government of Poland* (3) and *On the Social Contract*, book 2, chapter 7.

3. The language of "performative" and "constative" is Austin's (*How To Do Things with Words*) not Arendt's. I note in passing that Arendt's description of action as a form of utterance (The "doer of deeds is possible only if he is at the same time the speaker of words," *The Human Condition* 178–79), a de novo creation, her identification of this form of utterance with politics, and her characterization of politics as world-building, all lead me to believe that her account draws on the model of the originary performative, the divine utterance, "Let there be . . .," which, on the biblical account, is the first of a series of performatives whereby God created the world.

4. Arendt's distinction between an "argument in support of an action" and actions that "appear in words" implies that only performative utterances are speech acts. Austin began with this assumption but later found he could not maintain it and concluded that both performative and constative utterances are speech acts. Arendt is not the only one to make the interesting claim that the *written* document is the "perfect way for an action to appear in words." See Michael Warner's *Letters of the Republic* (chapter 4) on the importance of writing, printing, and textuality to the legitimation of the early American Republic.

5. Both the new conception of authority and the older Roman one are sustained by the foundings in which they originated. Arendt says that Roman authority was sustained by particular religious and traditional beliefs, but she does also claim that it was "the very coincidence of authority, tradition, and religion, *all three simultaneously springing from the act of foundation,* [that] was the backbone of Roman history from beginning to end" (*On Revolution* 199; emphasis mine).

6. Arendt makes no note of it, but the phrase, "in the presence of God and one another," instantiates the same "incongruous" unification of a constative and performative utterance as does Jefferson's "We hold these truths to be self-evident." Indeed, it suggests, contra Arendt, that the confidence the parties had in each other was not "granted and confirmed by no one"; it was guaranteed by "God" and his "Presence." It is also notable (although Arendt never mentions it) that the Mayflower Compact was drawn up in Britain, under the sanctioning and supporting gaze of Britain's legal and political institutions, *before* the colonists left for the uncertain and unknown New World. Moreover, the document was signed on the ship, *before* the colonists disembarked in America. In short, it would seem that the colonists' "confidence . . . in their own power" was perhaps a little less hardy than Arendt estimates. Cf. n. 12.

7. Arendt sometimes toys with the notion that a "principle" might save "the act of beginning from its own arbitrariness" (*On Revolution* 212–13; cf. *Be-*

tween Past and Future 156). At other times, however, she concedes that the arbitrariness of beginnings is "complete" (*On Revolution* 201).

8. And, as we know from Austin, discursive practices postulate a vast array of political and cultural institutions that set many of the conditions for discursive felicity: for example, they distinguish and sanction the distinction between those who are "in-authority" and those who are not; that is, they identify the authorized speaker of the performative, "I call this meeting to order" as the chair of the board, and they forbid, punish, fail to comprehend, or sanction the interrogation of anyone who impersonates the chair and usurps the chair's performative privilege.

9. On Austin's account, the felicity of promises/performatives is often secured by the use of formulaic or ritualistic utterance for performative purposes, as in "I declare this meeting adjourned."

10. The same point can be made with reference to Arendt's stories, which, Arendt assumes, are univocal, possessed of a force and meaning that are unproblematic. These are curious assumptions from one so insistent that plurality is the sine qua non of the public realm. Perhaps Arendt's account of the role of stories in politics is too influenced by the Greek model, in which an authoritative poet (Homer) gives the authoritative account of events.

11. Identity is the product not the condition of action, on Arendt's account (*The Human Condition* 193; Kateb 1–51; Honig, "Arendt, Identity, and Difference" 86–88).

12. This claim that signing requires *countersignatures* again renders problematic Arendt's faith in the power of the *we* to ensure its own action. In Arendt's process, there are only *cosigners,* but cosigners, on Derrida's account, are not sufficient to get us out of Sièyes's vicious circle. Hence, the parties to the Mayflower Compact combined "themselves together into a 'civil Body Politick'" not "*solely* by the strength of mutual promises," but (as Arendt well knows) "'in the Presence of God and one another'" (emphasis mine; cf. n. 6). The parties invoke the "Presence of God" because they need the validation of his witness and the security of his *counter*signature.

13. Arendt believes that this gap marks only the speech acts of her public realm; hence the risk and danger of public action, which she celebrates. Contra Derrida, she assumes that some language *is* "safe," unproblematic, or at least uninteresting: that which is not political, not productive, nonperformative speech, that which addresses "immediate, identical needs and wants." For this sort of thing, "Signs and sounds . . . would be enough" (*The Human Condition* 176).

14. Here Derrida refers to the phrase *We the people;* I take his argument to apply equally well to the *We hold.*

15. This identification of politics with resistibility is what leads Arendt to insist on her problematically severe distinction between the public and the private realms. The private realm is the realm of the body, whose demands upon us are, according to Arendt, necessarily irresistible. A footnote is hardly the

place for it, but let me suggest that Arendt's public/private distinction would lose some of its (problematic) force if instead of insisting on the inadmissibility of the irresistible to the public realm we responded to it with a Derridean strategy of intervention. I explore this idea in greater detail in "Toward an Agonistic Feminism: Hannah Arendt and the Politics of Identity."

16. Arendt is not the only one to note the etymological and conceptual connections between authority and augmentation (see Friedman, "On the Concept of Authority in Political Philosophy"; Peters, "Authority"; and Friedrich, "Authority, Reason, and Discretion"), but she alone reasons from them to an account of authority as deeply tied to a *practice* of augmentation.

17. The return to beginnings will be violent only in regimes that are corrupt, Pitkin argues. Others will respond to nonviolent forms of reinvigoration.

18. The absence in the American Republic of something like a ward system that would allow citizens to participate in the political activity of augmentation does not mean that the Republic lacks authority. It does mean that "the true seat of authority in the American Republic" is the Supreme Court, which is, "in Woodrow Wilson's phrase, 'a kind of Constitutional Assembly in continuous session.'" Consequently, Arendt argues, the American concept of authority is very different from that of Rome: "In Rome the function of authority was political, and it consisted in giving advice, while in the American republic the function of authority is legal, and it consists in interpretation" (*On Revolution* 200). This substitution of legal for political authority, together with the failure of the American Republic to vouchsafe spaces of freedom for popular participation in politics, marks, according to Arendt, the loss of the American Republic's revolutionary spirit.

11 Postmodernism and the Public Sphere

Dana R. Villa

Introduction

Much has been written about the transformation of the public sphere in America into a realm of spectacle: the sophisticated manipulation of images by media constantly incites desire in a way that renders public opinion ever more plastic, ever more responsive to the deployment of precoded cues bereft of context or argument. The "end of ideology/history" brings not the end of propaganda, but its *aufhebung:* a politics of images whose power is a function of its disconnection from the real or, better, its ability to elide totally the distinction between the symbolic and the real. The Reagan presidency was, of course, a bonanza for theorists schooled in Debord, Lacan, and Baudrillard, a pure example— courtesy of Micheal Deaver—of the absorption of the real by the image.

If, indeed, media currently produces reality as, in Baudrillard's words, "simulation effect," then "publicity"—the realm that Kant identified as crucial to the critical limitation of power—appears as little more than a hyperfunctionalized mechanism for generating legitimacy and manufacturing consent. It is therefore not surprising that the normative conception of a unified, coherent public sphere delineated by modern democratic theory has become the target of a corrosive postmodern skepticism. This "cynical consciousness" is partly a response to an increasingly fragmented and hierarchical society. In such a society, the best that can be hoped for is the politics of difference and multiculturalism. Hence postmodernism's embrace of a new, postliberal, pluralism.

Such pluralism repudiates the available (hegemonic) forms of publicity and views hopes for a revived, comprehensive, egalitarian public sphere as nothing short of reactionary.

There is much to the postmodern critique of our currently existing public sphere. Moreover, as I argue below, the criticisms directed by postmodern theory against the normative conception of the public realm are, in large part, persuasive. Nevertheless, the call for empowerment, which lies at the heart of the politics of difference, carries its own demand for new spaces for, and practices of, politics. Thus, as Nancy Fraser has recently argued, the *idea* of the public sphere, of an "institutionalized arena of discursive interaction," remains "indispensable" to a critical political theory ("Rethinking Public Sphere" 59). The precise nature of this indispensability is, however, an open question. What, exactly, is it that public realm theory can teach the postmodern unmaskers of the public sphere? Put another way: what positive role can the democratic ideal of the public sphere possibly play within the postmodern problematic?

This essay addresses these questions by juxtaposing the public realm theory of Arendt and Habermas with postmodern critics of the public sphere (Foucault, Lyotard, Baudrillard). While I agree with Fraser that the idea of the public sphere continues to play an absolutely essential theoretical role, I question the Habermasian assumption that this role is primarily normative. I contend that Arendt's agonistic, "pagan" stance shifts the critical weight of public realm theory away from issues of legitimation and consensus, and toward an appreciation of those initiatory, spontaneous, and "an-archic" practices typically bracketed as prepolitical by liberal democratic theory.[1] In addition, Arendt's public realm theory creates a narrative context for the postmodern turn to a politics of resistance, parody, and subversion. In this regard, her insistence upon the specificity of the political and her ontological approach to the public realm serve to trace the internal limits of a postmodern politics, a politics predicated upon the closure or fragmentation of the public sphere.

The Idea of the Public Sphere and Postmodern Skepticism

As a motto, "the recovery of the public realm" captures, more or less adequately, the primary goal of Hannah Arendt's political philosophy and the critical theory of Jurgen Habermas. Both Arendt and Habermas see the public realm as a specifically political sphere distinct from the state and the economy, an institutionally bounded discursive arena that is home to citizen debate, deliberation, agreement, and action. Yet they also see this space as overwhelmed by the antipolitical forces unleashed by modernity. For Arendt, it is the modern rise of "the social" which effaces what once was a strong distinction between the public and the private, which tears down the boundary between the realms of necessity and freedom (*Human Condition* 33 ff.). The result is that the public space is "devoured" by "household" concerns—the maintenance of life and economic reproduction—and politics is reduced to the function of "household administration," a function fulfilled by the state (Arendt, *Human Condition* 45–47).

For Habermas, modernity is essentially an epoch of rationalization, as Weber described it. Yet this rationalization is one-sided. The universalization of instrumental rationality—its application to all spheres of social life—converts practical/political questions into technical ones (Habermas, *Rational Society* 96). The result is the destruction of the space of democratic decision making, a realm now "colonized" by technical-administrative imperatives (Benhabib, *Critique, Norm* chap. 7; Habermas, *Communicative Action, Public Sphere*).

Reacting to these trends and the withdrawal of the political in the modern age, Arendt and Habermas refined their respective conceptions of the public sphere in order to provide rigorous criteria for determining a *genuine* public realm. By insisting upon the distinctiveness of this realm and the kind of interaction that occurs within it, Arendt and Habermas are able to elucidate the necessary minimal conditions for (to use Arendt's phrase) "the sharing of words and deeds"; that is, by theorizing the conditions necessary for uncoerced deliberation and decision amongst diverse equals, Arendt and Habermas provide an ideal of the public sphere that serves to highlight the forms of asymmetry, coercion, violence, and communicative distortion that presently characterize *our* public realm.

Poststructuralist and postmodern theory has increasingly raised objections to the fundamental presuppositions of the *type* of project in which Arendt and Habermas are engaged. In this essay I examine what I consider to be the three most basic and forceful objections raised by poststructuralism/postmodernism against Arendt and Habermas. The first, originating in the work of Foucault, I shall refer to as the *power* objection: it radically questions the idea/ideal of a coercion-free sphere by retheorizing the nature of power in the modern age (Foucault, *Discipline and Punish, History of Sexuality, Power/Knowledge*, "Subject and Power"). The second objection I label *epistemological:* it finds its most forceful formulation in the work of Lyotard, who challenges the very possibility of a unified, consensus-based public realm in an age that has witnessed the death of legitimating metanarratives and the corresponding fragmentation of the discursive realm into irreducibly heterogeneous language games (Lyotard, *Just Gaming, Postmodern Condition*). The third objection, in some ways the most telling, can be derived from the work of Deleuze or the popularization of certain Deleuzian themes in Baudrillard: it is *ontological* (Deleuze; Baudrillard, *Simulations; Selected Writings*, chaps. 5, 7). This objection questions the peculiar reality attributed to the public realm as a "common space of appearances" (Arendt), a *world* without transcendental or metaphysical support, yet one available to all its citizens/inhabitants. From the point of view of Deleuze or Baudrillard, the Arendtian conviction that "appearance . . . constitutes reality" betrays a "nostalgia for reality," for a world well lost (Arendt, *Human Condition* 57; Baudrillard, *Selected Writings*, chap. 7). This nostalgia appears to permeate Arendt's entire project (the analysis of modernity in terms of "worldlessness"), and Habermas is able to evade it only by offering an abstractly procedural account of political discourse.

While these objections are powerful, I believe they are also answerable, at least from the point of view of Arendt's project. Indeed, I will argue that the apparently obvious opposition between Arendt and Habermas, on the one hand, and poststructuralism/postmodernism, on the other, has been overdrawn, thanks in large part to the polemical stance taken by Habermas in *The Philosophical Discourse of Modernity*. In that work, Habermas creates a stark opposition between communicative and subject-centered reason, between the paradigms of mutual understanding or intersubjectivity and that of the philosophy of consciousness (chap. 11). In his view neither Hegel nor Marx succeeded in extricating themselves from the "horizon of the self-reference of the knowing and acting subject"; but then, neither do such critics of the philosophy of consciousness and the modern project as Heidegger, Derrida, and Foucault. All remain, from the Habermasian perspective, either caught up in the metaphysics of subjectivity (Hegel and Marx with their demiurgic conceptions of self-externalizing subjects) or endlessly tracing the transcendental/empirical bounds of the "humanist" paradigm (Heidegger, Derrida, Foucault). According to Habermas, the postmoderns, like their predecessors, fail to effect the transition to "the paradigm of mutual understanding" and remain locked within an exhausted episteme (295–96, 310).

This mapping of the world of modern/postmodern theory neatly locates Arendt's work on the intersubjective side of the divide. In the last section of this essay I question the adequacy of this mapping, suggesting that the Arendtian theorization of the public realm harmonizes in unexpected ways with the critics of the strong normative conception of the public sphere. This invites a rethinking of the relation between public realm theory and postmodernism/poststructuralism (Villa).

Arendt, Habermas, and the Normative Conception of the Public Realm

In his appreciation of Hannah Arendt's contribution to the theorization of power, Habermas emphasizes the way in which she "dissociates the concept of power from the teleological model of action" (*Philosophical-Political Profiles* 173). Contra Max Weber, who "defined power as the possibility of forcing one's own will, whatever it may be, on the conduct of others," Habermas argues that Arendt "understands power as the capacity to agree in uncoerced communication on some community action" (171). Habermas is referring to Arendt's "On Violence," where she draws a rigorous distinction between *power*, which she defines as "the human ability not just to act, but to act in concert," and strength, force and violence, all of which are uniquely instrumental (in *Crises of the Republic* 143). This definition points to a model of action quite different from the teleological one, whose means-end structure makes the achievement of a pregiven goal the organizing principle of all action. In contrast, Arendt understands action as "the sharing of words and deeds" amongst equals; in Habermas's formulation, action is essentially *communicative*. On this model—the communicative versus the teleological or instrumental—"the parties are oriented toward agreement and not just toward their respective success" (Habermas, *Philosophical-Political Profiles* 173). *Political* power—the power to act together, to act in concert—is generated through the common action of individuals whose interaction is structured in accordance with norms of reciprocity, respect, and equality, and for whom agreement or consensus stands "as an end in itself for all parties" (173).

   This reading of Arendt's theory of action and her concept of power stresses the parallels between her reassertion of the Aristotelian distinction between *praxis* and *poiesis* and Habermas's fundamental distinction between communicative and instrumental action. It focuses upon the dialogical dimension of Arendt's understanding of politics and asks us to view her notion of the public sphere as one that sets the basic conditions for what Habermas refers to as "coercion-free communication." This is important, for unless political action as communication is coercion-free, the consensus is that issues from it will have no binding force: it will simply be another expression of insidious or overt violence. Habermas sees the delineation of the public sphere presented in Arendt's *Human Condition* as a phenomenologically inspired attempt to "read off the general structures of unimpaired intersubjectivity in the formal properties of communicative action or *praxis*" (175). Unsurprisingly, Habermas interprets Arendt's conception of the public realm as a prefiguration of his own "ideal speech situation," the counterfactual elucidation of the formal conditions of coercion-free communication, abstracted, so he claims, from the very structure of communicative action (*Philosophical Discourse* 315). Theory functions, in both cases, to uncover the gap between current practice and the implicit *telos* of communicative interaction, the reaching of a "rationally motivated agreement" (315).

While I shall argue that the "consensus" model of politics Habermas attributes to Arendt is problematic, one must acknowledge that Habermas does capture an important dimension of Arendt's theorization of the public realm (Villa). In *The Human Condition* and *On Revolution*, Arendt consistently emphasizes the idea of the public realm as a space of "tangible freedom"; a space that is physically separate from those of work and labor; a space bounded or constituted by law; a space that can serve as an arena or stage for political action. Not only are coercion and violence excluded from this sphere, but so are all relations of hierarchy or command. The public realm is the space of freedom precisely because it creates an artificial *equality* amongst persons whose individual talents make them naturally unequal, and because it preserves the human condition of *plurality* by relating and separating persons simultaneously. The public realm is that artificial space or "world" common to us *qua* citizens, an "in-between" that makes both equality and individuality possible (*Human Condition* 7, 26, 52; *On Revolution* 31–32).

Here we encounter the irreducible *spatiality* of the public realm as conceived by Arendt. Unless this space has the power to gather us together, to remove each of us from the private while simultaneously guaranteeing each of us a distinct *place* in this "common world," genuine politics is not possible. Where this sphere is invaded by matters and ends that are not essentially open to debate, plurality is effectively neutered and the public realm loses its three-dimensionality: the "world" ceases to be constituted from a variety of perspectives (*Human*

Condition 55; Villa 286–87). Where this space is forcibly collapsed or eliminated as Arendt argues it is under totalitarianism, the "boundaries and channels of communication between individual men" are replaced by "a band of iron which holds them so tightly together that it is as though their plurality had disappeared into One Man of gigantic dimensions" (*Totalitarianism* 164). The space between individuals is destroyed, and, as a result, action is no longer possible. So long as the spatial dimension of the public realm is preserved and the "boundaries and channels of communication" remain intact, freedom in the distinctively Arendtian sense is possible.

Richard Bernstein has argued that Arendt's depiction of the public realm in terms of plurality and equality results in a normative conception of politics that is virtually indistinguishable from that of Habermas (*Philosophical Profiles* 221–37; *Beyond Objectivism* pt. 4). Plurality and equality open a space of deliberation oriented toward mutual agreement in which the "force of the better argument" (Habermas) can carry the day. Bernstein glosses Arendt's claim that "debate is the very essence of political life" by offering the following characterization of what happens in the Arendtian public space:

> [Politics] involves "no rule," the mutual and joint action grounded in human plurality and the isonomy of citizens where individuals debate and attempt to persuade each other. Persuasion, not force or violence, is the quintessence of political life. Persuasion is not the manipulation of others by image-making. Persuasion involves free, open debate among equals in which we seek to form, clarify and test opinions.
> (*Philosophical-Political Profiles* 224)

This gloss has the effect of identifying Arendt's public realm with an arena of communicative rationality in which opinion is gradually purified through the "non-coercively unifying, consensus-building force of a discourse in which participants overcome their at first subjectively biased views in favor of a rationally motivated agreement" (Habermas, *Philosophical Discourse* 315). While Arendt formally eschews Habermas's moral cognitivism, this reading finds support (as Bernstein points out) in her Kantian theory of "impartial" political judgment (*Philosophical-Political Discourse* 228–31; *Beyond Objectivism* 216–23).

If Bernstein reveals a fundamental continuity between the Arendtian and Habermasian conceptions of the public realm, Seyla Benhabib reinforces that assimilation by arguing that Arendt's concept of plurality must be seen in opposition to the Hegelian-Marxian model of a "super-subject" externalizing and reappropriating itself, a model that reduces plurality to transsubjectivity (*Critique, Norm* 243–44). The phenomenon of plurality, the basic constitutive condition of politics, is covered over by the "work model of action," Hegel and Marx's version of the traditional teleological concept. By emphasizing intersubjectivity and the communicative conception of action, the phenomenological ground of politics is recovered: "The communicative model of action does justice to the experiences of human plurality . . . for communication is the medium through which plurality is revealed. In acting and speaking we show who we are and our differences from each other" (244). The public realm, understood as a discursive space characterized by symmetry, nonhierarchy, and reciprocity, both presupposes and makes plurality possible, and so provides the opportunity for a politics based on mutual recognition and respect for difference.

Postmodern Objections to the Normative Conception of the Public Realm

The account of public realm theory offered thus far dwells on the similarities between Arendt and Habermas. In turning to postmodern objections to this type of theory I will continue to ignore, for the time being, the substantial differences between them.

Foucault's work can be understood as a sustained critique of public realm theory and its normative presuppositions (Fraser, *Unruly Practices* 29–30). As has been widely noted, Foucault's theorization of modern disciplinary power begins with what Nancy Fraser has called a "bracketing of the problematic of legitimacy" (*Unruly Practices* 19; Habermas, *Philosophical Discourse* chap. 10; Taylor). By setting aside the fundamental liberal distinction between legitimate and illegitimate power, Foucault brings to light the "local, continuous, productive, capillary and exhaustive" character of modern power (*Unruly Practices* 32; Foucault, *History of Sexuality* 93–108, 119). Power's "tightly knit grid of material coercions," its various microtechniques for the production of docile bodies and self-surveilling subjects, remain invisible so long as we treat it as sovereignty (Foucault, *History of Sexuality* 105). Yet it is just this anachronistic model of state power based on contract and intended for the preservation of rights that liberal theory asserts again and again by its imposition of the legitimacy problematic. In so doing, the liberal paradigm—the "juridical apparatus"—conceals the increasingly insidious forms of modern discipline and domination (Foucault, Power/Knowledge 81–91).

Neither Habermas nor Arendt relies upon the discourse of rights to make their critical points; nor can either be accused of holding a "sovereign model" of power. Both point to the possibility of a positive, as opposed to a merely negative or repressive, power: a power that arises from communicative interaction, from "acting together, acting in concert" (Arendt, *Crises of the Republic* 143; *Between Past and Future* 172).[2] The negative or repressive aspects are located elsewhere and identified with strength, violence, hierarchy, and so forth. However, from the Foucauldian point of view, this positive conception of power is too clean; it remains anachronistic, a democratic analogue to the state-centered liberal model. Both models of power—the positive one proposed by public realm theory, the negative one upheld by liberalism—blind us to the constitutive workings of modern power and its fundamental role in the production of subjects. Thus the liberal "bounding" of negative/repressive state power through the notion of rights finds its mirror image in public realm theory's specification of the necessary formal conditions for "unforced agreement." In other words, the public realm theory of Arendt and Habermas simply shifts the "power-free zone" of liberalism (power understood as legitimate coercion) from the private realm to the public, redefining power now as to the "ability to act." Indeed, insofar as the public realm is purified of subjective/strategic interests, it is more rigorously coercion-free than the "power-free" private sphere of liberalism. In both, however, the error is to pretend that we can use power without it using us.

The severe limitations of public realm theory in coming to grips with the nature of modern power are most apparent in its naive reliance upon conditions of symmetry, nonhierarchy, and reciprocity as adequate guarantees of a "coercion-free" space. As Fraser points out, in a "fully 'panopticized' society, hierarchical, asymmetrical domination of some persons by others would have become superfluous; all would surveil and police themselves" (*Unruly Practices* 49; Dews 157, 160–61). Foucault enables us to see the ways in which hierarchy and asymmetry—the two primary villains for public realm theory—are not essential to the smooth functioning of disciplinary power. The formation of autonomous individuals, their subjectification, is not so easily detached from their subjugation (Foucault, *Discipline and Punish* 29–30; *History of Sexuality* 98). Thus, while it is possible to imagine the realization of the ideal speech situation, this would be nothing more than

the achievement of "pseudoautonomy in the conditions of pseudosym-
metry" (Fraser, *Unruly Pratices* 49).[3] A Foucauldian would therefore
insist that public realm theory deal with the normalizing character of
communicative action. The criterion of consensus is too blunt an instrument for this task, since it leaves unexamined the self-surveillance
of the civically virtuous citizen (who has internalized the hegemonic
conception of the public good) or communicatively rational agent (who
has internalized the hegemonic conception of what constitutes "the
better argument").[4]

The second type of postmodernist objection to the normative conception of the public sphere also focuses upon the ideal of consensus, but
from an epistemological as opposed to a power perspective. Habermas's
strategy for rescuing practical/political questions from technocratic
usurpation, for preserving the public realm from system-colonization,
can be reduced to two basic theoretical moves. The first, which draws
on Arendt's distinction between acting and making, involves distinguishing between two types of rationalization in modernity, system and
communicative rationalization (Wellmer 35–66). This distinction enables us to view the "disenchantment" of practical discourse in the
modern age as a process separate from yet parallel to the growth of
purposive rationality: *communicative* rationalization consists in the
growing endorsement of the principle that validity claims can and
ought to be redeemed only through the medium of reflexive speech. The
reference to traditional grounds of validation, which presume a prediscursive legitimacy, is no longer possible.

The appeal to communicative rationality (to legitimation through
open dialogue and consensus) works, however, only if Habermas is able
to convince us that this rationality is universal (and so can guarantee
the possibility of reaching a *genuine* agreement) yet nonsubstantive.
Otherwise, he is open to the Nietzschean or Weberian objection that
any noninstrumental concept of reason is dogmatic. Habermas's deployment of what he believes is a philosophically viable procedural
account of rationality enables him (so he claims) to take full account of
the "disenchantment of the world" and the modern separation of value
spheres, while avoiding the Nietzschean/Weberian conclusion that will
or decision is the only possible source of meaning in a disillusioned age
(Benhabib, *Critique/Norm* 258ff.; Habermas, *Theory and Practice*). A
proceduralist account of discursive rationality enables escape from the
polytheism of values—Weber's "warring gods"—which characterizes
postmodernity. As long as there are standards of argumentative rationality implicit in speech, we will be able to distinguish a genuine

consensus from a false one and decisions based on reason from those based upon will or coercion, right from might.

Lyotard, in particular, is sympathetic to the Habermasian attempt to escape the universalization of functionalist reason, the legitimation of knowledge by power. Indeed, his analysis of the principle of performativity in *The Postmodern Condition* mirrors much of the standard Frankfurt School critique (xxiv, 47). Nevertheless, he is extremely skeptical of Habermas's attempt to transfer formal rules for what constitutes a genuine consensus from the scientific or theoretical community to the sphere of politics (30).

Lyotard is, first of all, dubious about the Habermasian picture of the legitimation of scientific discourse (the privileged model of argumentative rationality). "Paralogy" or "permanent revolution" is opposed to consensus (60ff.). Second, and more important for our purposes, he points out how Habermas's attempt to avoid an irreversible fragmentation of the discursive space by providing a procedural mechanism that mediates between the "warring gods" and specifies the formal characteristics of the "better argument" is, in fact, parasitic upon an Enlightenment metanarrative of emancipation. This metanarrative, Lyotard asserts, *was* capable of integrating the language games of science and politics through its deployment of consensus via open debate as *the* criterion of legitimate knowledge and institutions (32, xxiv). Yet once this metanarrative comes under suspicion—and, as Lyotard famously defines it, postmodernity *is* "incredulity toward metanarratives"—the idea that a model of argumentative rationality and agreement derived from science can provide context-independent criteria of validity is itself cast in doubt.

The Habermasian end-run around decisionism and the "polytheism of values" depends upon the availability of a metadiscourse that could, potentially, render the "heteromorphorous" language games of social life, each with their own context-dependent rules of legitimation, competence, and application, commensurable. Against the assumption that "discourse" holds the key to identifying context-independent criteria of validity, Lyotard states that "there is no reason to think that it would be possible to determine metaprescriptives common to all of these language games, or that a reasonable consensus like the one in force at a given moment in the scientific community could embrace the totality of metaprescriptions regulating the totality of statements circulating in the social collectivity" (47; Lyotard and Thébaud 58). Habermas cannot conceive of legitimation in terms other than a "search for universal consensus": as a result he *must* assume "that it is possible for all speakers to come to agreement on which rules or metaprescriptions are universally valid for language games" (*Postmodern Condition* 47).

For Lyotard, this assumption reduces the irreducible heterogeneity of language games; it attempts to neutralize the "diversity of discursive species," each subject to its own set of pragmatic rules. Moreover, Habermas assumes that "the goal of dialogue is consensus," that "humanity as a collective (universal) subject seeks its common emancipation through the regularization of 'moves' permitted in all language games, and that the legitimacy of any statement resides in its contributing to that emancipation" (*Postmodern Condition* 65–66). This assumption not only does violence to the heterogeneity of language games; it also does violence to the heterogeneity of the players—their plurality—by subjecting all to a regime of discursive practice designed to overcome what Lyotard sees as the *agonistic* dimension of those games (10). The spontaneity, initiation, and difference that characterize agonistic speech are repressed as a model of Kuhnian "normal science" is imposed upon the public sphere. It is for this reason—the flattening, antiagonistic, anti-initiatory, character of the consensus model—that Lyotard concludes that "consensus has become an outmoded and suspect value" and opts instead for a "pagan" politics that breaks decisively with all attempts to ground action and practical decision in a theoretical discourse of justice or legitimacy (*Postmodern Condition* 66; Lyotard and Thébaud 28).

For Lyotard, the fragmentation of the public sphere, the emergence of discordant language games that results from the postmodern death of totalizing metanarratives, opens the way to forms of political practice and judgment freed from the tyranny of science or *episteme* (Lyotard and Thébaud 27, 58; *Postmodern Condition* 28–29). *Paganism*—Lyotard's code word for an antifoundationalist politics of opinion, of judgment "without criteria"—rescues the political by unmasking the ideal of a grounded consensus and the theoricist/Platonist constraints it implies. Lyotard's epistemological rejoinder to the Habermasian construction of the public sphere parallels Foucault's objection in its bracketing of the legitimation problematic (for Lyotard this problematic encompasses any attempt to derive the political from the theoretical, the just from the true, even where "truth" is seen as a function of consensus) (Lyotard and Thébaud 25).[5] Public realm theory conceals the disciplinary underside of "acting together" and covers over the anti-agonstic, anti-initiatory implications that flow from the regularization of moves in any language game.

The final objection to public realm theory raised by postmodernism is ontological, so-called because it is directed against the specific reality claimed for the public space and the objects within it. It is more directly applicable to Arendt's theory, which attempts to construct an ontology of the public realm. Eschewing Habermas's attempt to delineate a public sphere in terms of a specific form of interaction and the rationality appropriate to it, Arendt defines the public phenomenologically, as a "common space of appearances." Plurality has a constitutive as well as consensual dimension: deliberation and debate from a diversity of perspectives constitutes a "shared world of appearance," a world whose reality is a function of incessant speech about that which lies between us (*Human Condition* 50ff.). From Arendt's point of view, that which "appears in public and can be seen and heard by everybody" is "real," a conviction expressed in her dictum that "for us, appearance—something that is being seen and heard by others as well as ourselves— constitutes reality" (50).

In making this claim, Arendt is self-consciously aligning herself with Nietzsche's undermining of the Platonic metaphysical distinction between appearance and reality (*Willing* 10). But where Nietzsche sees this distinction as expressing an ascetic devaluation of life, Arendt sees it as expressing a philosophic hostility to politics. Her desire to "save the phenomena," her insistence that meaning and reality reside *in* the appearances, not behind or above them, follows Nietzsche's revaluation of the world of becoming (Villa 287–88). However, Arendt backs away from the conclusion that Nietzsche drew when he traced the nihilistic logic set in motion by the institutionalization of the Platonic distinction, the 2,000-year process by which the "real world becomes a fable": "We have abolished the real world: what world is left? The apparent world perhaps? . . . But no! with the real world we have abolished the apparent world!" (*Twilight of the Idols* 41). For Nietzsche, try as we might to divorce it from any transcendental signified, our concept of appearances is irreducibly metaphysical. To presume, as Arendt does, that one can hold onto an "objective," shared world of appearances once all anchors to a transcendental reality are cut loose is, ultimately, to remain entangled in the web of metaphysics.

Arendt believes that the reality of the world, of a common space of appearances, is guaranteed as long as this in-between is the arena for spirited debate and deliberation. Where public spirit and "care for the world" animate a community, the *sensus communis* remains strong, providing a nontranscendental ground for action and judgment (Arendt, *Human Condition* 208–9, 274–85; *Between Past and Future* 221; *Lectures on Kant* 66–72). Such a "common feeling for the world" transcends the local, concretely contextual nature of Aristotelian *ethos*; at the same time, it makes no claim to providing a cognitive ground for moral/political judgment. Yet this "feeling for the world" is vulnerable, the easy victim of the modern subjectification of the real that Arendt traces in *The Human Condition* (chap. 6). Hence the mournful Arendtian leitmotif of modern "worldlessness," the peculiar alienation from the world that accompanies the withering away of "common sense."

Here Deleuze's interpretation of Nietzsche and Baudrillard's theorization of simulacra show us how the "loss of the world" remains trapped within the logocentric/metaphysical logic of the sign. From this perspective, Arendt does not overcome the terms, she merely inverts them. The Arendtian public sphere is a space of genuine appearances, of signs whose play and self-referentiality is restricted by their being "seen and heard by everyone." This implies and preserves an opposition between an authentic, real "in-between" and its inauthentic, manipulated counterpart, the former both condition and result of action and speech, the latter nothing more than the proliferation of signs/images, which only serve to destroy further our feeling for the world. Baudrillard's point in "Simulacra and Simulations" is that this way of looking at things, of seeing the "world" as increasingly "dimmed-down" or covered over, does not make a final break with the representational episteme. Postmodernity, on the other hand, has left the "order of appearance" behind: "reality"—which would include the reality of appearances that Arendt wants to preserve—is presently generated as a simulation-effect. The "decisive turning point," Baudrillard states, is "the transition from signs which dissimulate something to signs which dissimulate that there is nothing" (*Selected Writings* 170). Arendt's ontology of the public realm prevents us from seeing just how well and truly lost the world is. Her nostalgia for the "world," for worldliness, is a nostalgia for a common referent—a nostalgia that power is able to exploit for its own ends, in order to "rejuvenate the fiction of the real" (178).

Redrawing the Map: Responses and Repositionings

At the beginning of this essay I suggested that the relation between public realm theory and postmodernism/poststructuralism is more complex than Habermas's mapping of it allows. By starkly opposing the paradigm of the philosophy of consciousness and that of intersubjectivity, Habermas can present postmodernism/poststructuralism as the coda to an exhausted project, the closure of the philosophy of the subject rather than what comes after (*Philosophical Discourse* 296). Public realm theory stands, in contrast, ready to aid in the positive realization of the modern project, abandoning totalizing critique for the new paradigm.[6]

The danger of this polemical opposition is that it blinds us to the possibility of a different configuration. Once we detach the Arendtian conception of the public realm from the problematic that Habermas constructs, a more complex articulation of public realm theory and postmodernism/post-structuralism becomes possible. If we step back from the issues of legitimation and consensus, Arendt's theory reveals a narrative structure that hooks up, in unexpected ways, with the concerns of postmodern/poststructuralist critics.

With respect to Foucault's power objection, one must first acknowledge that Arendt and Foucault are simply talking about different things when they use the word *power*.[7] True, Arendt's related concepts of violence, strength, authority, and so forth are scarcely suited to capture the mechanisms Foucault wants to investigate. Nevertheless, it is obviously inappropriate to presume a common referent here, and then to argue that one theorist gets power "right," the other wrong. More important, however, is that Habermas is wrong to treat Arendt's definition of power—"the ability to act together, to act in concert"—as implying a consensus-centered conception of the public realm. From Arendt's point of view, plurality is not just a condition, but also an *achievement* of political action and speech: these activities give public expression to difference. The theory of political action presented in *The Human Condition* takes as its ideal an agonistic subjectivity that prizes the opportunity for individualizing action. *Contra* Habermas, action is an end in itself: for Arendt, it does not have as its goal the formation of a rational general will. Like Foucault and Lyotard, Arendt fears that the regularization/rationalization of communicative action leads to the creation of docile subjects. Thus, in her discussion of the "modern rise of the social" she states that

> it is decisive that society, on all its levels, excludes the possibility of action, which formerly was excluded from the household. Instead, society expects from each of its members a certain kind of behavior, imposing innumerable and various rules, all of which tend to "normalize" its members, to make them behave, to exclude spontaneous action or outstanding achievement. (*Human Condition* 40)

Once we see Arendt's public realm as a space for agonistic action denatured by the normalizing power of the social, we can make suggestive connections to the Foucauldian story about the takeoff of disciplinary power in the modern age. Arendt hardly shares Foucault's desire to develop a politics of everyday life. Nevertheless, they are both concerned to tell the story of how an essentially theatrical space (the agonistic public realm of Arendt, the premodern public realm of spectacle in Foucault) is colonized by a new form of disciplinary or "socializing" power, a power that substitutes an institutionally dispersed and normalizing regime of panoptic visibility for a centralized space in which *action* is seen and heard by all. The *telos* of this transformation, for both Arendt and Foucault, is the better preservation, cultivation, and management of the state's most precious resource, its populace. There is, I would suggest, a direct line to be drawn from Arendt's conception of the state as "national household" to Foucault's notion of bio-power (*Power/Knowledge* 140–43).

Foucault and Arendt are linked, moreover, by a concern to preserve forms and spaces of popular, spontaneous action ("counter-power") from encroaching bureaucratic structures (compare, for example, Arendt's emphasis on the spontaneous, popular nature of revolutionary action in *On Revolution* (chap. 6) to Foucault's defense of direct forms of popular justice in *Power/Knowledge*) (27–32). Reading Arendt and Foucault in this manner suggests that Arendt's highly specific, exclusive notion of political action is not *contradicted* by Foucault's account of power; rather, it suggests that they present complementary narratives about the closure of the space for action in the modern age. From this standpoint, the Foucauldian concept of "resistance," of local struggle against power/ knowledge regimes, can be seen as a successor concept to Arendt's notion of political action: where the space for action is usurped, where action in the strict sense is *no longer possible*, resistance becomes the primary vehicle of spontaneity and agonistic subjectivity.[8]

The reading I have just sketched moves Arendt's public realm theory from the problematic of legitimation/consensus to that of agonistic subjectivity. The "structures of unimpaired intersubjectivity" that Habermas stresses give way to a performance-centered conception of action, a conception framed in terms of a narrative about the closure of the public space in the modern period. This displacement reveals similar continuities with Lyotard's project. A consistent theme in Arendt's work is the hostility of truth to politics: at no point in her thought on the nature of political action does she embrace moral cognitivism or indicate a belief in *theoretical* criteria that could distinguish a genuine from an inauthentic consensus. For Habermas, the Arendtian repudiation of the will to truth in politics is evidence of an anachronistic (Aristotelian) conception of theory (*Philosophical-Political Profiles* 184). This objection, however, surely misses the point. The reason that Arendt sees "a yawning abyss between knowledge and opinion that cannot be closed by rational argument" is that her conception of political action is antiteleological (Habermas 184). Like Lyotard, she disputes the Habermasian assumption that "the goal of dialogue is consensus." Her account emphasizes action as an end in itself, the *performance* as opposed to the product of *praxis*.

Arendt, then, shares Lyotard's generally agonistic conception of speech: for both, "to speak is to fight, in the sense of playing, and speech acts fall within the domain of a general agonistics" (Lyotard, *Postmodern Condition* 10; cf. Arendt, *Human Condition* 41–42). Moreover, her emphasis on the initiatory dimension of action—"to act . . . means to take an initiative, to begin" (177)—parallels Lyotard's focus upon the speaker's ability and need to create new moves, invent new criteria (Lyotard and Thébaud 61). Arendt views the obsession with forming a rational general will as inevitably normalizing and destructive of plurality. In order to preserve this plurality from the regularizing force of consensus and theory she endorses a "pagan" politics of opinion, of judgment "without criteria." Lyotard's slogan that there can be no "derivation of the political from the theoretical" captures the spirit of Arendt's own vehement anti-Platonism (Lyotard and Thébaud 26–27).

But if Lyotard's idea of a politics founded "on the basis of opinion" seems largely derivative of Arendt, one seemingly irreconcilable difference remains. Lyotard celebrates the fragmentation of the public space; he glories in the heterogeneity that this fragmentation produces. The only criteria of legitimacy he recognizes are local and context-specific, first-order narratives as opposed to metanarratives/metadiscourses. In *Just Gaming* this position brings him very close to identifying the Aristotelian idea of an *ethos* as the sine qua non of a politics "without the Idea of Justice" (26). Arendt, whose own theory of political judgment presents a similar mix of Aristotelian, Kantian, and Nietzschean elements, avoids the relativist consequences of postmodern pluralism by appealing to the Kantian idea of a *sensus communis*, a common feeling for the world, which can provide a nontranscendental basis for judgments making a universal claim of validity (Villa 301–2). Lyotard views the appeal to the *sensus communis* as an act of bad faith: the withering away of common sense in postmodernity means, simply, that "there cannot be a *sensus communis*" (Lyotard and Thébaud 14). According to Lyotard, there is no escaping the fact that *we* "are in the position of Aristotle's prudent individual, who makes judgments about the just and the unjust without the least criterion" (14).

As in the case of Foucault, the opposition here is less dramatic than it first appears. Arendt does not dogmatically assert the existence of "a common feeling for the world" in a last-ditch effort to avoid acknowledging the inescapable fragmentation of the public sphere. If, as with Foucault, we see Arendt as essentially providing a narrative about modernity, then we also can see that she hardly disputes the postmodern assertion that reliance upon the *sensus communis* is no longer possible. The last part of *The Human Condition* is an extended meditation on how the energies of modernity have worked to dissipate our feeling for the world. The "worldliness" presupposed by the *sensus communis* is *not* a distinguishing characteristic of the *animal laborans* and the late modern polity. Indeed, Arendt would go further than Lyotard on this score: the "blurring of boundaries" effected by the modern rise of the social destroys the integrity of language games and local contexts. The ground necessary for anything approximating an *ethos* is lacking (chap. 2, sec. 6, and chap. 3, sec. 17).

This brings us, finally, to the ontological objection. If, as I have suggested, Arendt's public realm theory shares the Foucauldian/Lyotardian concern with the preservation of agonistic subjectivity; if we see her as calling for a politics that stresses plurality, difference, spontaneity, and initiation against the regularizing apparatus of consensus; then the relation between her theory and postmodernism/poststructuralism is quite different from that suggested by the Habermasian mapping. Can a similar "shift" be effected with respect to the ontological objection? I would answer no: here we confront *the* insurmountable difference between Arendt's public realm theory and postmodernism. This difference is not, as some might suggest, the result of a misplaced foundationalism or realism on Arendt's part. Rather, it is a question of profoundly different attitudes toward a single phenomenon, the "deworldling of the world" (to use Heidegger's phrase). Arendt mourns what the postmodern celebrates, the loss of certain ontological dimensions of human existence (action, the shared public world, the self as performance). The postmodern blurring of boundaries, the effacement of any meaningful distinction between the authentic and the inauthentic, reality and its simulacra, renders the Arendtian idea of the phenomenal integrity of a distinctly *political* realm simply nostalgic.[9] Arendt chooses, if not to recover the public realm, to at least preserve its memory; the "affirmative nihilists" of postmodernity wish to have done with such guilty nostalgia, viewing it as one more symptom of essentialism. There is a choice here, but it is not the one offered by Habermas. It is the choice between a politics of mourning and a politics of parody, a politics that remembers the *res publica* and a politics engaged in the endless subversion of codes.

Conclusion: Politics and the Ghost of the Public Sphere

In her essay "Rethinking the Public Sphere," Nancy Fraser criticizes Habermas's conception of the public sphere along lines similar to Foucault. Like him, she is skeptical of Habermas's tendency to view exclusionary practices as perverting, rather than constituting, the bourgeois-liberal model of the public sphere. Drawing upon alternative histories of the public sphere, Fraser shows how, in practice, the "bourgeois public sphere" functions as "the prime institutional site for the construction of the consent that defines the new, hegemonic mode of domination" (62). This hegemonic function is no accident, and the ability of the "bourgeois public sphere" to get the job of legitimation done is facilitated by a set of assumptions built into the ideal of the "public" formulated by Enlightenment political theory and upheld by Habermas. Chief among these assumptions are: (a) the idea that it is possible to create an institutionalized space for discursive interaction in which status differentials are bracketed and actors deliberate "as if" they were social equals; (b) the notion that a single, comprehensive public sphere is to be preferred over a nexus of multiple publics, the proliferation of multiple publics being viewed as a step away from greater democracy (62). Taken together these assumptions make it possible for what Fraser calls a "bourgeois-masculinist" paradigm of deliberation to present itself as neutral and universal: the bourgeois public sphere perpetuates domination via discursive means, monopolizing the space of publicity at the expense of the relatively disempowered.

Fraser chooses, for these reasons, to opt out of the strong normative conception of the public sphere offered by Habermas. She argues, instead, for a more flexible theorization of the public sphere, one that would make room for a plurality of competing publics. Moving from a singular, normative conception of the public sphere to a plural, more phenomenological account would do justice to the very real differences of class, gender, and race and expand our view of available and politically relevant discursive spaces by including "subaltern counterpublics" as crucial alternative forms of publicity (67). *Pace* Habermas, participatory parity is, Fraser believes, better achieved by cultivating multiple publics. Yet the critique of a singular, comprehensive public sphere does not require the embrace of fragmentation or the repudiation of an inclusive, participatory politics. The model proposed by Fraser enables the theorization of a "contestatory interaction of different publics," that is, a view of the public sphere as decentered, highly articulated, and essentially agonistic in its "inter-public" relations (66, 70).

Whether or not one finds Fraser's quasi-Lyotardian attempt to split the difference between postmodernism and public realm theory persuasive, it does serve to highlight one important consequence of Arendt's shift away from the legitimation problematic. For with this shift, the idea of the "public sphere" ceases to function in an essentially normative capacity: public realm theory no longer sets the standards for genuine agreement or a just being-together, except in a minimal and largely negative way (e.g., the prohibition of force and violence). With the abandonment of this (Platonic) paradigm, public realm theory transforms itself into narrative, telling a story that keeps alive the memory of an agonistic public sphere. Narratives such as those offered by Arendt in *The Human Condition* and *On Revolution* enable us to identify practices and spaces that would otherwise be overlooked: wherever we find agonistic spontaneity, resistance, and theatricality, there we find a *political* practice. By promoting the memory of an agonistic public space, public realm theory helps save political phenomena from a "night in which all cats are gray," a night brought on by the closure of the public realm and the postmodern blurring of boundaries.

Fraser's essay points to an alternative beyond the purely mournful or subversive attitudes sketched above. Her vision of a plurality of competing publics reveals how the fragmentation of the public sphere need be neither the cause of mournful withdrawal nor uncritical, "Nietzschean" celebration. If we view contemporary American politics in terms of a proliferation of publics, we see that the task at hand is not rebuilding consensus, recovering shared values, or imposing a civic identity; rather, the task before us is the creation of discursive networks between publics and the expansion of contexts for agonistic subjectivity. We are, it seems to me, at the very beginning of this process, one greatly inhibited by the production and consumption of media spectacle. As long as this circuit monopolizes our "public sphere," the light of the public will, in Heidegger's phrase, obscure everything (*Being and Time* sec. 38).

Arendt agrees with this pessimistic assessment of our current public sphere (*Men in Dark Times* ix). However, the theoretical thrust of her agonistic, pagan view of the public realm is to impel us to seek out new spaces and practices of politics, rather than simply shake our heads at how far we fall beneath the ideal. At the same time, her thought denies us the comforts of a smug postmodern pluralism. The analysis of the "withering away of common sense" underlines the stakes of acting and judging in a world stripped not only of normative "banisters," but also of *worldliness* itself. To uphold the ethos of the agonistic political actor where "care for the world" has been deprived of its phenomenological ground is a sobering burden from which neither apocalypticism nor impertinence will free us.[10]

Notes

I thank Bill Connolly, Fred Dolan, Bob Gooding-Williams, and Austin Sarat for their comments and criticisms.

1. The phrase "an-archic" action, borrowed from Reiner Schürmann, refers to action exempted from the rule of first principles or ends pregiven by reason. See Schürmann 6–11.

2. In this regard see the interview between Foucault and Rabinow, Charles Taylor, Martin Jay, and Richard Rorty in *The Foucault Reader*, ed. Paul Rabinow (New York: Pantheon, 1984), 373–80. Foucault is asked to comment upon the "Arendtian/Habermasian" conception of power (377). His response is minimal: he admits the need to hold onto the notion of "consensual politics" as a regulatory principle, a statement that echoes his view in "The Subject and Power," where he takes a stand against nonconsensual power relations while remaining wary of the concept of consensus *überhaupt*. He fudges the question with specific regard to Arendt by stating that "it seems to me that in many of the analyses that have been made by Arendt, or in any case from her perspective, the relation of domination has been constantly dissociated from the relation of power. Yet I wonder whether this distinction is not something of a verbal one" (378).

3. I should add that Fraser rejects this possibility.

4. Hence Foucault's ambivalent or ironic attitude toward the notion of consensuality. See "On Politics and Ethics" 373–80, and Dumm, "The Politics of Postmodern Aesthetics."

5. This bracketing leads Seyla Benhabib to mount a criticism of Lyotard parallel to Fraser's critique of Foucault. See Seyla Benhabib, "Epistemologies of Postmodernism" 114–15.

6. In fairness to Habermas, it should be noted that this mapping—at least as regards public realm theory—has been largely accepted by postmodernist/poststructuralist critics.

7. Janicaud points out that the critique Habermas offers of Foucault's theory of power substitutes the German *macht* for the French *pouvoir*, thereby eliding the distinction between *puissance* (strength) and *pouvoir* (power). This elision, similarly found in the English translation, facilitates the critique of Foucault as "normatively confused," a charge made by Habermas (*Philosophical Discourse*), Fraser (*Unruly Practices*), and Taylor ("Foucault on Freedom and Truth"). But, as Janicaud points out, *pouvoir* is typically reserved for "specific juridical-political forms and moralities" (284). Thus, while Foucault and Arendt use "power" to designate different phenomena (the juridical-disciplinary apparatus on the one hand, concerted popular action on the other), there is hardly the generalized conflation of power, strength, violence, and so forth in Foucault that some of his critics charge. As he makes clear in a number of places (particularly in "Subject and Power" 220), Foucault is sensitive to the kind of distinctions Arendt makes in "On Violence"; indeed, he considers them essential. The fact that he prefers to call popular action à la Arendt "counter-power" needs to understood against the background of his thesis concerning the ubiquitous, capillary, and productive nature of disciplinary power.

8. I should note that, for Arendt, resistance *is* a form of action. See *Between Past and Future*, Preface.

9. There is an obvious parallel here to Derrida's charge that Heidegger, while deconstructing the metaphysics of presence, nevertheless betrays a nostalgia for presence in his employment of the metaphorics of nearness and farness (of Being). See Derrida, *Of Grammatology* 22, 143; *Margins of Philosophy* 130, 133. For a response to Derrida's critique, see White 65.

10. For the deficiences of postmodern "impertinence" as an ethicopolitical stance, see White.

12 Democracy and Territoriality

William E. Connolly

The New American State

Nothing, it seems, is more un-American than the Hegelian state. The latter embodies world spirit, regulates the market closely, fosters gender inequality, gives collective ethical life priority over individual rights and conscience, and treats the state as the foundation of life, while America embodies pragmatism, the creativity of the market, a struggle for gender equality, the priority of rights over common ends, and a limited government. Yet when it comes to the claim of sovereignty, in both its internal and its external faces, the Hegelian character of the American state becomes manifest. Indeed, today America is the only place in the world that can aspire to be a Hegelian state.

The Hegelian state is a sovereign, self-subsistent whole. The "members" recognize their dependence upon the fundamental substance of the state by giving highest allegiance to it when fundamental issues arise; the state governs all political relations with forces outside its territory; war is an occasion to rescue the internal unity of the state from disruptive influences; and a "world historical state" properly exercises hegemony over other states lacking its significance. The world historical state is, in a sense, the only sovereign state, the only state that secures its own preconditions for self-subsistence by adapting the activities of other states to its priorities.

> The nation to which is ascribed a moment in the Idea . . . is entrusted with giving complete effect to it in the advance of the self-developing

self-consciousness of the world mind. This nation is dominant in world history during this one epoch, and it is only once that it can make its hour strike. In contrast with this its absolute right . . . the minds of other nations are without rights, and they, along with those whose hour has struck already, count no longer in world history. (Hegel, *Philosophy of Right* 218)

The burden of this essay is that most theorists of the American democratic state are far more Hegelian than they acknowledge, that these Hegelian proclivities reflect and exacerbate dangerous currents in American politics, that they specifically threaten the democratic ethos in the late-modern time, and that a timely revivification of the democratic imagination requires a compromise of sovereignty in both its "internal" and its "external" manifestations. We live during a time when asymmetries between the globalization of life and the confinement of democracy to the territorial state foster state chauvinism abroad and the suppression of fundamental issues internally. It is thus necessary to challenge American nostalgia for a "politics of place" in which territoriality, sovereignty, foreign relations, electoral accountability, and belonging correspond to each other in one political place. It is timely to revivify democracy, not by replacing the state that proclaims itself to be the guardian of a new world order with a supersovereign, world democratic state, but through a creative disaggregation of elements in the contemporary democratic imagination, one that extends the democratic ethos beyond the territorial state even while institutions of electoral accountability remain confined within it. To move there from here, it is first necessary to review ways in which the American political unconscious restricts democratic energies to a sovereign, territorial state with world historical responsibilities. It is timely to think critically about how nostalgia for an integral politics of place puts the squeeze on democracy.

The Paradox of Sovereign Democracy

Rousseau understood the founding of a general will to be implicated in paradox. He located the paradox in time (perhaps to imagine another time when it could be resolved):

> In order for an emerging people to appreciate the healthy maxims of politics and follow the fundamental rules of statecraft, the effect would have to become cause; the social spirit, which should be the result of the in-

stitution, would have to preside over the founding of the institution itself; and men would have to be prior to the laws what they ought to become by means of laws. (Rousseau, *The Social Contract* 46)[1]

For a general will to be brought into being, effect (social spirit) would
have to become cause and cause (good laws) would have to become
effect. The problem is how to establish either condition without previous attainment of the other upon which it rests. This is the paradox of
political founding.

But Rousseau then conceals the legacy of this paradox in the operation of the general will after it has been founded by the creative intervention of a wise legislator. If the pure political will is to function as a
regulative ideal (unattainable in actuality but essential as a standard
against which to appraise actuality), the legacy of violence in the founding must be concealed. To note merely one instance of concealment:
Rousseau's artful efforts to legitimize the subordination of women can
be seen, first, to express the necessity of subordination (of either men or
women) within the family so that the will of a unified family can
contribute a single will to the collective quest for a general will, and,
second, to conceal the violence lodged within those practices that secure this effect by treating them as suitable for women as such. The
appearance of a general will (which must be common and singular)
requires the covert subordination of that which would otherwise cloud
its appearance. The strategy succeeds if violence in the founding is
treated by the hegemonic political identity to have no continuing existence in the present: acting as if, for instance, the subordination of
women is both essential to the general will and natural to them, or as if,
on another plane, the systematic violence against indigenous inhabitants in the American founding carries no continuing effects into the
present. The paradox of sovereignty is dissolved into a politics of forgetting. Rousseau's double relation to the paradox of sovereignty is not
unique. It is built into his theory of sovereignty as a self-sufficient
practice.

Paul Ricoeur explicitly delineates this paradox. He reads it as a paradox of politics as such. A political act is legitimate if it reflects the
previous consent (or will or decision or tacit agreement or rational
consensus, etc.) of a sovereign authority (a people, an elected assembly,
a ruler following the dictates of a constitution, etc.). But, Ricoeur persuasively argues, no political act embodies such a standard perfectly
prior to its institution. If it did it would not be a *political* act, but one of
administration or execution; because it does not, a political act always

lacks full legitimacy at the moment of its production. It always invokes in its retrospective justification standards and judgments incompletely thematized and accepted prior to its production. The paradox of politics/sovereignty resides in this temporal gap between act and consent and between the intentions of the act and the effects it engenders; and the temporal gap contains an element of arbitrariness not eliminatable from political life. Ricoeur states the indispensability and corrigibility of political acts through the language of consent: "it is of the nature of political consent, which gives rise to the unity of the human community organized and oriented by the state, to be able to be recovered only in an act which has not taken place, in a contract which has not been contracted, in an implicit and tacit pact which appear as such only in political awareness, in retrospection, and in reflection" ("The Political Paradox" 254).

If Ricoeur is right, the very structure of sovereignty compromises the integrity and coherence that idealists of democratic politics demand. Its logic corresponds to Alice's realization in Wonderland that there is always "jam yesterday and jam tomorrow, but *never* jam today." And it recalls, too, the experience of a "divided will" in Christian conceptions of sin, where the sinning agent is responsible because the will is ones's own, but the will is never completely one's own because it always contains anterior elements evading self-control. If I read Ricoeur correctly, it is not primarily that the practice of sovereignty/politics reveals the human truth of the Christian concept of divided will but that the early Christian conception of will contains a dark premonition of the "labyrinth of politics" that fixes the paradigmatic site of the paradox.[2]

How does one prove (or disprove) the "paradox of sovereignty"? Such an issue is likely never to be settled definitively. But, perhaps the best way to make the case for its persistence and significance is to examine paradigmatic studies that presuppose its absence and then run into difficulties because they do so.

(Schumpeterian) Realism and (Walzerian) Idealism

Joseph Schumpeter has widely been treated as a "father" of American, realist theories of democracy. Criticisms of his theory, elaborated in the United States during the 1960s, concentrated on its reduction of democracy to a method for electing officials, its demolition of the common good, and its devaluation of participation as a means to educate citizens to the common good.[3] Schumpeter does criticize theories of the common good and the general will. But he does not quite reduce democracy to a method.

The "general will" cannot express the will of the people, says Schumpeter. Rather, it is the effect of strategic and rhetorical devices such as "affective reasoning," "reiterated assertion," "evasions," "principles of association," the "psycho-technics" of exalting "certain propositions into axioms" and putting "others out of court." In manufacturing a general will, leaders deploy "pleasant associations . . . of a sexual nature"; they associate their objectives with "pretty girls"; they draw upon "ideology," "sentimentality," and "fits of vindictiveness"—to create a common will, or, at least, to "manufacture" the majority will they purport to follow. This is all "realistic," since it is simultaneously impossible to discover a general will as the "classic theorists of democracy" imagined it and impossible in modern life to achieve legitimate rule for long without subjecting potential leaders to competitive elections.

Still, this demolition of the general will as the magic source of democratic legitimacy does not reduce Schumpeterian democracy to a mere method for electing officials. The method must still be legitimated. Schumpeter legitimates it by calling it a rational mode of governance, more closely, by condemning conceptions of democracy that involve popular activism and agitation as irrational and by supporting the sober, cool, detached governance of leaders accountable to citizens only on election day. Throughout his textualization of the irrational production of the general will flows a subtext of contrast to rational democratic governance. Thus, in the manufacture of a general will, "there is indeed nearly always some appeal to reason. But mere assertion, often repeated, counts more than rational argument and so does the direct attack upon the sub-conscious, which takes the form of . . . pleasant associations of an entirely extra-rational character" (Schumpeter 257).

Schumpeter invokes a specific code of rationality to vindicate a realist democratic method. The method contains a variety of rules such as the imperative of periodic elections, the necessity of slogans in electoral competition, the insulation of governors from the vicissitudes of public opinion between elections so that they can promote the "long-term interest," a split between foreign and domestic policy that insulates leaders even further from the electorate, the cultivation of an independent civil service, the education of citizens into the wisdom of patience and forbearance between elections, and so forth. Just to take one example: "The voters . . . must respect the division of labor between themselves and the politicians they elect. They must not withdraw confidence too easily between elections and they must understand that, once they have elected an individual, political action is his business and not theirs" (Schumpeter 295). These are the musts of political rationality, and deviation from them is irrational. Now that a code of rationality has displaced the general will as the core of democratic politics, how is this code redeemed?

The text does not iterate a conception of rationality and then show how it succeeds in placing these conclusions on the upper side of a divide between rational and irrational government. Rather, it places rationality, bosses, experts, "words as bullets," maturity, efficiency, periodic elections, the insulation of elites, and the national interest alone one line of equivalences and domestic politics, vote trading, sexual associations, reiteration, sentimentality, fits of vindictiveness, the general will, manipulation, indulgence, voters, evasion of reality, "the nursery," repetition, and "degeneration of foreign policy into domestic politics" along another as a contrary set of equivalences.

How is each item associated with the others on its line and each line differentiated from the other? By the same ("extra-rational") tactics Schumpeter detected in the production of the general will. Items on the first list are unified by a traditional code of masculinity (bosses, bullets, maturity, efficiency, etc.) that is never named but always insinuated, while those on the second are united by a corollary code of femininity (pretty girls, vote trading, reiteration, sentimentality, fits of vindictiveness, indulgence, evasion, etc.). The text is sprinkled with formulations of the following sort: a "rational treatment" of crime "requires that legislation . . . should be protected from both the fits of vindictiveness and the fits of sentimentality in which the laymen in the government and in the parliament are alternatingly prone to indulge" (Schumpeter 292).

Capitalism, Socialism, and Democracy exalts a realist model of political rationality by enclosing it within a traditional cultural code of masculinity, and it exalts political realism by associating it with this masculinist economy of rationality. It then contrasts this network of associations with a feminine line of associations equilibrated through inversion of the same tactics. This intertextualization of political rationality and masculinity follows the same logic that Schumpeter identifies in the production of the general will: it "attempts to evoke and crystallize pleasant associations of an entirely extra-rational, very frequently sexual nature." Here, too, "we find the same evasions and reticences and the same trick of producing opinion by reiterated assertion that is successful precisely to the extent it avoids rational argument" (Schumpeter 254, 263). The text deploys feminine stratagems to produce the superiority of masculine equivalences, inadvertently revealing the dependence of masculine/realist/rationalist equivalencies on a feminine practice of equilibration said to be alien to them. Schumpeter is a cross-dresser with a deep voice. He is a realist.

The realist textualization of democracy forgets the paradox of politics by slipping a silver bullet of political rationality into the opening just vacated by the general will. To reiterate (yes): democratic realism instantiates masculine rationality through feminine strategems while simultaneously denying the indispensability of these tactics through masculinist imperatives. It conceals the paradox (the gaps) it opens by recourse to tactics it ridicules.

Michael Walzer's *Spheres of Justice* opposes this valorization of universal reason. It evinces suspicion of any powerful drive to universalization, whether Schumpeterian, Kantian, or Rawlsian in character. It unfolds through the warm words of plurality, diversity, spheres, complex equality, membership, belonging, shared understandings, and connected intellectuals, contrasting these spherical shelters to a barren world of abstract reason, external standards, simple equality, strangers, and disconnected intellectuals who would insert standards "from nowhere." If Walzer forgets/evades the paradox of politics it cannot be in the name of Schumpeterian standards. For Schumpeter imposes, while Walzer belongs.

Walzer views the democratic state through the optics of a plurality of "spheres" such as the market, the family, education, religion, medical care, and citizenship, each with internal understandings of justice in its sphere that can be brought to bear whenever (a) an injustice is discovered within it or (b) its internal principles illicitly leak into other spheres. Thus: selling consumer goods is fine, but selling votes or sex exceeds the bounds of justice; the home is a place of privacy, but its confines must not become an excuse to exclude children from education; intellectuals are judged by reasonable standards of scholarship but not by standards of faith and heresy appropriate to a religion. These delineations, richly developed and exemplified, will play a role in any theory that evinces respect for diversity and individuality in contemporary life.

The book, however, is replete with general qualifications not applied to particular cases and particular criticisms/concessions not allowed to accumulate to disperse its central theme. No detailed accounting can be presented here. But a series of fundamental divisions between having a job and pursuing a career, between having a high school education or less and having a college education or more, between being constituted as a normal adult and as abnormal in some way, between being a black male in the inner city and a white male in the suburbs, between being a criminal and a law-abiding member of the community, and between being an illegal alien and a citizen—these fundamental breaks scramble the spheres both as descriptions of actuality and as norms capable of integrating outcasts, abnormals, marginal workers, and aliens. Constituencies that bring a couple of these liabilities to a particular sphere encounter expectations, resentments, demands, and cruelties that demean, confine, and depoliticize them systemically. Explorations of these divisions might preserve the idea that different standards of justice come into play in different domains of life, but it would also disperse the warm vocabulary of membership, spheres, belonging, and shared understandings through which the Walzerian textualization of contemporary life proceeds. The world of spheres is cracked.

Two themes in this book do the most to conceal paradox and to confine the scope of democratic energies. They revolve, first, around the presentation of "shared understandings" and, second, around the delineation of the master line dividing the world inside the state from the one outside. Shared understandings do for Walzer what political rationality did for Schumpeter. They reinstate sufficient standards of judgment jeopardized by the devaluation of abstract rationality; they provide the glue that holds each sphere together; and they contain this spherized diversity within the boundaries of the territorial state. Belonging not only protects you from a cold world, but also it provides you with bearings through which to be a moral agent within the warm world of the state.

Walzer must locate enough coherence in the understandings of each sphere to provide "us" with sufficient leverage to identify a set of "violations" and "deviations" within it, and (though this is not emphasized) this coherence must then be compelling enough ethically so that "we" do not feel compelled to oppose the standards identified. This delicate distribution of emphasis is discernible in a summary statement advanced in *Political Theory* shortly after publication of the book:

> We can say that a (modern, complex, differentiated) society enjoys both freedom and equality when success in one institutional setting isn't convertible into success in another, that is, when the separations hold, when political power doesn't shape the church or religious zeal the state, and so on. There are, of course, constraints and inequalities within each institutional setting, but we will have little reason to worry about them if they reflect the internal logic of institutions and practices (or as we have already argued in *Spheres of Justice*, if social goods like grace, knowl-

edge, wealth, and office are distributed in accordance with shared understandings of what they are and what they are for). But all too often the
separations don't hold. (Walzer, "Liberalism and the Art of Separation"
321)

How is this textual balance maintained? Consider an example in the
territory of crime, punishment, and imprisonment. "Similarly, our understanding of the purpose of a prison (and the meaning of punishment
and social roles of judges, wardens, and prison guards) sets limits to the
exercise of power within its walls. I am sure those limits are often
violated" (Walzer, *Spheres of Justice* 289). A statement about prison
walls itself divided by a grammatical wall. "Our," "purpose," "understanding," and "limits" are placed on one side; "I," "am sure," "violated," and "often" on the other. The dominant theme locates laudatory
standards in shared understandings; the subtheme communicates a
subtext of realism in Walzer's understanding. The subtheme is communicated under his breath, so to speak, to the very constituency ("us")
who putatively share the first set of understandings. The grammatical
wall stems the flow of understandings to knowledge, of norm to violation, and of our to us; but it also allows them to seep surreptitiously
through this barrier to the other side. The Walzerian wall is a membrane. This porous wall, created by a period and a one-eighth-inch gap
on the printed page, gives Walzer the kind of deniability/implication
with respect to our shared understandings that wardens and police
chiefs practice with respect to prison and police violence. For *everyone*
"is sure" that these "understandings" are "often violated," broken so
regularly and systematically that the logic of violations forms part of
the understandings. We, like Walzer, live on both sides of the Walzerian
wall between understandings/knowledge, I/we, practices/violations;
our understandings, like his, contain a series of walls/membranes
within them.

There are, for instance, nationally televised programs in which juve-
nile offenders are graphically informed by hardened prisoners exactly
what will happen to them inside those walls if they are sent to prison.
"We" view these programs, ambivalently rooting for the youths to get
the message and for the prospective agents of revenge to teach them a
lesson if they fail to do so. This folk wisdom—this shared understanding—of prison life forms part of the strategy of deterrence by the state;
it functions, too, to construct walls of sentiment dividing those outside
prison walls from those inside.

An alternative formulation might read:

> Our understanding of the purpose of a prison . . . simultaneously sets
> limits to the exercise of power within it and sanctions deniable violence
> behind its walls. The walls perform a triple function for us: they protect
> us from offenders; they organize our ambivalences about crime and
> punishment into a psychically tolerable structure; and they offer us de-
> niability during those rare moments when prison violence becomes too
> visible to ignore.

The revised formulation—breaking down walls that Walzerian grammar constructs—intensifies pressure to respond in new ways to old
ambivalences. It carries Foucauldian resonances. It might press some of
us to pull further away from the old "we" in our interpretations and
proposals; this reconstituted "we" might listen more closely to muffled
sounds behind prison walls, partly so we can better hear ambivalences
outside them too. We might engage more actively the powerful role that
revenge and resentment play in practices of crime, responsibility, punishment, and imprisonment; and we might ponder more closely how
prevailing spheres of understanding foment and channel these powerful
forces.[4]

What one could no longer do is assert easily that shared understandings suffice to characterize prison violence as a "violation," a violation
that would be removed once a preestablished "we" is informed of it and
lives up to its understanding. These walls—and thus those gaps—exist within the understanding. They are not exterior to it. "We" must
change ourselves to reconfigure the walls, and vice versa. With that
recognition we find ourselves contesting some dimensions of prison
practice/understanding.[5] In doing so, our operational conception of
politics becomes more complex, less colonizable by the discourse of
belonging, sharing, connectedness, and spheres. We remain implicated
in practices we endorse or contest, but not in a way that coordinates
smoothly with belonging and sharing. Shared understandings no longer
cover political life with a blanket; the gaps, porosities, and ambivalences they contain become constitutive elements in politics. So do the
textual strategies by which they are consolidated and concealed.

Walzerian "understandings" protect the legitimacy of his normative
vision by attributing it to us; its attribution to us proceeds through a
series of divisions and excisions that conceal/forget the paradox of
politics.[6] But Walzerian understandings are not bound by time alone.
They are also bounded in space. The spheres protect horizontal divisions within the state, but the territorial state establishes a more basic
division between its inside and its outside. Here are formulations that
construct this wall of walls:

The primary good that we distribute to one another is membership in some human community. And what we do with regard to membership structures all our other distributive choices: it determines with whom we make those choices, from whom we require obedience and collect taxes, to whom we allocate goods and services.

Statelessness is a condition of infinite danger.

(W)e who are already members do the choosing, in accordance with our own understanding of what membership means in our community and of what sort of community we want to have.

What precisely [strangers] owe to one another is by no means clear, but we commonly say that positive assistance is required if (1) it is needed or urgently needed by one of the parties; and (2) if the risks and costs of giving it are relatively low for the other party. . . . This is our morality; conceivably his too.

Here I only want to point to mutual aid as a (possible) external principle for the distribution of membership. . . . The force of the principle is uncertain, in part because of its own vagueness, in part because it comes up against the internal force of social meanings. And these meanings can be specified . . . through the decision-making processes of the political community. (Walzer, *Spheres of Justice* 31–34)

The text explores fruitfully a variety of difficulties that arise when a state debates its terms of membership. But the line of demarcations it constructs between we/them, inside/outside, protection/danger, community/stranger, and our morality/conceivably his is not confined to this issue. Inside the wall of walls there is the rich, warm world of we, community, primary goods, membership, internal understandings, our morality, meanings, distributive mechanisms, mechanisms of state security, democratic accountability, obligations, and obediences. On the other side there are alternative worlds of strangers, danger, external principles, uncertain obligations of mutual aid, and conceivable moralities. Many of these others live in other states (with, conceivably, their own warm meanings that are luke-cold to us), while others of these others exist in the infinite coldness of statelessness. But not very much connects either set to us politically, morally, temporally. That's just the way it is, baby. The very thought of democratic currents flowing over state lines draws the Walzerian mind back to the (hopeless) issue of *timeless* principles.

This fusion of shared understandings with the territorial state as the fundamental unit of political membership constitutes the Walzerian space for democratic action. Beyond this boundary there are interstate and state/stateless relations. But not democratic politics.[7] Since the hypothetical alternatives overtly conceived to this division are the anarchy of a universal market without states or the oppression of a world state, the reader (in a rich, powerful, democratic state) settles back into the comforting rhetoric of democratic politics inside a territorial state governed by shared understandings and common principles of membership. The threat of anarchy and coldness outside intensifies the pressure, first, to treat "shared understandings" as sufficient standards of political judgment within the state and, second, to treat the territorial state as the highest unit of political loyalty, identification, and democratic participation.

This representation of a wall guarding the warm inside from the cold outside occludes ways in which the outside forms part of the inside in many contemporary states. In the United States, for example, there is a third world inside every city (the "inner city") that corresponds rather closely to the third world outside the state. And the policies that the state applies to its external/internal world of third-world minorities, drug addicts, criminals, welfare clients, and homeless wanderers approximates those it applies to the third world outside.[8] There is also a discernible affiliation between "shared understandings" applied by dominant constituencies to outsiders both inside and outside the borders of the state. The earlier reflection on prison life exemplifies this. But such a proliferation of inside/outside divisions does not mesh smoothly with the presumption of alignment among belonging, territory, state, sovereignty, and shared understandings.

We are now in a position to gather these bits and pieces together by asking, How do Rousseau, Schumpeter, and Walzer stand with respect to Ricoeur's paradox? Ricoeur poses powerful objections to the sufficiency of general will, political rationality, and shared understandings in these respective presentations of democracy and sovereignty. These constructions function to conceal the paradox of politics; they depoliticize life just where a more active politicization is needed. But, when it comes to the wall dividing democratic politics inside the state from the outside, Ricoeur joins Rousseau, Schumpeter, and Walzer in underlining the boundary of the territorial state (numerous others could be named on this latter list—including my former self—but who's counting?). Walzer, indeed, is almost the only one among contemporary political theorists who explicitly tries to justify the boundary.

None of the theorists on this list considers the possibility of disaggregating the democratic imaginary so that democratic energies already exceeding the boundaries of the state might be mobilized and legitimized more actively. All, moreover, give too much priority within the state to practices of democratic rule; none gives sufficient attention to the positive role played by a *democratic politics of disturbance* in projecting new challenges to old relations of identity and difference, disrupting the dogmatism of settled understandings, and exposing violences and exclusions in fixed arrangements of democratic rule. The "internal" pluralism of each—admirable to the differential extent it is elaborated, with Rousseau at one end and Ricoeur/Walzer at the other—is too closed in its internal articulation and too dichotomous in its definition of externality.

The Democratization of Territorial Security

If political theory is the academic field where questions of individuality, loyalty, community, rights, belonging, democracy, justice, and freedom are debated inside the contours of the state, international relations is the field where diplomacy, subversion, order through anarchy, war, low-intensity conflict, economic interdependence, diplomacy, and national security are observed through the optics of interstate relations. It is not just the differences between them but how these two fields produce one another that now requires attention.

John Herz provides an illuminating example here because he wrote one book focusing on the declining role of territoriality in the politics of security and then another essay taking much of the first study back. These two studies, when juxtaposed to the three theories of territorial democracy just reviewed, expose the tenacity of state territorialization in contemporary politics. They may also inadvertently expose a need to pluralize the spatializations of democratic practice.

The first Herzian analysis seeks to maintain coherence between epistemic realism and political realism while calling the strategic/political primacy of territoriality into question.[9]

> What is it, ultimately, that accounted for the peculiar unity, coherence, or compactness of the modern nation-state, setting it off from other nation-states as a separate unit and permitting us to characterize it as an "independent," "sovereign," "power"? It would seem that this underlying something is to be found neither in the sphere of law, nor even in that of politics, but rather in the ultimate, and lowest, substratum where the state unit confronts us, in, as it were, its physical corporeal capacity: as

an expanse of territory, encircled for its identification and defense by tangible, military expressions of statehood, life fortifications, and fortresses. (Herz, *International Politics in the Atomic Age* 40)

The epistemic realism of this passage is contained within the terms *underlying, ultimate, lowest, substratum, physical corporeal capacity, tangible*. These contrast to surface, secondary, ideational, incorporeal, and intangible dimensions lodged, apparently, in such practices as law, sovereignty, democracy, and ideology.[10] The key to the consolidation of the territorial state between the sixteenth century and the middle of the twentieth century resided in its growing capacity to protect populations inside these borders from external enemies. The state became "the ultimate unit of protection" because in the long run people "will recognize that authority, any authority, which possesses this power of protection" (Herz, *International Politics* 40–41).

The state became a sovereign unit because it was able to create a relatively "impermeable shell" around its territory; other virtues of the state, including its provision of possible space for democratic institutions, flow from this: "everything . . . reflects the internal pacification of the new territorial state and its external defensibility" (Herz, *International Politics* 52).

But by 1959 the old link between territory and security had broken. The old-world system depended upon vast "open" (!) areas outside the European theater of sovereign states, areas that were open to exploration, exploitation, and colonization by dominant states.[11] Also, in the old days (within "the family" of states) states were often defeated, but seldom "wiped out as such." Since World War II, though, a state can be wiped out due to advances in military hardware; and the motive to do so expands with the depletion of virgin areas for colonization. The emergence of new ideologies that stretch across territorial lines makes states more vulnerable to unrest fomented from outside, and international media of communication ("radio broadcasting") exacerbate this process. The introduction of "air war" is pivotal: "With it . . . the roof blew off the territorial state" (Herz, *International Politics* 104). And, finally, the possibility of nuclear devastation has upset the whole logic of state security through territorial impermeability. "Now that power can destroy power from center to center everything is different" (Herz, *International Politics* 108). In general, the postwar state cannot establish its economic self-sufficiency, national security, or ideological unity with the same confidence it did in the past.

These tendencies toward state interdependence and boundary permeability have intensified radically since 1959. Nonetheless, by 1967 Herz withdrew most of the political implications he had detected in these patterns. Against his expectation, the old territoriality failed to dissolve into collective security and international organizations. Rather, a "new territoriality" inscribed itself rapidly upon the old and extended itself into new areas; everywhere the "territorial urge and the urge to maintain (or establish or regain) one's 'sovereignty' and 'independence'" (re)asserted themselves (Herz, "The Territorial State Revisited" 15).

Here is the new Herzian analysis of territorialization in a nutshell: A "nation" is at home with itself only if it governs itself; nation-states need internal legitimacy to promote stability, external security, and economic efficiency; the most legitimate mode of self-governance today is democracy; and modern democracy must be organized within a bounded territory if it is to be. Thus the new territoriality becomes an effect of causes it used to produce. Here are a few formulations expressing these linkages:

> In a positive way, nations, in order to be effective actors in international relations, must prove to be "legitimate" units, that is, entities which . . . can be . . . considered as basic and "natural" for the fulfillment of essential purposes, such as protection and welfare of the people. (Herz, "Territorial State Revisited" 21)

> What, then, renders a nation-state legitimate? Legitimacy originates from feelings and attitudes of the people within as well as neighbors and others abroad in regard to the unit, its identity and coherence, its political and general "way of life." (Herz, "Territorial State Revisited" 24)

> Being compelled to fight for or defend one's territory generates true nationhood. (Herz, "Territorial State Revisited" 25)

> *Internal* legitimacy (without which . . . the unit as such can provide little solidity) in our day is closely related to democracy in the broad sense of people having the conviction that they control their destinies and that government operates for their welfare. (Herz, "Territorial State Revisited" 25)

And so you have it. Herz and Walzer. Schumpeter and Herz. Sovereignty and democracy. Legitimacy and security. Nostalgic realism and nostalgic idealism. Nationality and shared understandings. The democratization of territorial security. The stratification of democratic identity. All grounded in the mystique of territorial democracy. The pull of the democratic imaginary holds the territory together despite those (un)real forces that threaten to blow its roof off. Herz, Walzer, and Schumpeter together produce correspondences among state, territoriality, nationality, sovereignty, democracy, belonging, and legitimacy. Do they conceal/forget gaps, cruelties, exclusions, and dislocations within this set of correspondences?

Today the territorial/security state forms the space of democratic liberation and imprisonment. It liberates because it organizes democratic accountability through electoral institutions. It imprisons because it confines and conceals democratic energies flowing over and through its dikes. The confinement of democracy to the territorial state—to a (paradoxical) sovereign place where (ambiguous) understandings (dis)organize the common life—consolidates and exacerbates pressures to exclusive nationality. Every protean nation demands a state, and every state strives to become a nation—often in the name of territorial democracy. If competing demands for nationhood do not fit well together on the same territory—they often do not, as the examples of Ireland, Israel, South Africa, Spain (the Basques), Maine, Canada, Iraq/Turkey/Syria (the Kurds) and states of the former Soviet Union testify—a crisis is fomented or a set of suppressions is transcribed into the background noise of territorial politics. And in more settled territorial democracies, when the reach of issues affecting people exceeds its bounds, the stomach of the state digests the excess into strategic interests, diplomatic issues, or political excrement. The territorial state too often stifles democratic energies or translates them into national chauvinist sentiments.

The Disaggregation of Democracy

What these theorizations of territorial democracy by Rousseau, Ricoeur, Schumpeter, Walzer, and Herz share is the demand that all the elements of the democratic imaginary fit together on the same space. This is the imperative that imprisons democracy through state territorialization. But if the practice of modern democracy involves shared understandings, formal institutions of electoral accountability, and the capacity to act in concert within a sovereign state, does it not therefore require state territorialization to be? Yes and no. Yes, institutions of electoral accountability do form a key condition of democracy, and the territorial state is the modern site upon which this institutionalization is built; but, no, institutions of electoral accountability do not exhaust the affirmative possibilities built into a democratic ethos.

Democracy does not require shared understandings in the storng sense of that phrase, but—as I have already suggested—it needs public spaces and points of reference through which issues can be defined and pressures for action can be organized. Democracy, moreover, is a form of *rule* or *governance*, but it is much more than that as well: It is an egalitarian constitution of cultural life that encourages people to participate in defining their own troubles and possibilities, regardless of where these troubles originate and how narrow or broad they are in scope; it is, moreover, an ethos through which newly emerging constellations might reconstitute identities previously impressed upon them, thereby disturbing the established priorities of identity/difference through which social relations are organized; it is, therefore, a social process through which fixed identities and naturalized conventions are pressed periodically to come to terms with their constructed characters, as newly emergent social identities disturb settled conventions and denaturalize social networks of identity and difference; it is, thereby, a distinctive culture in which many constituencies respond politically and affirmatively to modern pressures to problematize those final markers (God, natural law, the divine right of kings, the natural basis of traditional identities, a fictive contract) that might have governed their foremothers and fathers, a political culture in which a variety of constituencies responds affirmatively to uncertainties, diversities, heterogeneities, and paradoxes of late-modern life by participating in the construction and reconstruction of their own identities.

Democracy is, among other things, an affirmative cultural/political response to the problematization of final markers that marks the late-modern condition. It contests authoritarian and totalitarian modes of response to this same condition because they draw upon contemporary instruments of surveillance, repression, and social mobilization to reinstate coercively old markers or their new equivalents.[12] It treats the contestation of final markers as a contribution to freedom, self-formation, and self-governance among constituencies no longer required to believe that how they have been constituted historically is what nature requires them to be. And it cultivates a politics of agonistic respect among multiple constituencies who respond differentially to mysteries of being while acknowledging each other to be worthy of respect partly because they are implicated in *this* common condition. A democratic ethos balances the desirability of governance through democratic means with a corollary politics of democratic disturbance through which any particular pattern of previous settlements might be tossed up for grabs again.

The ethos of democracy, understood in these terms, has territorial/institutional conditions of existence, but it also embodies a crucial cultural disposition: at least a significant minority of those implicated in it understand that the porous understandings they share rest upon contestable foundations, that there are numerous differences among them grounded in a matrix of uncertainty, and that a laudatory way to respond to these uncertain commonalities and shared uncertainties is to cultivate respect for a politics of democratic governance and contestation that limits ways in which contested changes are to be initiated and disturbed traditions are to be retained. The ethos of democracy both fosters a perpetual problematization of final markers (for they constantly tend to reinstate themselves) and foments a culture of agonistic respect among those who *affirm* this "alienated" world.

The key to a culture of democratization is that it embodies a productive ambiguity at its very center, never allowing one side or the other to achieve final victory: *its role as a mode of governance is balanced and countered by its logic as a cultural medium of denaturalization of settled identities and conventions.* In a world where the paradox of politics is perpetually susceptible to forgetfulness, there is a perpetual case to be made on behalf of renewing democratic energies of denaturalization.[13] For if the second dimension of democracy ever disappeared under the weight of the first, state mechanisms of electoral accountability would become conduits for fascist unity.[14]

The copula in the above formulations condenses a host of contestable issues into the rhetoric of assertion. This is my condensation of the democratic imaginary in which we participate differentially. My formulation intersects with those that link democracy to political paradox in governance, to the problematization of final markers, and to maintenance of productive tension between the functions of governance and disturbance. It deviates from those that give singular hegemony to democracy as a mode of rule, sufficiently governed by shared understandings or timeless principles, confined within the borders of a sovereign state. In defense of my "is," I can say that these expectations float within the ethos of democracy wherever it has established a significant cultural presence, and that, when thematized, these elements are likely to be appreciated by many in themselves and in their close connections to other valued dimensions of democratic life.

To disaggregate elements in the democratic imaginary is to identify features that can exceed its state territorialization. Territorial democracy and the pluralization of democratic spaces are drawn together today through mutual relations of dependence, but the scope of the second is not strictly confined by the spatial institutionalization of the first. Some elements in the democratic ethos can extend beyond the walls of the state.

Take social movements. A gay/lesbian rights movement, for instance, challenges the dominant configuration of gender and sexual identity by striving to reconstitute definitions of difference through which those identities are secured. To the extent that it succeeds, "heterosexuals" are less able to assume that their sexual orientations reflect nature or normality, more pressed to acknowledge the role of contingency in the formation of sexual identity, less able to find grounds for discriminating against gays or lesbians on a variety of fronts. A gay rights movement is not impelled to halt at the boundaries of a particular state. Activists may extend the movement beyond the state, establishing alliances with others of similar orientation in a variety of states, developing connections across state lines that exert pressure on those states that imprison gays or treat them as psychologically abnormal or disqualify them as teachers, parents, soldiers, or intelligence agents. It might, for instance, press financial institutions that invest in homophobic states to divest those holdings. It might hold international conferences that expose globally homophobic state/corporate policies, publicizing the fragility of the evidence upon which these practices are based as well as the injuries and cruelties they impose, and mobilizing new energies inside and outside particular states against these practices. It might exert pressure on a nonstate, cross-national organization such as Amnesty International to expand its scrutiny of states engaging in torture and political detention to include those that imprison or punish individuals for homosexuality.

Or take state secrecy. To the extent that states classify political information, they deprive citizens of knowledge needed to hold officials accountable. But democratic pressures against secrecy inside any particular state are blunted by the state's monopoly over the classification process and political symbols of allegiance, danger, and security. Global, nonstate political organizations can increase knowledge of state secrecy and its effects by drawing together a variety of locals who are objects of these practices or witnesses to them. These cross-national, nonstate networks of information and leads dig global channels through which to publicize state practices of secrecy and manipulation, helping to delegitimate them in several states simultaneously. They crack through the walls of the state. Such a nonstate, international movement might help to invigorate democratic energies within states, exert external pressure upon the secret practices of states, and contribute to destatification of the symbols of danger and security in the late-modern time.

And such issues can be proliferated indefinitely, engaging the state's monopoly over definitions of security and danger, gender rights, nuclear proliferation, the earth's ecological balances, the production of poverty, state immigration policies, and so on. Cross-national, nonstate democratic movements not only exert internal/external pressures upon states and corporations with respect to specific issues, but they also challenge a state's monopoly over the allegiances, identifications, and energies of its members. They ventilate democratic politics inside the state by extending action beyond it. They scramble the constitution of the inside by extending identifications to constituencies inside and outside. Most fundamentally, such movements contest the cultural assumption of alignment between a citizen's commitment to democracy and her commitments to the priorities of a particular state, thereby attenuating those nationalist sentiments flowing from the state as the only legitimate site of democratic action. To the extent such movements unfold—taking advantage of the globalization of markets, transportation, and communications that enable them to be—a fundamental imperative of the late-modern time becomes more apparent to more people: today a decent democrat must sometimes be disloyal to the state that seeks to own her morally and politically; and she must sometimes do so in the name of allegiances to a global condition that transcends the confines of any state. As things stand now, corporate elites, financial institutions, criminal networks, communication media, and intelligence agencies exercise considerable independence in this regard. Only democratic citizens remain locked behind the bars of the state in the late-modern time.

But, it might reasonably be objected, if the democratic state does not form the only space of political allegiance and identification (the place of "belonging," the site of "shared understandings"), what else does? Timeless principles and standards seem too abstract and general to perform this function sufficiently. (These insufficiencies inspired the reformulations by Walzer and Herz.) An appropriate response requires first a critique of the question. Theories (and practices) of pluralism *within* the state acknowledge how loyalties move from one place to another as issues and concerns shift. You may be loyal to the faith of your church, but not necessarily to its legal proposals in the domains of capital punishment, abortion, or gender relations. You may be loyal to your union with respect to the issue of dues checkoff, but not necessarily to its endorsement of candidates for election. Similarly, with respect to the state, one might be loyal to its institutionalization of democratic elections and to rights it endorses constitutionally, but not to its war policies, its strategic course, its classification practices, its resources dependencies, its constitution of criminality, or its ecological practices. Most pertinently, there is no a priori reason why deep differences with respect to these state priorities must be expressed only within the parameters of state politics. In a multidimensional, pluralist world, every particular allegiance is contingent because the occasion might occur when it collides with another one you have found to be even more fundamental at this time.

But where is the place that might, if not supplant loyalty to the state, compete with it so that sometimes a new "we" finds itself bestowing allegiance to constituencies and aspirations in ways that contest the state's monopoly over political allegiance? There is no such place—at least if "place" is implicitly defined through the optics of political nostalgia. Today, though, a series of new we's might come to terms with limitations to democratic action generated by the demand for symmetry between state-territory and democratic institutions. We might extend political identifications to a distinctive *global time* that impinges upon us in fundamental ways even while it is not organized into a (non)soverign political place. We match the understanding of how sovereignty has been traditionally overplayed as a coherent practice within the state to one that appreciates how it poses too stringent a limitation to identifications and loyalties extending beyond it.

Late modernity is a distinctive political time without a corresponding place of collective political accountability. It is marked by the globalization of markets, communications, monetary exchanges, transportation, disease transmission, strategic planning, acid rain, greenhouse effects, resource depletion, terrorist activity, drug trade, nuclear threats to civilization, and tourism—just to list a familiar miscellany. Late modernity is not brand-new in these respects. Its distinctiveness is that in its time these interactions have become intensed, extended, and interlocked more tightly, while the speed at which the whole complex circulates has accelerated. The web of the world is spun smaller, tighter, closer, and faster than it used to be. We all impinge upon each other more densely and actively than we did in the past, and the numerous networks of discordant interdependencies in which we are implicated generate aggregate effects with impressive consequences for the global future. Moreover, there are distinctive cultural developments in the late-modern time, with respect to the problematization of final markers, the generalization of the drive to economies of rapid growth, the spread of democratic aspirations, the rise of nationalist sentiments, the drives to universalize rights, the tendencies of states to monopolize symbols of danger and democracy, and so forth. These trends intersect with those interdependencies densely enough to provide global democrats, not with shared understandings to realize, but with convergent points of reference through which timely political issues can be defined and pursued. They provide the need and the condition of possibility—not for the globalization of democratic elections or the liquidation of territorial democracy—but for the pluralization of democratic energies, alliances, and spaces of action that exceed the closures of territorial democracy.

To refuse to develop political allegiances and identifications with this global time as a time would be to fail to elevate democratic sensibilities and spaces of action to levels reached by other components of late-modern life. That would be unrealistic democratism. To define timely global and regional issues is to identify with others living in this time through political engagements that cross the boundaries of states. It is to recognize—and to legitimize the recognition—that today democratic politics flow below, through, and above the level of the state.

The extrastate pluralization of democratic spaces stands to the state today as state-territorial organization stood to city-states in sixteenth-century Italy or feminism stood to the structure of gender relations as recently as the early 1960s. It is protean, unformed, and unrealistic from the perspective of fixed identities and conventional boundaries. Epistemic realists will always find it difficult to conceptualize new energies if they demand the solidification of possibilities into fixed objects prior to representation in their theories.

The aura of unreality in the extension of democratic energies resides in the inevitable inchoateness from which new formations are (sometimes) created out of old identities, spaces, and energies. But one aspect of this cloudy condition can be addressed now. Culturally stabilized terms of comparison between territorial democracy and extrastate democratization can be revalued by coming to terms more bluntly with corollary limitations imposed upon democracy by the contemporary territorial state. For today statist democracy is pervaded by its own cloud of unreality. Its historically received mode of territorialization no longer responds sufficiently to the aspiration to have a hand in shaping corporate, strategic, distributive, ecological, military patterns that enable, regulate, and endanger global life. Territorial democracy will become a late-modern anachronism unless it is challenged and exceeded by a new pluralization of democratic spaces and allegiances. And even that may not be enough.

Notes

1. I discuss this quotation in the context of Rousseau's general thought in *Political Theory and Modernity,* chapter 3.

2. Ricoeur deals with these issues much more extensively in *The Symbolism of Evil.* Here he examines the "tragic myth," the "Orphic myth," and the "Adamic myth" comparatively to explore what together they tell us about the human experience of evil. He privileges the Adamic myth. But he also opposes the conception of Original Sin that Augustine draws from it, in which there was initially a pure act of will by Adam followed by a history of human beings with divided wills. He also tries to fold elements from the other two myths into the Adamic myth, claiming that they complete the insights built into it. Thus he makes a lot of the role of the serpent in Eden, a being that represents the anterior presence of evil even in the original condition. He thereby tries to fold an element of the tragic experience (where evil resides in the formation of good) within the Adamic myth. It is uncertain (to me) whether this tragic structure is retained once "Christology" is introduced by Ricoeur into the picture. To keep the issues as well defined as possible, I will simply say that I would give priority to the tragic myth and try to build a vision of democratic politics around appreciation of that experience. I suspect that Ricoeur and I part company somewhere in the territory of this divergence in prioritization of mythic experiences.

3. The classic response here is advanced by Peter Bachrach, *The Theory of Democratic Elitism.* Other critiques can be found in William E. Connolly, ed., *The Bias of Pluralism,* particularly in the essays by Arnold Kaufman and David Kettler.

4. Thomas L. Dumm has advanced this effort impressively in *Democracy and Punishment.*

5. *Spheres of Justice* continues this politics of concealment through admission in the way it interprets the work of Michel Foucault. The Walzerian reading of *Discipline and Punish* construes Foucault to say that a series of bureaucratic elites have acquired unaccountable power over prisons (and other institutions), while I read it to say that disciplinary power operates through and over these agents as well in ways that render the recurrent cycles of prison discipline and prison reform part of the "success" of the prison. These cycles maintain ambivalence inside shared understandings, rather than contesting the code itself.

6. Near the end of the book, this uninterpreted formulation appears: "Social meanings need not be harmonious; sometimes they provide only the intellectual structure within which distributions are debated" (314). Assuming that "social meanings" correspond to "shared understandings," and that "sometimes" means more than rarely and reaches to fundamental issues, this concession, if pursued closely, would require the text to move onto a plane it tries to avoid. One could continue to use Walzerian language once such a concession is made, but to do so the text would have to move onto a metaphysical plane and endorse a

teleological philosophy. Walzer, though, signals in the Preface that this book does not wish to move onto the ontological plane. After announcing how the book coheres with arguments by William Galston and Nicholas Rescher, Walzer says, "But, in my view, the pluralism of these two arguments is vitiated by Galson's Aristotelianism and by Rescher's utilitarianism. My own argument proceeds without these foundational commitments" (xviii). The upshot of the preceding critique is that the Walzerian argument expresses its social ontology in the vocabularies it selects and conceals their significance through a reading of "shared understandings" that cannot bear the weight placed upon it. I have tried to deal with this issue (not, however, with respect to Walzer) in *Identity\Difference: Democratic Negotiations of Political Paradox.*

7. There is a crucial proviso to this, one that links politics and the "connected intellectual" to issues in other states. One might, Walzer knows, have identifications that bind one to another state, as a Jewish-American might be tied to Israel, an Irish-American to Ireland, a French-Palestinian to the idea of Palestine, and so forth. Walzer extends connectedness beyond the state. But even here it seems that the lines separating connected intellectuals from those unconnected to the issues in question are drawn too tightly. In an exchange between Walzer and Edward Said, Walzer acknowledges the significance of issues with respect to Palestinians inside Israel and then seems to use the law of connectedness to make them his issues rather than Said's. "The battle over the Jewish tradition is my battle; in that sense I am a parochial intellectual. But it is also a *battle;* it doesn't involve, as Said charges, 'just going along with one's own people for the sake of loyalty and "connectedness" ' " ("An Exchange: 'Exodus and Revolution'" 250). It *is* Walzer's battle, and one imagines him to be an effective warrior in it, ready to oppose those traditions that subvert other understandings that he takes to be fundamental. But if the battle involves the way Israel treats Palestinians, it is Said's battle too. Just as Said's battles are Walzer's too. (This inevitability helps to explain why the debate between these two is so vitriolic and how its terms may embody a tragic dimension difficult for the disputants to assert independently, but detectable to those listening to them together). And if those battles impinge upon contemporary considerations of peace and justice that implicate a large variety of others, then we others, too, are implicated in them, though to differential degrees. The line here is not between the connected and the unconnected or disconnected intellectual, with the former having rights and obligations and the latter stuck in an abstract world of empty formulations. Connectedness, in the late-modern world, is a complex relation, embodying variable degrees of implication and distantiation. It is because Walzer underplays the interconnectedness of peoples, issues, and contingencies in the late-modern world that he is tempted by dichotomies where complex gradations are needed.

8. Michael Shapiro and Deane Neubauer explore these connections/disconnections creatively in "Spatiality and Policy Discourse: Reading the Global

City." The essays by R. B. J. Walker and Warren Magnusson in the same collection, *Contending Sovereignties: Redefining Political Community*, are also very pertinent to themes developed here. Walker, in "Sovereignty, Identity, Community," poses a series of problems surrounding "spatiotemporal" definitions of politics and Magnusson, in "The Reification of Political Community," explores how social movements exceed the boundaries of the state.

9. By "epistemic realism" I mean (a) a mode of analysis that gives (putative) privilege to independent objects not deeply contaminated by ideas, beliefs, and ideologies; and (b) a model that treats entities to have greater causal efficacy the more "material" and the less "ideational" they are. By "political realism" I mean a normative conception of politics that treats as most real/normal/necessary those entities epistemically endowed with status (a) and that adjusts its political imaginary to correspond to persistent features of political life. In the first study Herz's epistemic and political realism cohere nicely; in the second, he retains a semblance of political realism by giving up large chunks of epistemic realism.

10. There are several issues posed by this quotation that I will bypass. One of them is a corollary issue involving models of interpretation such as hermeneutics, rational choice theory, and discursive theory, which do incorporate ideational dimensions into their accounts of practice but sometimes implicitly dematerialize these practices, treating them as if they were constituted simply as conversations rather than as discursive practices that have become materialized in bodies, territories, dispositions, obdurate habits, identities, unconscious presumptions, institutional intersections, and so forth. These two typologies constantly seem to reproduce each other.

11. "In particular, it made it easier for the members of the family [of sovereign states] to observe self-denying standards 'at home' by providing them with an outlet for their warlike and expansionist inclinations in the vast realm outside Europe" (Herz, *International Politics* 67).

12. A presentation of the "problematization of final markers" must be balanced eventually by one that explores how the politics of naturalization and denaturalization circulates, encountering disturbances and reconsolidating itself on new terms. This balance is short-circuited in the present essay in the interests of concentrating on key ingredients in the democratic ethos. I have tried to follow this circuit further in *Political Theory and Modernity* and *Identity\Difference*. Nietzsche is the hero here. He does not, as some of his followers and critics suggest, contend that the self can simply create itself out of nothing once the challenge to old "idols"/markers has succeeded. For the density of language, the dictates of social coordination, the small size of the human "chamber of consciousness," psychic pressures to consolidate identity, and the fact that an identity is impressed upon one before one has the resources to examine it genealogically, set limitations to the scope of self and social reconstruction. To treat the self, for instance, as a work of art is not to create

oneself from scratch, but to work creatively and modestly on a set of contingent characteristics that have already become entrenched in the self as "second nature."

13. The phrase "dissolution of final markers" is coined by Claude Lefort (*Democracy and Political Theory*). I prefer "problematization of final markers," first, because they have not been dissolved but more actively problematized in modern life, and second, because my conception of democracy includes the contestation of markers you may take to be final, but not their necessary elimination.

14. One way to test what happens when the sovereignty side of democracy suffocates the disturbance side is to examine a theory of democracy that actively supports this priority. Carl Schmitt made this implication clear while he was (in 1922) still a theorist of democratic sovereignty. "Every actual democracy rests on the principle that not only are equals equal but unequals will not be treated equally. Democracy requires, therefore, first homogeneity and second—if the need arises—elimination or eradication of heterogeneity" (*The Crisis of Parliamentary Democracy* 9). The text makes clear that it does not take much for the need to arise in Schmitt's mind.

Bibliography

Abraham, Nicolas, and Maria Torok. *The Wolf Man's Magic Word.* Minneapolis: U of Minnesota P, 1986.

"After the Coup, What Role for the KGB?" *New York Times* 6 October 1991: E9.

Althusser, Louis. *Lenin and Philosophy.* Trans. Ben Brewster. New York: Monthly Review P, 1971.

Anderson, Benedict. *Imagined Communities: Reflections on the Origin and Spread of Nationalism.* Rev. ed. New York: Verso, 1991.

Anson, George. *Voyage Around the World.* London, 1748.

Arendt, Hannah. *Between Past and Future.* Enl. ed. New York: Penguin, 1977.

———. *Crises of the Republic.* New York: Harcourt Brace Jovanovich, 1972.

———. *The Human Condition.* Chicago: U of Chicago P, 1958.

———. *Lectures on Kant's Political Philosophy.* Ed. Ronald Beiner. Chicago: U of Chicago P, 1982.

———. *The Life of the Mind.* 2 vols. Ed. Mary McCarthy. New York: Harcourt Brace Jovanovich, 1977.

———. *Men in Dark Times.* New York: Harcourt Brace Jovanovich, 1968.

———. *On Revolution.* New York: Penguin, 1963.

———. *On Violence.* New York: Harcourt Brace Jovanovich, 1970.

———. *Totalitarianism* (Part 3 of *The Origins of Totalitarianism*). New York: Harcourt Brace Jovanovich, 1968.

———. "Understanding and Politics." *Partisan Review* 20:4 (1953): 377–92.

———. *Willing.* Vol. 2, of *The Life of the Mind.*

Arizona Republic. "The National Guard and the War on Drugs." 7 April 1989: A1.

Austin, J. L. *How to Do Things with Words.* Cambridge: Harvard UP, 1962.

Avrich, Paul. *The Haymarket Tragedy.* Princeton: Princeton UP, 1984.

Bachrach, Peter. *The Theory of Democratic Elitism: A Critique.* Boston: Little, Brown, 1967.

Balibar, Etienne. "The Paradox of Universality." *The Anatomy of Racism.* Ed. David Theo Goldberg. Minneapolis: U of MP, 1990. 283–94.

Barker, Francis. *The Tremulous Private Body.* London: Methuen, 1984.

Baudrillard, Jean. *America.* Trans. Chris Turner. New York: Verso, 1989.

———. "Revolution and the End of Utopia" *Jean Baudrillard: The Disappearance of Art and Politics.* Ed. William Stearns and William Chaloupka. New York: St. Martin's, 1991. 233–43.

———. *Selected Writings.* Ed. Mark Poster. Stanford: Stanford UP, 1988.

———. *Simulations.* Trans. Paul Foss, Paul Patton, and Philip Beitchman. New York: Semiotext[e], 1983.

Benjamin, Walter, *Critique of Violence.* In *Reflections: Essays, Aphorisms, and Autobiographical Writing.* Ed. Peter Demetz. New York: Harcourt Brace Jovanovich, 1978.

Beinin, Joel. "Origins of the Gulf War." *Open Magazine Pamphlet Series* 3 (February 1991).

Bell, Rudolph. *Holy Anorexia.* Chicago: U of Chicago P, 1985.

Benhabib, Seyla. *Critique, Norm, Utopia.* New York: Columbia UP, 1986.

———. "Epistemologies of Postmodernism." *New German Critique* 33 (1984): 103–26.

Benvenuto, Bice, and Roger Kennedy. *The Works of Jacques Lacan: An Introduction.* New York: St. Martin's, 1986.

Bercovitch, Sacvan. *The American Jeremiad.* Madison: U of Wisconsin P, 1978.

Berman, Marshall. *All That Is Solid Melts into Air: The Experience of Modernity.* New York: Simon and Schuster, 1982.

Bernstein, Richard. *Beyond Objectivism and Relativism.* Philadelphia: U of Pennsylvania P, 1983.

———. "If They've Won, Can Conservatives Still Be Important?" *New York Times* 14 January 1991: E24.

———. *Philosophical Profiles.* Philadelphia: U of Pennsylvania P, 1986.

Black, George. "The Dearth of Suitable Villians." *Los Angeles Times* 25 September 1990: B7.

———. *The Good Neighbor.* New York: Pantheon, 1988.

Boyte, Harry C. *The Backyard Revolution.* Philadelphia: Temple UP, 1980.

Bradlee, Ben. *Guts and Glory: The Rise and Fall of Oliver North.* New York: Donald Fine, 1988.

Branch, Taylor. *Parting the Waters: America in the King Years 1954–1963.* New York: Simon and Schuster, 1988.

Brooke, James. "Gaviaria's Gamble." *New York Times Magazine* 19 October 1991: 38–44.

Brooks, Geraldine, and Tony Horwitz. "Shaken Sheiks." *Wall Street Journal* 28 December 1990: A1.

Burke, Kenneth. *Language as Symbolic Action.* Berkeley: U of California P, 1966.

Bush, George. Address to the Commonwealth Club of San Francisco. White House Office Text. 7 February 1990.

———. "1991 State of the Union Address." *Vital Speeches* 57:9 (1991): 1–3.

Butler, Judith. *Gender Trouble: Feminism and the Subversion of Identity.* New York: Routledge, 1990.

Butler, Judith, and Joan Scott, eds. *Feminists Theorize the Political.* New York: Routledge, 1992.

Campbell, David. *Writing Security: United States Foreign Policy and the Politics of Identity.* Minneapolis: U of Minnesota P, 1992.

Camus, Albert. *The Rebel: An Essay on Man in Revolt.* Trans. Anthony Bower. New York: Vintage, 1951.

Casteneda, Jorge. "ABC World News Tonight." 24 April 1990.

Chalmers, Alexander. *The Works of the English Poets from Chaucer to Cowper.* 21 vols. London: N.p., 1810.

Chaloupka, William. *Knowing Nukes: The Politics and Culture of the Atom.* Minneapolis: U of Minnesota P, 1992.

Chambers, Ross. "Narratorial Authority and 'The Purloined Letter.' " Muller and Richardson, *The Purloined Poe: Lacan, Derrida, and Psychoanalytic Reading.* 285–306.

Clarke, Stewart Alan, "Fear of a Black Planet: Race, Identity Politics, and Common Sense." *Socialist Review* 9:1 (1991): 3–4.

Clines, Francis X. "100,000 Join Moscow Rally, Defying Ban By Gorbachev To Show Support For Rival." *New York Times* 29 March 1991: A-1.

Con Davis, Robert. "Lacan, Poe, and Narrative Repression." *Lacan and Narration: The Psychoanalytic Difference in Narrative Theory.* Ed. Robert Con Davis. Baltimore: Johns Hopkins UP, 1983. 983–1005.

Conley, Tom. "A Trace of Style." Krupnick, *Displacement: Derrida and After.* 74–92.

Connolly, William E. *Identity\Difference: Democratic Negotiations of Political Paradox.* Ithaca: Cornell UP, 1991.

———. *Political Theory and Modernity.* New York: Basil Blackwell, 1988.

———, ed. *The Bias of Pluralism.* New York: Atherton, 1969.

Cott, Nancy. *The Bonds of Womanhood.* New Haven: Yale UP, 1977.

Cramer, Richard Ben. "How Bush Made It: A Portrait of the President as a Young Man." *Esquire* June 1991: 74–88, 128–34.

Dallek, Robert. *The American Style of Foreign Policy: Cultural Politics and Foreign Affairs.* New York: Oxford UP, 1989.

Davis, Mike. *City of Quartz: Excavating the Future in Los Angeles.* London: Verso, 1990.

———. *Prisoners of the American Dream.* London: Verso, 1986.

Debord, Guy. *Comments on the Society of the Spectacle.* Trans. Malcolm Imrie. London: Verso, 1990.

Deleuze, Giles. *Nietzsche and Philosophy.* Trans. Hugh Tomlinson. New York: Columbia UP, 1980.

DeLillo, Don. *Libra.* New York: Vintage, 1988.

de Man, Paul. *Allegories of Reading: Figural Language in Rousseau, Nietzsche, Rilke, and Proust.* New Haven: Yale UP, 1979.

"Democrats Propose Diverting Funds from SDI." *Washington Times* 18 May 1989: 2.

Der Derian, James. "Arms, Hostages and the Importance of Shredding in Earnest (II)." *Social Text* 22 (1989): 79–91.

———. "The (S)pace of International Relations: Simulation, Surveillance, and Speed." *International Studies Quarterly* 34 (1990): 295–310.

Der Derian, James, and Michael Shapiro, eds. *International/Intertextual Relations: Postmodern Readings of World Politics.* Lexington, MA: Lexington Books, 1989.

Derrida, Jacques. "Declarations of Independence." *New Political Science* 15 (1986): 7–15.

———. "Deconstruction in America: An Interview With Jacques Derrida." *Critical Exchange* 17 (1985).

———. "Devant la loi." *Kafka and the Contemporary Critical Performance.* Ed. Alan Udoff. Bloomington: Indiana UP, 1987. 128–49.

———. *Disseminations.* Chicago: U of Chicago P, 1981.

———. "Le Facteur de la vérité." *The Post Card: From Socrates to Freud and Beyond.* Trans. Alan Bass. Chicago: University of Chicago Press, 1987. 411–96.

———. "Force of Law: The Mystical Foundation of Authority." Trans. Mary Quaintance. *Cordoza Law Review* 11:5–6 (1990): 921–1045.

———. "Fors: The Anglish Words of Nicholas Abraham and Maria Torok." Introduction to Abraham and Torok, *The Wolf Man's Magic Word.*

———. *Margins of Philosophy.* Trans. Alan Bass. Chicago: U of Chicago P, 1982.

———. "My Chances/Mes Chances: A Rendezvous with some Epicurean Stereophonies." *Taking Chances: Derrida, Psychoanalysis and Literature.* Trans. Irene Harvey and Avital Ronell. Ed. Joseph H. Smith and William Kerrigan. Baltimore: Johns Hopkins UP, 1984. 1–32.

———. *Of Grammatology.* Trans. Gayatri Chakravorty Spivak. Baltimore: Johns Hopkins UP, 1974.

———. "Psyche: Inventions of the Other." *Reading De Man Reading.* Ed. Lindsay Waters and Wlad Godzich. Minneapolis: U of Minnesota P, 1989. 25–66.

———. "The Purveyor of Truth." Muller and Richardson, *The Purloined Poe.* 173–212.

———. "Two Words for Joyce." *Post-Structuralist Joyce: Essays from the French.* Ed. Derek Attridge and Daniel Ferrer. Cambridge: Cambridge UP, 1984. 145–59.

Dews, Peter. *Logics of Disintegration.* New York: Verso, 1987.

Dolan, Frederick M. "Hobbes and/or North: The Rhetoric of American National Security." *Canadian Journal of Political and Social Theory* 12:3 (Fall 1988): 1–19.

———. "Representing the Political System: American Political Science in the Age of the World Picture." *Diacritics* 20:3 (1990): 93–108.

Donner, Frank. *Protectors of Privilege: Red Squads and Police Repression in Urban America.* Berkeley: U of California P, 1990.

Douglas, Mary, and Aaron Wildavsky. *Risk and Culture: An Essay on the Selection of Technological and Environmental Dangers.* Berkeley: U of California P, 1982.

Drew, Elizabeth. "Washington Prepares for War." Sifry and Cert, *The Gulf War Reader.* 180–93.

Drinnon, Richard. *Facing West: The Metaphysics of Indian Hating and Empire Building.* New York: Schocken Books, 1990.

Dumm, Thomas L. *Democracy and Punishment: Disciplinary Origins of the United States.* Madison: U of Wisconsin P, 1987.

———. "The Politics of Post-modern Aesthetics: Habermas Contra Focault." *Political Theory* 16:2 (1988): 209–28.

Eco, Umberto. *Travels in Hyperreality.* New York: Pantheon, 1983.

Edelman, Murray. *Constructing the Political Spectacle.* Chicago: U of Chicago P, 1988.

Edsall, Thomas. "The Reagan Legacy." *The Reagan Legacy.* Ed. Sidney Blumenthall and Thomas Edsall. New York: Pantheon, 1988. 1–24.

Ehrenreich, Barbara. "Who Wants Another Panama?" Sifry and Cerf, *The Gulf War Reader.* 299–302.

Elshtain, Jean Bethke. *Women and War.* New York: Basic, 1987.

Ewald, Francois. "Insurance and Risk." *The Foucault Effect: Studies in Governmental Rationality.* Ed. Graham Burchell, Colin Gordon, and Peter Miller. Chicago: U of Chicago P, 1991. 197–210.

Executive Order 9835. "Prescribing Procedures for the Administration of an Employee Loyalty Program in the Executive Branch of the Government." *Code of Federal Regulations Title 3—The President 1943–1948 Compilation.* Washington D.C.: Government Printing Office, 1957.

Executive Order 10450. "Security Requirements for Government Employment." *Code of Federal Regulation Title 3—The President 1949–1953 Compilation.* Washington, D.C.: Government Printing Office, 1958.

Felman, Shoshana. "On Reading Poetry: Reflections on the Limits and Possibilities of Psychoanalytic Approaches." Muller and Richardson, *The Purloined Poe.* 133–56.

Fields, Barbara. "Ideology and Race in American History." *New Left Reader* (1991): 95.

Fish, Stanley. "Withholding the Missing Portion: Psychoanalysis and Rhetoric." Fish, *Doing What Comes Naturally.* Durham, N.C.: Duke UP, 1989. 525–55.

Flathman, Richard E. *Authority and the Authoritative: The Practice of Political Authority.* Chicago: U of Chicago P, 1980.

——, ed. *Concepts in Social and Political Philosophy.* New York: Macmillan, 1973.

Foucault, Michel. *Discipline and Punish: The Birth of the Prison.* Trans. Alan Sheridan. New York: Pantheon, 1977.

——. *The History of Sexuality.* Vol. 1. Trans. Robert Hurley. New York: Random House, 1980.

——. "Interview Between Foucault, Rabinow, Taylor, Jay, and Rorty." *The Foucault Reader.* Ed. Paul Rabinow. New York: Pantheon Books, 1984. 381–90.

——. "On Politics and Ethics." *The Foucault Reader.* 373–80.

——. "Politics and Reason." *Michel Foucault: Politics, Philosophy, Culture.* Ed. Lawrence D. Kritzman. New York: Routledge, 1988. 57–86.

——. *Power/Knowledge: Selected Interviews and Other Writings, 1972–1977.* Trans. Colin Gordon, Leo Marshall, John Mepham, and Kate Soper. New York: Pantheon, 1980.

——. "The Subject and Power." *Michel Foucault: Beyond Structuralism and Hermeneutics.* Hubert L. Dreyfus and Paul Rabinow. Chicago: U of Chicago P, 1982. 208–26.

Fraser, Nancy. "Rethinking the Public Sphere." *Socialtext* 8:3–9:1 (1990): 56–80.

——. *Unruly Practices.* Minneapolis: U of Minnesota P, 1989.

Fraser, Russell. *The War Against Poetry.* Princeton: Princeton UP, 1970.

Freud, Sigmund. *Three Case Histories.* New York: Collier, 1963.

Friedman, Lawrence. *A History of American Law.* New York: Simon and Schuster, 1973.

Friedman, Richard B. "On the Concept of Authority in Political Philosophy." Flathman, *Concepts in Social and Political Philosophy.* 121–45.

Friedrich, Carl J. "Authority, Reason, and Discretion." Flathman, *Concepts in Social and Political Philosophy.* 167–83.

Gadamer, Hans Georg. *Philosophical Hermeneutics.* Trans. David Linge. Berkeley: U of California P, 1977.

Gaddis, John Lewis. *Strategies of Containment: A Critical Appraisal of Postwar American National Security Policy.* New York: Oxford UP, 1982.

Gaines, John. "War Games Succeed in Capture of Mock Drug Lord." *San Diego Union* 20 April 1990: B1.

Gates, Robert. "Testimony to Senate Intelligence Committee." *New York Times* 3 October 1991: A12–14.

Gelb, Leslie. "Not Another Summit." *New York Times* 3 November 1991: E15.

Genette, Gerard. *Figures of Literary Discourse.* New York: Columbia UP, 1984.

Girard, René. "Discussion." *Violent Origins: Ritual Killing and Cultural Formation.* Ed. Robert G. Hamerton-Kelly. Stanford: Stanford UP, 1987. 106–45.

———. "Generative Scapegoating." Hamerton-Kelly, *Violent Origins: Ritual Killing and Cultural Formation*. 73–105.

———. *Violence and the Sacred*. Baltimore: Johns Hopkins UP, 1979.

Gitlin, Todd. *The Whole World Is Watching: Mass Media in the Making and Unmaking of the New Left*. Berkeley: U of California P, 1980.

Glacken, Clarence J. *Traces on the Rhodian Shore: Nature and Culture in Western Thought from Ancient Times to the End of the Eighteenth Century*. Berkeley: U of California P, 1967.

Goldfield, Michael. "The Color of Politics in the United States: White Supremacy as the Main Explanation for the Pecularities of American Politics from Colonial Times to the Present." *The Bounds of Race: Perspectives on Hegemony and Resistance*. Ed. Dominick LaCapra. Ithaca: Cornell UP, 1991. 25–48.

Goldstein, Robert Justin. *Political Repression in Modern America: From 1870 to the Present*. New York: Schenkman, 1978.

Gordon, Colin. "Governmental Rationality: An Introduction." *The Foucault Effect: Studies in Governmental Rationality*. Ed. Graham Burchell, Colin Gordon, and Peter Miller. Chicago: U of Chicago P, 1991. 1–51.

Gracie and Zarkov. "Electronic Guerilla Warfare." *Mondo 2000*. No. 3 (1990): 105–08.

Greenblatt, Stephen. *Marvelous Possessions: The Wonder of the New World*. Chicago: U of Chicago P, 1991.

Groening, Matt. "How to Be a Sensitive Poet." *Love Is Hell*. New York: Random House, 1985.

Gusfield, Joseph R., ed. *Protest, Reform, and Revolt: A Reader in Social Movements*. New York: Wiley, 1970.

Habermas, Jurgen. *The Philosophical Discourse of Modernity*. Trans. Frederick G. Lawrence. Cambridge, Mass.: MIT P, 1987.

———. *Philosophical-Political Profiles*. Trans. Frederick G. Lawrence. Cambridge, Mass.: MIT P, 1983.

———. *The Structural Transformation of the Public Sphere*. Trans. Thomas Burger. Cambridge, Mass.: MIT P, 1989.

———. *Theory and Practice*. Trans. John Viertel. Boston: Beacon, 1973.

———. *The Theory of Communicative Action*. 2 vols. Trans. Thomas McCarthy. Boston: Beacon, 1985.

———. *Toward a Rational Society*. Trans. Jeremy Shapiro. Boston: Beacon, 1970.

Halberstam, David. "When 'Civil Rights' and 'Peace' Join Forces." *Martin Luther King, Jr.: A Profile*. Ed. C. Eric Lincoln. New York: Hill and Wang, 1970. 187–212.

Hall, Stuart. "Ethnicity: Identity and Difference." *Radical America* 23:4 1989: 9–23.

———. *The Hard Road to Renewal*. London: Verso, 1988.

Halliday, Fred. "The Ends of Cold War." *New Left Review* 180 (March/April 1990): 5–23.

Hamowy, Ronald. *Dealing with Drugs: Consequences of Government Control.* Lexington, Mass: Lexington, 1987.

Hartz, Louis. *The Liberal Tradition in America.* New York: Harcourt Brace Jovanovich, 1955.

Harvey, David. "D.C. National Guard and Washington's Drug War." *Rotor and Wing* 40 (March 1990): 40–42.

Havel, Vaclav. *Disturbing the Peace.* New York: Knopf, 1990.

———. *Power of the Powerless.* New York: Sharpe, 1990.

Hawking, Stephen. *A Brief History of Time.* New York: Bantam, 1988.

Haywood, Ian. *The Making of History.* London: Associated University Presses, 1986.

Heale, M. J. *American Anticommunism: Combatting the Enemy Within 1830–1970.* Baltimore: Johns Hopkins UP, 1990.

Heberle, Rudolph. *Social Movements: An Introduction to Political Sociology.* New York: Appleton-Century-Crofts, 1951.

Hegel, G. W. F. *Hegel's Philosophy of Right.* Trans. T. M. Knox. New York: Oxford UP, 1975.

———. *The Philosophy of History.* Trans. J. Sibree. New York: Dover, 1956.

Heidegger, Martin. "The Age of the World Picture." *The Question Concerning Technology and Other Essays.* 115–54.

———. *Being and Time.* Trans. John Macquarrie and Edward Robinson. New York: Harper and Row, 1962.

———. *Nietzsche.* 4 vols. Trans. David Farrell Krell. San Francisco: Harper and Row, 1979–1987.

———. *The Question Concerning Technology and Other Essays.* Trans. William Lovett. New York: Harper and Row, 1977.

———. "The Question Concerning Technology." *The Question Concerning Technology and Other Essays.* 3–35.

———. "The Word of Nietzsche: 'God Is Dead.'" *The Question Concerning Technology and Other Essays.* 53–112.

Herman, Edward S. *The Real Terror Network: Terrorism in Fact and Propaganda.* Boston: South End, 1982.

Herz, John H. *International Politics in the Atomic Age.* New York: Columbia UP, 1959.

———. "The Territorial State Revisited: Reflections on the Future of the Nation-State." *Polity* 1 (Fall 1968): 11–34.

Herzl, Theodore. *The Jewish State.* New York: Freeman Press, 1896.

Hicks, John, and Robert Tucker, eds. *Revolution and Reaction: The Paris Commune.* Amherst: U of Massachusetts P, 1973.

Hitchens, Christopher. "How Neoconservatives Perish." *Harper's* November 1990: 282:1686.

Hobbes, Thomas. *De Cive.* Oxford: Clarendon, 1983.

———. *Leviathan.* Ed. Michael Oakeshott. New York: Collier Macmillan, 1962.

———. *Man and Citizen.* Ed. Bernard Gert. New York: Doubleday, 1972.

Honig, B. "Arendt, Identity, and Difference." *Political Theory* 16:1 (1988): 77–98.

———. "Declarations of Independence: Arendt and Derrida on the Problem of Founding a Republic." *American Political Science Review* (March 1991).

———. "Toward an Agonistic Feminism: Hannah Arendt and the Politics of Identity." Butler and Scott, *Feminists Theorize the Political.* 215–38.

Howard, Donald R. *Chaucer.* New York: Fawcett, 1987.

Hughes, Langston. *Selected Poems.* New York: Vintage, 1959.

Jacobs, Jane. *The Death and Life of Great American Cities.* New York: Random House, 1961.

Jaeger, Werner. *Paidea.* Vol. 1. New York: Oxford UP, 1945.

Janicaud, Dominique. "Rationality, Force and Power: Foucault and Habermas's Criticisms." *Michel Foucault, Philosopher.* Trans. Timothy J. Armstrong. New York: Routledge, 1992. 283–301.

Jehl, Douglas. "U.S. Agents in Combat to Defend Base in Peru." *Los Angeles Times* 13 April 1990: A5.

Jehlen, Myra. *The American Incarnation: The Individual, the Nation, and the Continent.* Cambridge: Harvard UP, 1986.

Johnson, Barbara. "The Frame of Reference: Poe, Lacan, Derrida." *The Critical Difference.* Ed. Barbara Johnson, Baltimore: Johns Hopkins UP, 1980. 110–47.

Kalinich, Lila. "Where Is Thy Sting? Some Reflections on the Wolf-man." *Lacan and the Subject of Language.* Ed. Ellie Ragland and Mark Bracher. New York: Routledge, 1991. 167–87.

Kammen, Michael. *People of Paradox: An Inquiry Concerning the Origins of American Civilization.* New York: Oxford UP, 1980.

Kant, Immanuel. "Perpetual Peace." *Perpetual Peace and Other Essays.* Trans. Ted Humphrey. Indianapolis: Hackett, 1983. 107–43.

Kantorowitz, Ernst. *The King's Two Bodies.* Princeton: Princeton UP, 1957.

Kateb, George. *Hannah Arendt: Politics, Conscience, Evil.* Oxford: Rowman and Allanheld, 1983.

Kelley, Kitty. *Nancy Reagan: The Unauthorized Biography.* New York: Simon and Shuster, 1991.

Kibbey, Ann. *The Interpretation of Material Shapes in Puritanism: A Study of Rhetoric, Prejudice, and Violence.* London: Cambridge UP, 1986.

King, Martin Luther, Jr. " 'I Have a Dream' Speech." Gordy Records, n.d.

Klapp, Orrin. *Collective Search for Identity.* New York: Holt, Rinehart, 1969.

———. *Symbolic Leaders.* Chicago: Aldine, 1965.

Klein, Richard, and William B. Weaver. "Nuclear Coincidence and the Korean Airline Disaster." *Diacritics* 16 (Spring 1986): 2–21.

Kopkind, Andrew. "Imposing the New World Order at Home." *The Nation* 8 April 1991: 446–48.

Kovic, Ron. *Born on the Fourth of July.* New York: McGraw-Hill, 1976.

Kristeva, Julia. "Stabat Mater." *The Kristeva Reader.* Ed. Toril Moi. New York: Columbia UP, 1986. 160–87.

Kroker, Arthur, and Marilouise Kroker. "Panic Sex in America." *Body Invaders.* Ed. Kroker and Kroker. New York: St. Martin's, 1987. 10–20.

Krupnick, Mark, ed. *Displacements: Derrida and After.* Bloomington: Indiana UP, 1983.

Kuberski, Philip. "Charles Olsen and the America Thing: The Ideology of Literary Revolution." *Criticism* 27:2 (1985): 175–93.

Kunkel, David, ed. *Campaign for President: The Managers Look at '88.* Dover, Mass: Auburn House, 1989.

Kuttner, Robert. *The Life of the Party.* New York: Viking, 1987.

Kwitney, Jonathan. *Crimes of Patriots.* New York: Viking, 1989.

Lacan, Jacques. "The Purloined Letter." *The Seminar of Jacques Lacan: Book II The Ego in Freud's Theory and in the Technique of Psychoanalysis 1954–1955.* Trans. Sylvana Tomaselli; ed. Jacques-Alain Miller. New York: Norton, 1988. 191–205.

Laplanche, J., and J.-B. Pontalis. *The Language of Psychoanalysis.* Trans. Donald Nicholson-Smith. New York: Norton, 1973.

Le Carré, John. *The Secret Pilgrim.* New York: Knopf, 1991.

Lee, Patrick. "Addiction to Oil Still Drives U.S." *New York Times* 24 March 1991: A1.

Lefort, Claude. *Democracy and Political Theory.* Trans. David Marcy. Minneapolis: U of Minnesota P, 1988.

Lewis, David L. *King: A Biography.* 2d ed. Urbana: U of Illinois P, 1978.

Lewy, Guenter. *The Federal Loyalty-Security Program: The Need for Reform.* Washington, D.C.: American Enterprise Institute, 1983.

Lipset, Seymour Martin. *Political Man.* New York: Doubleday, 1959.

Lipset, Seymour Martin, and Gerald M. Achaflander. *Passion and Politics: Student Activism in America.* Boston: Little, Brown, 1971.

Locke, John. *Two Treatises on Government.* Ed. Peter Laslett. Cambridge: Cambridge UP, 1970.

Lofland, John. *Protest: Studies of Collective Behavior and Social Movements.* New Brunswick, N.J.: Transaction Books, 1985.

Lyotard, Jean-Francois. *The Differend: Phrases in Dispute.* Trans. George Van Den Abbeele. Minneapolis: U of Minnesota P, 1988.

———. *The Postmodern Condition: A Report on Knowledge.* Trans. Geoff Bennington and Brian Massumi. Minneapolis: U of Minnesota P, 1984.

Lyotard, Jean-Francois, and Jean-Loup Thébaud. *Just Gaming.* Trans. Wlad Godzich. Minneapolis: U of Minnesota P, 1985.

Maas, Peter. *Manhunt: The Incredible Pursuit of a CIA Agent Turned Terrorist.* New York: Random House, 1986.

Machiavelli, Niccolo. *The Prince and The Discourses.* 1532 and 1531. Ed. Max Lerner, trans. Luigi Ricci. New York: Modern Library, 1950.

Magnusson, Warren. "The Reification of Political Community." Mendlovitz, *Contending Sovereignties: Redefining Political Community.* 45–61.

Marshall, Jonathan, with Peter Dale Scott and Jane Hunter. *The Iran-Contra*

Connection: Secret Teams and Covert Operations in the Reagan Era. Boston: South End, 1987.

Mason, Peter. *Deconstructing America: Representations of the Other.* London: Routledge, 1990.

Massing, Michael. "Dealing with the Drug Horror." *New York Review of Books* 30 March 1989: 22–26.

———. "The War on Cocaine." *New York Review of Books* 22 December 1988: 61–67.

May, Elaine Tyler. *Homeward Bound: American Families in the Cold War Era.* New York: Basic, 1988.

McCoy, Alfred. *The Politics of Heroin in Southeast Asia.* New York: Harper and Row, 1972.

Mendlovitz, Saul H., ed. *Contending Sovereignties: Redefining Political Community.* London: Lynne Reiner, 1990.

Miller, Judith, and Laurie Mylroie. *Saddam Hussein and the Crisis in the Gulf.* New York: Random House, 1990.

Mollenkopf, John. *The Contested City.* Princeton: Princeton UP, 1983.

"Moscow Embassy Telegram #511." *Containment: Documents on American Policy and Strategy, 1945–1950.* Ed. Thomas H. Etzold and John Lewis Gaddis. New York: Columbia UP, 1978. 50–63.

Muller, John. "Negation in 'The Purloined Letter': Hegel, Poe, and Lacan." Muller and Richardson, *The Purloined Poe.* 343–69.

Muller, John P., and William J. Richardson, eds. *The Purloined Poe.* Baltimore: Johns Hopkins UP, 1988.

Myers, Robert J. "The Carnegie Poll on Values in American Foreign Policy." *Ethics and International Affairs* 3 (1989): 296–312.

Mylne, Vivienne. *The Eighteenth-Century French Novel.* Cambridge: Cambridge UP, 1981.

Nadelmann, Ethan. "The Case for Legalization." *The Public Interest* 92 (Summer 1988): 3–31.

Nancy, Jean-Luc. "Guerre, droit, souveraineté—Techné." *Les Temps Modernes* 539 (Juin 1991): 1–42.

———. *The Inoperative Community.* Ed. and trans. Peter Connor. Minneapolis: U of Minnesota P, 1991.

———. "Our History." *Diacritics* 20:3 (Fall 1990): 96–115.

National Public Radio. "All Things Considered." August 21, 1991.

National Security Council 68. "United States Objectives and Programs for National Security, April 14, 1950." 1978. *Containment: Documents on American Policy and Strategy, 1945–1950.* Ed. Thomas H. Etzold and John Lewis Gaddis. New York: Columbia UP, 1978. 385–442.

National Security Council 5602/1. "Basic National Security Policy." 15 March 1956. Record Group 273. National Archives.

National Security Council 5906/1. "Basic National Security Policy." 5 August 1959. Record Group 273. National Archives.

Navy News and Undersea Technology 16 April 1990.

Nietzsche, Friedrich. *On the Genealogy of Morals.* 1887. Ed. Walter Kaufmann, trans. Walter Kaufmann and R. J. Hollingdale. New York: Vintage, 1969.

———. *Twilight of the Idols.* Trans. R. J. Hollingdale. New York: Penguin, 1979.

———. *The Use and Abuse of History.* 1872. Trans. Adrian Collins. Indianapolis: Bobbs-Merrill, 1957.

———. *The Will to Power.* Trans. Walter Kaufmann. New York: Vintage, 1968.

Nin, Anais. *Diary of Anais Nin.* Vol. 1 (1934–1939). New York: Harcourt, 1978.

Noonan, Peggy. *What I Saw at the Revolution: A Political Life in the Reagan Era.* New York: Random House, 1990.

Norton, Anne. *Republic of Signs: Governing Representations in American Political Culture.* Forthcoming.

O'Gorman, Edmundo. *The Invention of America: An Inquiry into the Historical Nature of the New World and the Meaning of Its History.* Bloomington: Indiana UP, 1961.

Omi, Michael, and Howard Winat. *Racial Formation in the United Kingdom from the 1960's to the 1980's.* London: Routledge and Kegan, 1986.

Pack, Robert. "Lyric Narration: The Chameleon Poet." *Hudson Review* 37:1 (Spring 1984): 54–70.

Pagels, Heinz R. *Perfect Symmetry.* New York: Bantam, 1986.

Pateman, Carole. *The Sexual Contract.* Stanford: Stanford UP, 1988.

Patterson, Thomas E. *The American Democracy.* Hightstown, N.J.: McGraw-Hill, 1990.

Penley, Constance, and Andrew Ross, eds. *Technoculture.* Minneapolis: U of Minnesota P, 1991.

Peters, R. S. "Authority." Flathman, *Concepts in Social and Political Philosophy.* 146–83.

Pitkin, Hanna Fenichel. *Fortune Is a Woman.* Berkeley: U of California P, 1984.

Plato. *Gorgias.* Harmondsworth, Middlesex: Penguin, 1960.

"Play a Prank for Freedom!" *Spy Magazine* January 1990: 52–54.

Pocock, J. G. A. *The Machiavellian Moment: Florentine Political Thought and the Atlantic Republican Tradition.* Princeton: Princeton UP, 1975.

———. *Virtue, Commerce, and History: Essays on Political Thought and History, Chiefly in the Eighteenth Century.* Cambridge: Cambridge UP, 1985.

Poe, Edgar Allan. *The Tell Tale Heart and Other Stories.* New York: Random House, 1988.

Rand, Nicholas. *Le Cryptage et la vie des oeuvres.* Paris: Aubier, 1989.

Rapaport, Herman. "Staging: Mt Blanc." Krupnick, *Displacement: Derrida and After.* 59–74.

Reed, Adolph, Jr. "The 'Black Revolution' and the Reconstruction of Domination." *Race, Politics, and Culture: Critical Essays on the Radicalism of the 1960's.* Ed. Adolph Reed. Westport: Greenwood Press, 1986.

Reed, Adolph, Jr, and Julian Bond. "Equality: Why We Can't Wait." *The Nation* 9 December 1991: 733–737.

Regan, Donald. *For the Record: From Wall Street to Washington.* New York: St. Martin's, 1988.

Reich, Robert. *Tales of New America.* New York: Basic Books, 1987.

Reider, Jonathan. *Canarsie: The Jews and Italians of Brooklyn Against Liberalism.* Cambridge: Harvard UP, 1985.

Ricoeur, Paul. "The Political Paradox." *Legitimacy and the State.* Ed. William E. Connolly. New York: New York UP, 1984. 250–72.

———. *The Symbolism of Evil.* Boston: Beacon, 1967.

Roberts, Steven V. "Reagan Endorses Bush as Successor." *New York Times* 12 May 1988: A32.

Robinson, Walter V., and Philip Bennett. "Amid Ruin, Residents Cheer GI's." *Boston Globe* 24 December 1989: A1.

Roediger, David R. *The Wages of Whiteness: Race and the Making of the American Working Class.* London: Verso, 1991.

Rogin, Michael P. *Fathers and Children: Andrew Jackson and the Subjugation of the American Indian.* New York: Knopf, 1975.

———. " 'Make My Day': Spectacle As Amnesia in Imperial Politics." *Representations* 29 (Winter 1990): 99–123.

———. *Ronald Reagan, the Movie.* Berkeley: U of California P, 1987.

Ronell, Avital. *Crack Wars: Literature, Addiction, Mania.* Lincoln: U of Nebraska P, 1992.

———. *Dictations: On Haunted Writing.* Bloomington: Indiana UP, 1986.

———. "The Differends of Man." *Diacritics* 19:3–4 (1989): 63–75.

———. *Finitude's Score: Essays for the End of the Millennium.* Forthcoming from U of Nebraska P.

———. *The Telephone Book.* Lincoln: U of Nebraska P, 1989.

Rorty, Richard. "Habermas and Lyotard on Postmodernity." *Habermas and Modernity.* Ed. Richard Bernstein. Cambridge: MIT P, 1985. 161–175.

Ross, Andrew. "Containing Culture in the Cold War." *Cultural Studies* 1 (1987): 328–48.

Rousseau, Jean-Jacques. *Emile.* Trans. Alan Bloom. New York: Basic, 1979.

———. *The Government of Poland.* 1770. Ed. and trans. Willmore Kendall. Indianapolis: Hackett, 1985.

———. *On the Social Contract: With Geneva Manuscript and Political Economy.* 1762. Ed. Rogers Masters, trans. Judith Masters. New York: St. Martin's, 1978.

Rubenstein, Diane. "This Is Not a President: Baudrillard, Bush, and Enchanted Simulation." *The Hysterical Male: New Feminist Theory.* Ed. Arthur Kroker and Marilouise Kroker. New York: St. Martin's, 1991. 253–68.

Rudé, George. *The Crowd in History.* New York: Wiley, 1964.

Safire, William. "The Big-Government Right." *New York Times* 25 November 1991: A19.

Saxton, Alexander. *The Rise and Fall of the White Republic: Class Politics and Mass Culture in Nineteenth-Century America.* London: Verso, 1990.

Schmitt, Carl. *The Crisis of Parliamentary Democracy.* 1926. Cambridge: MIT P, 1988.

Schumpeter, Joseph. *Capitalism, Socialism, and Democracy.* New York: Harper and Row, 1942.

Schürmann, Reiner. *Heidegger on Being and Acting: From Principles to Anarchy.* Trans. Christine-Marie Gros. Bloomington: Indiana UP, 1987.

Sciolino, Elaine. "In Rebuttal to Senate Committee, CIA Nominee Is Truthful but Incomplete." *New York Times* 13 October 1991: A24.

Seery, John Evan. *Political Returns: Irony in Politics and Theory from Plato to the Antinuclear Movement.* Boulder: Westview, 1990.

Shapiro, Michael, and Deane Neubauer. "Spaciality and Policy Discourse: Reading the Global City." Mendlovitz, *Contending Sovereignties: Redefining Political Community.* 97–125.

Showalter, English. *The Evolution of the French Novel 1641–1782.* Princeton: Princeton University Press, 1972.

Sifry, Micah, and Christopher Cerf, eds. *The Gulf War Reader.* New York: Random House, 1991.

Simmons, William S. "Conversion from Indian to Puritan." *New England Quarterly* 52 (1979): 197–218.

Simms, Paul. "How to Become President." *Spy* November 1988: 118–28.

Sleeper, Jim. *The Closet of Strangers: Liberalism and the Politics of Race in New York.* New York: W. W. Norton, 1990.

Sloterdijk, Peter. *Critique of Cynical Reason.* Trans. Michael Eldred. Minneapolis: U of Minnesota P, 1987.

Slotkin, Richard. *The Fatal Environment: The Myth of the Frontier in the Age of Industrialization, 1800–1890.* Middletown, Conn.: Wesleyan UP, 1986.

———. *Regeneration Through Violence: The Mythology of the American Frontier, 1600–1860.* Middletown, Conn.: Wesleyan UP, 1987.

Smith, Eric. *By Mourning Tongues: Studies in English Elegy.* London: Boydell, 1977.

Smith, James Morton. *Freedom's Fetters: The Alien and Sedition Laws and American Civil Liberties.* Ithaca: Cornell UP, 1956.

Sonenshine, Tara. "The Revolution Has Been Televised." *Washington Post National Weekly Edition* 8–14 October 1990: 29.

Speakes, Larry, with Robert Pack. *Speaking Out: The Reagan Presidency from Inside the White House.* New York: Avon, 1988.

Stephanson, Anders. "Regarding Postmodernism: A Conversation with Fredric Jameson." *Universal Abandon? The Politics of Postmodernism.* Ed. Andrew Ross, Minneapolis: U of Minnesota P, 1988. 3–31.

Stewart, Philip. *Imitation and Illusion in the French Memoir-Novel, 1700–1750.* New Haven: Yale UP, 1969.

Stewart, Susan. "The Marquis de Meese." *Critical Inquiry* 15:1 (Autumn 1988): 162–92.

Strauss, Leo. *Thoughts on Machiavelli.* Chicago: U of Chicago P, 1978.

Susman, Warren, with Edward Griffin. "Did Success Spoil the United States? Dual Representations in Postwar America." *Recasting America: Culture and Politics in the Age of the Cold War.* Ed. Larry May. Chicago: U of Chicago P, 1989. 19–38.

Takaki, Ronald T. *Iron Cages: Race and Culture in Nineteenth Century America.* Seattle: U of Washington P, 1979.

Taking the Stand: The Testimony of Lieutenant Colonel Oliver North. New York: Pocket Books, 1987.

Tayacan. *Psychological Operations in Guerilla Warfare* (The CIA Manual). New York: Vintage, 1985.

Taylor, Charles. "Foucault on Freedom and Truth." *Political Theory* 12:2 (May 1984): 152–83.

Thompson, Hunter S. *Fear and Loathing: On the Campaign Trail '72.* San Francisco: Straight Arrow, 1973.

Thucydides. *The Peloponnesian War.* Trans. Alex Warner. Harmondsworth, Middlesex, England: Penguin, 1954.

Tocqueville, Alexis de. *Democracy in America.* Trans. George Lawrence, ed. J. P. Mayer. New York: Doubleday, 1969.

Todorov, Tzvetan. *The Conquest of America: The Question of the Other.* Trans. Richard Howard. New York: Harper and Row, 1984.

Tolkien, J. R. R. *The Return of the King.* New York: Ballantine, 1981.

Toner, Robin. "New Political Realities Create Conservative Identity Crisis." *New York Times,* 13 May 1991: A1.

Tower, John, et al. *The Tower Commission Report.* New York: Bantam Books and Time Books, 1987.

Uncapher, Williard. "Trouble in Cyberspace:Civil Liberties at Peril in the Information Age." *The Humanist* 51:5 (September/October 1991): 10–11.

Unger, David. "Ferment in the Think Tanks: Learning to Live with No Global Threat." *New York Times* 5 January 1991: A1.

U.S. Congress. *Report of the Congressional Committees Investigating the Iran-Contra Affair.* New York: Random House, 1988.

U.S. Department of Health and Human Services. *Vital Statistics of the United States 1987: Volume II, Mortality Part A.* Hyattsville, MD.: Government Printing Office, 1990.

U.S. Department of State. *The International Narcotics Control Strategy Report.* Washington D.C.: Department of State Publication, March 1989.

Villa, Dana R. "Beyond Good and Evil: Arendt, Nietzsche, and the Aestheticization of Political Action." *Political Theory* 20: 2 (1992): 275–309.

Virilio, Paul. *Speed and Politics.* Trans. Mark Polizzotti. New York: Semiotext(e), 1986.

Wakoski, Diane. "Justice Is Reason Enough." Diane Wakoski, *Trilogy* 11. New York, 1974.

———. *Toward a New Poetry.* Ann Arbor: U of Michigan P, 1980.

Walker, Martin. "Green Berets Train Peru Anti-drug Units." *Manchester Guardian* 23 April 1990: 6.

Walker, R. B. J. "Sovereignty, Identity, Community." Mendlovitz, *Contending Sovereignties: Redefining Political Community.*

Walzer, Michael. "Exodus and Revolution." *Commentary* 83 (1987): 25–35.

———. "Liberalism and the Art of Separation." *Political Theory* 12: 3 (1984): 315–30.

———. *Spheres of Justice: A Defense of Pluralism and Equality.* New York: Basic, 1983.

———. "What Does It Mean To Be An 'American'?" *Social Research* 57 (1990): 591–614.

Warner, Michael. *Letters of the Republic: Publication and the Public Sphere in Eighteenth-Century America.* Cambridge, Mass.: Harvard UP, 1990.

Washington Post-ABC Poll. "Many in poll say Bush plan is not stringent enough." 8 September 1989: A1.

Wellmer, Albrecht. "Reason, Utopia, and Enlightenment." In *Habermas and Modernity.* Ed. Richard Bernstein. Cambridge, Mass.: MIT P, 1985. 35–67.

White, Stephen K. *Political Theory and Postmodernism.* Cambridge: Cambridge UP, 1991.

Whitfield, Stephen J. *The Culture of the Cold War.* Baltimore: Johns Hopkins UP, 1991.

Wilson, William Julius. *The Truly Disadvantaged: The Inner City, the Underclass, and Public Policy.* Chicago: U of Chicago P, 1987.

Wines, Michael. "Gates's Task: Restoring Confidence and Purpose." *New York Times,* 7 October 1991: A12.

Wolfe, Alan. *America's Impasse: The Rise and Fall of the Politics of Growth.* New York: Pantheon, 1981.

Woodward, Bob. *The Commanders.* New York: Simon and Schuster, 1991.

Yarmolinsky, Adam, ed. *Case Studies in Personnel Security.* Washington, D.C.: Bureau for National Affairs, 1955.

Young, Edward. "The Complaint, or Night Thoughts." *Works of the English Poets.* Ed. Alexander Chambers. London, 1810.

Zizek, Slavoj. *The Sublime Object of Ideology.* London: Routledge, 1989.

Zone 3–5. New York: Urzone, 1989.

Notes on Contributors

DAVID CAMPBELL is assistant professor of political science at The Johns Hopkins University, where he teaches international political theory and American foreign policy. He is the author of *Writing Security: United States Foreign Policy and the Politics of Identity.*

WILLIAM CHALOUPKA teaches political science at the University of Montana. He is the author of *Knowing Nukes: The Politics and Culture of the Atom,* and he edited (with William Stearns) *Jean Baudrillard: The Disappearance of Art and Politics.*

STUART A. CLARKE teaches political science at Williams College.

WILLIAM E. CONNOLLY is professor of political science at The Johns Hopkins University, where he teaches political theory and edits the book series *Contestations: Cornell Studies in Political Theory.* He is the author, most recently, of *Political Theory and Modernity* and *Identity\Difference: Democratic Negotiations of Political Paradox.*

JAMES DER DERIAN teaches international relations at the University of Massachusetts at Amherst. He is the author of *On Diplomacy: A Genealogy of Western Estrangement* and *Antidiplomacy: Spies, Terror, Speed and War,* and be edited (with Michael Shapiro) *International/Intertextual Relations: Postmodern Readings of World Politics.*

FREDERICK M. DOLAN is assistant professor of rhetoric at the University of California at Berkeley, where he teaches political theory. He has published essays on Nietzsche, Heidegger, Foucault, and Derrida, as well as on American political discourse. He is the author of the forthcoming *Allegories of America.*

JOHN DOLAN, senior lecturer at Otago University in Dunedin, New Zealand, has published poetry as well as articles on the history of English lyric.

THOMAS L. DUMM is associate professor of political science at Amherst College, where he teaches American politics and contemporary theory. He has written essays on law, political theory, and poststructuralism for various journals, as well as several books, including *Democracy and Punishment, Michel Foucault and the Politics of Freedom,* and the forthcoming *United States: Representations of Political Experience.*

LARRY N. GEORGE teaches in the Department of Political Science of the California State University at Long Beach. He has published articles on political theory and foreign policymaking, interamerican relations, and mimetic readings of the cold war.

KIARAN HONDERICH, assistant professor of economics at Williams College and a staff economist at the Center for Popular Economics, works on international trade and political economy.

BONNIE HONIG is assistant professor of government at Harvard University, where she teaches modern political theory. She is the author of *Political Theory and the Displacement of Politics.*

ANNE NORTON is professor of political science at the University of Pennsylvania. She is the author of *Alternative Americas: A Reading of Antebellum Political Culture, Reflections on Political Identity,* and *Republic of Signs.*

AVITAL RONELL teaches theory at the University of California at Berkeley. Her most recent books are *The Telephone Book: Technology, Schizophrenia, and Electric Speech* and *Finitude's Score: Essays for the End of the Millenium.*

DIANE RUBENSTEIN, associate professor of political science at Purdue University, has published Lacanian readings of American politics and is the author of *What's Left? The Ecole Normale Supériure and the Right.*

DANA R. VILLA is assistant professor of political science at Amherst College, where he teaches political theory. He has published articles on Arendt, Nietzsche, and Heidegger and has written the forthcoming *Arendt and Heidegger: Overcoming the Tradition.*

Index